Value-based Human Resource Strategy:
Developing your consultancy role

D0896811

Value-based Human Resource Strategy:
Developing your consultancy role

Tony Grundy and Laura Brown

ELSEVIER
BUTTERWORTH
HEINEMANN

AMSTERDAM BOSTON HEIDELBERG LONDON NEW YORK OXFORD
PARIS SAN DIEGO SAN FRANCISCO SINGAPORE SYDNEY TOKYO

Elsevier Butterworth-Heinemann
Linacre House, Jordan Hill, Oxford OX2 8DP
200 Wheeler Road, Burlington, MA 01803

First published 2003

British Library Cataloguing in Publication Data
A catalogue record for this book is available from the
British Library

Library of Congress Cataloging in Publication Data
A catalog record for this book is available from the Library
of Congress

ISBN 0 7506 5769 3

For information on all Butterworth-Heinemann
publications visit our website at www.bh.com

Typeset by Genesis Typesetting Ltd, Rochester, Kent, UK
Printed and bound in Great Britain

Contents

Preface

Human Resource Strategy is becoming a 'must-have' for many organizations, but unfortunately many HR managers and line managers do not actually have much of a clear idea as to what it looks like. Even fewer are confident in how to set about getting one, and yet fewer then know what to do with it, and how to show that it has genuinely added shareholder (or 'economic' value).

HR strategy is thus in grave danger of ending up alongside so many management trends – like TQM, BPR, organizational transformation, and the learning organization – as half-implemented, unsuccessful and ultimately disappointing initiatives. To avoid it becoming a distracting management ornament, we felt it imperative to write this book in order to give both HR and line managers the frameworks, the tools, and the practical illustrations so that they can do all of the above things.

We have not been HR managers ourselves – which is probably an advantage, as we hope we bring to the topic a more objective and analytical perspective. This perspective has been refined over the years through research, facilitation experience, and consulting with many major organizations – including Abbey National, BP, BT, CGNU, the Metropolitan Police, Royal Bank of Scotland, Serono (Pharmaceuticals), Tesco, and many others. Many of these organizations have incorporated our processes within their approach to HR strategy.

This book is also aimed not merely at the HR managements (and consultants), but also at all line managers who wish to manage organizational strategy for both competitive and financial value. Whilst it is not a comprehensive academic text, being mainly practical in focus, it should be an essential read for MBA students studying HR resources/HR strategy and for those who are about to do projects on softer, organizational topics. It will also provide a complementary perspective to conventional texts on strategic management.

We bring to HR strategy our knowledge of and training in many disciplines, including strategic management, organizational behaviour and finance. We hope that you will enjoy this book as much as we enjoyed creating and completing it – which was finally accomplished on the Sun Princess, Princess Cruises, August 2002.

This book provides a unique pathway into being a strategic HR consultant, providing many processes and a complete toolkit for taking issues from diagnosis through options to implementation.

Dr Tony Grundy and Dr Laura Brown
August 2002, Alaska

PART 1

HR strategy

CHAPTER 1

Introduction

Human Resource (HR) strategy is now widely recognized as being an important – and perhaps essential – way of developing organizations to meet increased competitive challenges. Yet many managers (including HR managers) have only a broad, and at times vague, notion of what it actually is.

Even fewer managers have much of an idea of how to derive an HR strategy, and of how it will be used – and in practice, an even higher proportion have only the vaguest concept of how it can add value, especially in economic terms.

'HR strategy' thus seems currently to fall into the category of being a 'nice-to-have' management process. In many companies it appears to fall into the zone of 'MBO' ('Management by Ornaments'), its role being principally to make HR departments feel more comfortable about their direction and position, or as something to tick off as 'done' by the Chief Executive.

Indeed, the very assumption that HR strategy is principally 'owned' by HR departments is itself something to be challenged. In this book we take the view that HR strategy is not something to be owned solely or primarily by HR departments, but rather by senior line management collectively. The HR department's role is therefore to *facilitate* its development and then help to project manage it, and to support its implementation.

Our other main propositions are that:

- HR strategy must play a key role in developing the organization's competitive advantage, not merely to support the business strategy but also to develop it proactively.
- HR strategy can and must play a major contribution to the creation and capture of shareholder value, or 'economic value'. This means that we should be able to trace some very clear links between HR strategy and short-, medium- and long-term incremental cash generation, directly or indirectly.
- HR strategy is actually best developed on an integral part of the business strategy, rather than separately, or as an add-on afterthought.
- The Number One owner of the HR strategy should be the Chief Executive.
- To facilitate HR strategy, to project manage and support its implementation to add value, requires a somewhat different mind-set and processes, priorities and skills within most HR departments.

Here the leadership development process worked back from the objective (which was to get the value out of leadership behaviours at an everyday level) by delivering this in the least time and at the least cost.

To illustrate the significance of the 'cunning plan', while working with the Royal Bank of Scotland HR managers we found that if they were not exposed to continual reinforcement to the 'cunning plan' idea, they would generally produce average plans for implementation. These average plans would then turn out to have lots of difficulties and uncertainties, and uneven stakeholder support. However, by spending a little time up front to be 'cunning', these barriers were typically much reduced.

Having demystified and upgraded our idea of 'strategy' generally, we can now move onto the idea of 'HR strategy'.

WHAT IS HR STRATEGY?

HR strategy can be defined as being:

The plans, programme, and intentions of developing an organization to meet its present and future competitive challenges in order to generate superior economic value.

This definition is pictured visually in Figure 1.1, which shows how competitive challenges are posed by the wider environment, and by changes in customer needs, distribution methods, technology and competitor activity.

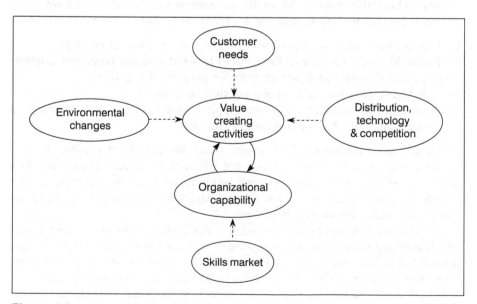

Figure 1.1
HR strategy – the key influences

There is also increasing competition in the labour market for scarce skills. These factors are all tied into the generation of economic value, which in turn feeds back into organizational capability to meet these challenges as a virtuous cycle.

The various components of HR strategy can be described as follows:

- *Plans* – these include the overall direction of the organization in terms of size, scope activities, structure, style, skills and values, and also the specific priorities for supporting these developments.
- *Programmes* – these are the specific bundles of HR-related projects that will deliver either organizational breakthroughs (step changes) or continuous improvements in capability.
- *Intentions* – these are the areas where, although some deliberate intent exists, it has not (as yet) crystallized into specific plans and projects.
- *Organization* – this embraces the formal and informal arrangements for ongoing exchange through an internal division of labour. It also includes alliances, outsourcing and virtual working. This more fluid model of organizations takes HR strategy beyond the more tangible definition of traditional organizational boundaries.
- *Economic value* – this is the additional cash flow generated either for customers or for rewarding the superior skills or performance of staff; a fair proportion of this accrues ultimately to the shareholders. Even where some of this economic value is relatively intangible, we can often find ways of putting an approximate value on it (for example, in Chapter 12 we take a look at how it might be possible to put a value on strategic thinking – which can make a major contribution towards creating economic value).

Whilst there are plenty of guides on HR strategy, these are predominantly written by people who (quite naturally) are HR professionals. This means that they may be less likely to have a clear focus on its deliverables, and particularly on how this can be targeted to create and harvest economic value. Our own interest is much more business-focused. We believe that by giving HR strategy a more value-based focus, it is much more likely to both win over line managers and also to make it a success. Because of the (assumed) less tangible nature of the human or people element (which we find odd, as we persistently see people and sometimes touch them on a day-to-day basis), it is perhaps thought not possible to target their value. However, just because something is not easy to measure with precision, this does not mean that it does not have an economic value – as we see in the next graphic case from everyday personal life ('Putting an economic value on people'), where the value is of a protective nature.

As an example of putting an economic value on HR strategy, let us turn to a case study in the football industry, namely Arsenal Football Club. We chose football because people (players) are self-evidently crucial, and clubs do need to put a value on organizational resource and its development. It is therefore a useful learning benchmark for other organizations.

Having defined HR strategy and illustrated how it can add economic value, it is now time to explore what forms it can take. This introduces us to the idea of 'the HR strategy mix' of deliberate, emergent, submergent, emergency and detergent strategies.

THE HR STRATEGY MIX

From the 1960s through to the 1980s, a very strong theme in strategic management generally was the importance of 'deliberate strategy' – which involved thinking in detail about where you are, where you want to be in the future, and how you will get there.

As the rationalist strategic thinkers became more advanced in prescribing conceptual frameworks (culminating in Michael Porter's *Competitive Strategy*, 1980, and *Competitive Advantage*, 1985), managers themselves seemed to be stuck in a kind of strategic Stone Age, reticent in employing these new techniques (until the late 1990s). Dubbed the 'Design School' by Henry Mintzberg (1993) (a term propagated in his aptly-titled book *The Rise and Fall of Strategic Planning: Reconceiving Roles for Planning, Plans, Planners*), by the mid-1990s rationalist thinking seemed to have reached the summit of its development, with nowhere else to go.

Mintzberg suggested that most of the manifestations of strategy are very much implicit, fragmented and fluid. Whilst formal strategic plans sometimes existed, they were infrequently acted upon and most strategic action manifested itself in more haphazard behaviour. Usually the only real way of defining a strategy (for Mintzberg) was to look at strategic actions *after* the event, and then to try to discern if there had been any pattern. Mintzberg's definition of strategy was thus one of 'a pattern in a stream of decisions or actions', usually discovered largely after or during the event, rather than before.

Let us now therefore go one stage further, paraphrasing Mintzberg as:

Strategy is a pattern in a stream of explicit and implicit strategic decisions designed to create a specific competitive positioning through deploying organizational resources.

This point that 'strategy' (whether it is business strategy or HR strategy) is effectively a collection of mutually aligned decisions designed to create a specific competitive positioning is a most important and helpful one. It is important because it shifts much of our frame of reference in strategic management from the 'Very Big Picture' to a more tangible and everyday management level. In effect, this recognizes that most strategic thinking should be done at a smaller scale than is typically appreciated. We call this level that of the 'mini strategy'. This approach is helpful because it enables management (at all levels) to get a better grip on HR strategy, especially so that they *actually get on and implement it.*

Mintzberg cleverly called strategies that are not obvious until they have actually happened, 'emergent strategies'. Whilst Mintzberg's extension of the types of strategy from one to two (deliberate and now emergent) is laudable, these two forms simply do not, in our view, go far enough. We have therefore added three additional forms – the 'submergent', the 'emergency' and the 'detergent' – giving a total set of:

1. *Deliberate* – a detailed, analytical framework for both the rationale and the 'how' of the strategy.
2. *Emergent* – a strategy that emerges from a pattern on a stream of decisions or actions.
3. *Submergent* – a deliberate or emergent strategy that is not working, but one that managers are still committed to and is drawing in more resources. Here, managers often redouble their efforts, putting in more time and resources without questioning the original scope of the strategy and its rationale.
4. *Emergency* – a strategy that has 'lost the plot'; one where there is so little coherence to action that there is no real sense of direction at all.
5. *Detergent* – a strategy that has not worked in the past but is now being rethought, re-engineered, transformed into something relatively different, or simply abandoned.

These five forms of HR strategy are depicted in Figure 1.2. This shows a deliberate strategy at the start, often moving into an emergent phase. Unless its direction and implementation is steered, it may drift into submergent or 'emergency' phases, or even the 'detergent' phase (where it is tidied up).

Any HR strategy can be analysed to discern which stage of its evolution it is presently at. A strategy that is in two or more of the above phases simultaneously is said to have a 'strategy mix'.

Besides asking where the HR strategy is within the strategy mix, it is also imperative to examine the strategy mix as it changes over time. Figure 1.3 shows a typical example of a major change project within HR strategy.

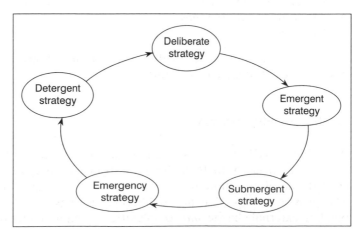

Figure 1.2
The strategy mix

An example of submergent strategy is the attempts by Marks & Spencer in 1998 to turn its business around under the existing management team (see Chapter 5 for a case study of Marks & Spencer).

Emergency HR strategy

Emergency HR strategies are characterized by very little in the way of a longer-term pattern, being mainly reactions to short-term pressures or temptations. Emergency strategies are 'off the highway' of achieving longer-term strategic direction. An emergency strategy would hardly count as a strategy at all, except that it is so prevalent in everyday reality.

An example of an 'emergency' business strategy (controversially) is the attempt by Marks & Spencer in 2000 to rejuvenate its clothing strategy by launching designer sub-brands (but without attributing them to named designers) in an effort to make up for not being seen as a trendy brand (see Chapter 5).

Detergent HR strategy

A 'detergent' HR strategy is sometimes called a 'refocusing' strategy. The expression 'detergent strategy' is perhaps more powerful, as it links directly to cleaning up a mess left after an emergent, submergent or emergency strategy. A detergent strategy can be found either as part of a major and dramatic organizational turnaround, or as a more localized attempt to prepare a more solid basis for new deliberate strategies.

An example of a detergent business strategy is IBM's downsizing of its hardware businesses, which entered the 1990s as over-manned, unwieldy operations, and entered the millennium as a much leaner operation.

A key conclusion from the notion of the 'strategy mix' is that no single form of strategy is therefore appropriate to managing HR strategies in differ-

The HR strategy mix – diagnostic questions

For one area of your HR strategy (e.g. performance management, better team working, career pathing, commercial awareness):

1. Which of the strategy forms did this HR mini-strategy originate in? (Consider especially deliberate, emergent or detergent.)
2. Which forms of strategy did it move through?
3. Where is it now?
4. What is the 'so-what' from this, in terms of example of future options, or for future HR strategy development process? What should you do better/avoid doing again in future?

ent contexts. Deliberate, emergent (and even detergent) strategies need to be managed together in a deliberate juggling act. Often a strategy appears to be a blur between two or more forms, or in transition between two.

Summary

The above forms of strategy are all extremely important to HR projects, as (a) the HR strategy mix may be predominantly of an emergent, submergent or emergency nature (meaning that it is very difficult, if not impossible, to make linkages between a specific HR project or programme and its higher level HR strategy), and (b) the project itself may be in a more emergent, submergent or 'emergency' state.

Before we leave the strategy mix for a while, let us do a brief recap, and expand on our earlier ideas further.

First, the various levels of strategy are often loosely interconnected, meaning that it is often not straightforward to link HR strategy with business strategy. Second, the business strategy itself might be fluid and ambiguous, making it hard to develop and link in the HR strategy. Third, the HR strategy might be at a lower point in the strategy mix cycle (a blend of submergent, emergency or detergent strategies), and here there will be very little to link HR projects back to – so they get developed as stand-alone initiatives. This makes it also much harder to target their economic value, as at least some of this future is manifested through their being part of an interrelation set. Fourth, different HR initiatives themselves might be at different phases of their own strategy mix: they may be mainly deliberate or emergent, or perhaps mainly at the submergent/emergency phases, or maybe mainly detergent.

To make life just slightly more complex, HR strategies might be developed primarily for strategic positioning (for example, to define an overall, future organization), or they may be mainly concerned with HR strategy implementation. This raises the possibility of strategies being 'deliberate' in terms of strategic positioning, but 'emergent' in terms of their implementation planning (the internal 'how' of the HR strategy).

Having defined what HR strategy is and the forms that it can take, let us now make sure we know what it *is not*. HR strategy is not just about the sum total of personnel-related initiatives that are at present being pursued in the organization. It is much more focused on the future rather than on remedial initiatives. It should also define an integrated set of actions and the set of necessary and sufficient organizational skills that will together deliver the future organizational vision.

HR STRATEGY – POSSIBLE CONTENT

In our search for HR strategy it is worth illustrating a good format for the content of a deliberate HR strategy plan, so that you can work backwards from that plan when project managing its creation – especially when establishing a deliberate HR strategy. Whilst the main headings are pretty standard the sub-heading content obviously varies depending on the context, and may include:

1. Organizational goals, and their links to business strategy
   - Competitive: responsiveness to external challenge
   - Future capability
   - Innovation: speed of decision-making and change rate of value-added new ideas
   - Efficiency
2. Key HR issues and gap analysis (see below)
   - Skills gap/shortages
   - Cost gap
   - Innovation gap
   - Mind-set gap
   - Behavioural gap
3. HR strategic breakthroughs (see below)
   - Leadership/strategic competencies
   - Morale shift
   - Major restructurings
   - Flexible working patterns
4. Value added and interdependencies
   - Summary business cases
   - Major interrelationships
5. HR continuous improvements
6. Key uncertainties
7. Appendices
   - Organizational diagnosis
   - HR breakthroughs – project plans and detailed business cases.

The above format for an HR strategy must be considered with an important caveat. This format assumes that HR strategy is to be framed in a separate document from the business strategy. In the next chapter we will argue that it is preferable *not* to have it as a separate document as such, although this format can form a useful appendix and summary of action for HR.

The following examples of HR strategy outputs (by project area for Crawley Borough Council) arose through our facilitation, and have been provided by Peter Wiles, the Council's Head of Personnel.

HR strategy outputs: Crawley Borough Council

Vision and values

The prime purpose of the HR strategy is to achieve the Council's social, environmental and economic objectives, which are set out fully in its Corporate Plan and in the annual service plans. This strategy is a key part of the Corporate Plan in setting out how to achieve the best from staff and how we should act as an employer in facilitating this process.

Employee communications and involvement

The Council's aim is to provide open, honest, two-way communication and, most importantly, full involvement and empowerment. We aim to develop and improve our appraisal and team briefing systems. To see how we are progressing, we will repeat the staff attitude survey every two years.

There is a key role for managers in building the climate in which the changes we are seeking can be achieved, in making clear what is expected, and in helping to release the full potential of every member of staff.

Employee relations

It is vital that we develop a culture that encourages new ideas, accepts that mistakes are a natural part of the learning process, and avoids blame. We expect staff to play their part by acting responsibly and adhering to procedures. Whilst we encourage risk-taking, risks should be measured and taken with appropriate professional caution.

Inevitably in such an environment differences and problems will arise, but we will support staff where appropriate and provide fair and effective mechanisms for dealing with such difficulties.

We demand the highest standards of conduct and behaviour, and have introduced a confidential 'whistle blowing' procedure to highlight and root out any breaches of these standards.

Pay and conditions/recruitment and retention

We welcome the national Single Status Agreement, which aims to break down the traditional demarcation of 'staff' and 'manual workers'. We will work to provide fair and competitive pay and conditions to attract and retain staff who are competent and have the right attitude to deliver Crawley's vision. Having said that, it has to be recognized that a pay system that fairly rewards similar levels of skill and responsibility equally cannot at the same time match market rates in individual areas. Major market problems will be tackled separately on a temporary basis.

We will also examine how to develop greater flexibility within service conditions so that we provide services when and how the customers require them. Current skill shortages and recruitment difficulties point to the vital importance of a professional and systematic recruitment process. We have already introduced core training requirements for those who are part of the recruitment process. We would aim to equip staff to compete to the best of their ability for promotion opportunities that occur. Most posts will be advertised externally so that underrepresented groups can have the opportunity of competing for the posts, but managers will have the discretion to advertise internally where they are satisfied that this will produce a competitive response.

Equality

We believe that our services are enhanced by having staff from diverse backgrounds and cultures. There is also a duty on employer and employees to ensure a workplace free from unfair discrimination in relationships between members, managers, employees, colleagues and customers.

We must also ensure that all of our staff have equal access to training and development opportunities.

We will continue to improve our standards of equal opportunity practice and have thorough monitoring and review systems in place to check our progress.

The Council's employee structure has very few young people to form the base for future qualified and experienced staff. We therefore need to attract younger people, including school leavers.

OWNERSHIP AND POSITIONING OF HR STRATEGY

The choice of ownership of HR strategy is a very important issue. When corporate planning developed in the 1960s and 1970s, it followed a very hierarchical model – a more traditional and bureaucratic model of the organization. The various levels of strategy were:

1. Corporate strategy (what business the group was in, and how shareholder value would be created)
2. Business strategy (how the strategic business units were going to compete)
3. Functional strategies (for example marketing, operations, logistics, IT, finance and HR).

With the exception of marketing strategy, which was felt to be pivotal in developing business strategy, the other functional strategies were seen as being more in a supportive and perhaps even a reactive role. Whilst operations and IT strategy were developed to have a more proactive role, especially in the 1980s, and finance did the same in the 1990s, HR strategy was left to bring up the rear. Hence, even in much of the more developed literature on HR strategy, it was seen as following on from the business strategy. Our view, which is a central theme of this book, is that HR strategy should be *at least* as proactive in developing businesses strategy as the other functional strategies. HR strategy should play a particularly proactive role as it is very much there to challenge the organizational mind-set, *which is perhaps the biggest single constraint on developing innovative business strategies.*

Owing to this significance, we felt (and this is supported by our later research in Chapter 2) that HR strategy is too important to be left in the hands of the HR department, *however innovative and competent.* Indeed, in our view it can (and must) be championed by the Chief Executive. The role of HR is not peripheral at all in this; the CE needs to facilitate both its development and its implementation.

This implies a major shift in the role of HR, which can be summed up as in Table 1.1:

Table 1.1
The shift in the role of HR

	From	To
Business strategy	Little role	A much more proactive role
HR strategy	Creating it	Facilitating its development
Business role	Peripheral	Equal top team member
Major concerns	Procedural	Change management
Skills	Operational personnel	Problem solving/advisory

In your company, where are you on this continuum?

THE HR STRATEGY PROCESS AND ROLES

It is widely agreed in the literature that HR strategy is crucial in delivering real competitive advantage. However, as shown in the previous section, HR issues still appear to be relegated to a secondary position when compared to marketing strategy, financial strategy and to operational tactics. They are often given even less prominence in actual organizations.

It is both a mystery and a puzzle that so few organizations appear to have an HR strategy of some kind, let alone get tangible value out of it. At one major conference on HR strategy (run by one of the authors), over 50 delegates were asked if they had an explicit HR strategy. Only a few hands went up. A few more hands went up when asked whether, even if they lacked an explicit, *deliberate* HR strategy, they had an *emergent* strategy (and probably they meant an 'emergency' strategy).

An important limitation on HR strategy is the prevalence of excessively short-term thinking on resource allocation generally in many companies. As many of the cost drivers in organizations are people-related, this can greatly inhibit the development of an effective HR strategy. This underlines the very real importance of positioning it as *value-based HR strategy*.

A further factor limiting the development of effective HR strategies is the lack of a well-defined process and integrated techniques for delivering it. Whilst HR management appears awash with intricate competency frameworks and psychometrics, there appears little to integrate the HR strategy 'big picture' with the plethora of HR programmes, which may often appear

Shareholder value has become an increasingly important concept in modern management thinking. Shareholder value theory came into prominence in the mid- to late 1980s, with Alfred Rappaport (1986) and a number of other theorists (including Bennett Stewart, who first coined the expression of 'Economic Value Added' or 'EVA').

Whilst there is a considerable literature on shareholder value, most of this is of a fairly technical, financial value, dealing with the valuation of business and corporate strategy. Shareholder value theory came from a variety of sources, including:

1. Corporate finance/financial economics, which helped managers to understand how to calculate and use the 'cost of capital'. This was the minimum return required by providers of finance to cover (a) business risk; (b) the rate of inflation, and (c) the 'time value of money' (i.e. the return still required for risk-free investment where there is no inflation to cover the deprival costs of not having the money for the period of investment).
2. The theory of strategic investment decisions – the use of the cost of capital to trade off long- versus short-term cash flows, or their 'residual value' (and after deducting the cost of capital, the 'net present value' or 'NPV').
3. Strategic management – the understanding of product markets and relative competitive position to help generate these cash flows in the very first place.

This book focuses on the first two points listed above, as applied to organizational investment – for instance in organizational change, expansion, or acquisition of new management resource.

Because of the perceived 'less tangible' nature of investment in organization and people, HR strategy has not traditionally been the land of targeting shareholder (or 'economic') value creation. When researching strategic investment decisions several years ago (Grundy, 1992), one of the authors discovered that 'intangibles' were not necessarily impossible to quantify at all, especially if targeted economic value were to be considered indicative. For example, investment in customer service could be evaluated, using a step-by-step process, by:

- Measuring shifts in customer perception
- Evaluation (in broad terms) of what this was worth to them (financially)
- Estimating approximately how much value could be captured through more sales, higher prices, discounts avoided and through avoidance of the loss of customers
- Ensuring that the intended improvement was of a sufficient quantum difference to genuinely make a real difference – sufficient to affect customer behaviour for the positive (a quantum improvement rather than an incremental improvement).

These ideas were then developed to look at putting a value on strategic change, valuing acquisitions (Grundy, 1994), and on the value of alignment in team behaviour (Grundy, 1998; see also Chapter 11). This was followed by further research into the value of strategic thinking (Grundy and Brown, 2002b; see also Chapter 12).

Table 1.2 can help us to put a base-appropriate value on intangibles, and is based on an example of culture change at BP (see Chapter 8).

Table 1.2
Organization of intervention – culture change

Areas of value	Manifestation	Economic value
'Detergent' value	Stopping doing things/doing things in old ways	The costs avoided (and disruption) of old ways
Shifts in underlying values, attitudes, etc.	Critical incidents – immediate changes	The value of better decision-making, faster/more efficient execution
Sustainable change	Demonstrable shift between the 'old' world and the 'new'	The value of ongoing better, quick decision-making
Emergent change	World-class capability	Value-based management implemented – with results
	Successfully integrated acquisitions	Successful, value-added expansion

In each of these cases it is possible at least to put a range of value on the final column; working from less tangible to more tangible (i.e. left to right) it is then possible to find a way through the complexity. However, trying to do it in one step (i.e. simply putting numbers on the left-hand column) would be almost meaningless.

Focusing on putting a value on HR strategy more specifically, and drawing from these ideas, the following insights emerge:

- Many of the softer and more distinctive aspects of competitive advantage can be ultimately traced back to how organizations actually behave
- At root, the majority of value and cost drivers (which generate net cash flow) are behavioural in nature
- To generate a surplus economic value over and above the cost of capital requires a combination of superior development and deployment of organizational resources, and also better alignment within the organization than in competitors
- Using the 'critical incident' methodology, which identifies specific positive or negative events that create or destroy shareholder value, we can generally estimate the economic effect of to key organizational drivers – not necessarily precisely, but in an indicative and approximate way. These indicative measures are illuminating both before, during and after implementing organizational change (for example through a deliberate HR strategy). This is illustrated in Chapter 8, with a short case study on culture change at BP.

- Emergent
- Submergent
- Emergency
- Detergent?

2. How is its economic value correlated with the form it takes?
3. Where it is emergent, how do you prioritize HR initiations?
4. Where it is emergent, is there a danger of it becoming 'submergent', or even 'emergency'?
5. To what extent does your HR strategy document cover the areas suggested in the 'HR strategy – possible content' section? In particular, does it actually contain summary business cases and major interdependencies/interrelationships?
6. Who is the ultimate owner of HR strategy? (HR? line management? Your CEO?)
7. If everyone were suddenly to have amnesia regarding HR strategy, what potential economic value would be lost or destroyed?

CHAPTER 2

The links of HR strategy and corporate strategy

■ INTRODUCTION

As seen in Chapter 1, human resources (HR) strategy can be defined as:

> The plans, programmes and intentions to develop the human capability of an organization to meet the future competitive challenges in order to generate superior economic value.

Chapter 1 also showed that the role of HR strategy is by no means self-evident. To address its value, two key questions are addressed in this first section:

1. What are the links between HR strategy and corporate strategy?
2. What role do these links play in determining organizational effectiveness?

Organizational effectiveness can be defined as:

> The capacity of the organization to adapt rapidly to its external environment and to meet market and other external demands with good resulting business performance and thus economic value.

In this chapter we will first look at the key linkages needed between HR strategy and corporate strategy to help close the people gap, and we also look at some of the key linkages with the organizational structure.

Next, we will begin to examine the lessons from case study material regarding the linkage of HR and corporate strategies, especially for value creation and destruction, from two large and prominent international financial services organizations (which must remain anonymous). Here we make the radical proposals that (a) HR strategy is probably not best developed as a separate process from business strategy, and (b) it is also probably best not called 'HR' strategy at all, as inevitably this will be associated just with HR strategy rather than with the total organization.

operations, in the value chain.) Not calling it 'HR strategy' might actually be to its advantage.

3. *Theme three: emergence.* HR strategy formulation may be inhibited because those managers involved may be 'awaiting a deliberate business strategy' rather than being prepared to work with an emergent strategy.

4. *Theme four: the intangible.* The core strategy process may be overly concerned with more tangible strategic issues, rather than the less tangible aspects of human capability. It may thus result in a situation of there being 'too little', within competitive strategy, to graft HR strategy onto.

5. *Theme five: turbulence.* Organizational politics and organizational turbulence may simply prevent links from cementing, however fluid and flexible these may be.

6. *Theme six: ownership and structure.* Who should HR strategy be owned by, and how does it sit in the organizational structure? This appears to be absolutely central to linking corporate and HR strategy.

These themes of complexity, identity, emergence, the intangible, turbulence, and ownership and structure, suggest that linking HR strategy to corporate strategy is likely – even in the most favourable environment – to be very difficult. But how do these difficulties manifest themselves? This is discussed now, and the effects of these difficulties at work are illustrated. The central thesis is:

> To make effective linkages in practice between corporate strategy and Human Resources strategy and to thus close the people gap requires an ongoing shift from a separate HR strategy in which the HR department is responsible for developing and coordination, to a unified 'organization and people' or 'HR' strategy owned and developed by line managers with facilitation by the HR department.

Table 2.1 highlights the evolutionary phases that span from traditional personnel management through to HRM, HR strategy and 'organization and people' strategy. It helps to explain the evolution of HR strategy, and is also useful as a diagnostic tool.

To be genuinely effective, an HR strategy process must not be based on out-of-date, bureaucratic planning processes that are there to cover everything, so that it all looks 'ticked off'. Instead, an issue-based process that has a more selective focus and is championed by top management, facilitated by HR, and integrally linked to corporate strategy/business strategy development, might be far more fruitful.

Equally, HR strategy (or organization and people strategy, as it might be redefined) could well be a joint starting point for developing at least some areas of corporate strategy. For example, IKEA's central competence is in flat-pack assembly furniture at unbelievably low prices. Given that, would not an interesting strategic line of enquiry be self-assembly of flat-pack cheap housing, to alleviate the housing crisis for the young in the UK and elsewhere?

Table 2.1
Evolution of HR strategy

	Personnel management Stage 1	HR management Stage 2	HR strategy Stage 3	HR strategy Stage 4
Main focus	Stability	Improving performance strategy	Reactive to business	Proactive and interactive with business strategy
Status	Fragmented and routine	Partially integrated programmes	Fully integrated HR programmes	HR programmes integrated with operational change
Plan process	Short-term reactive	HRM planning: short/medium term	Short-, medium-, longer-term separate strategy	Interwoven with operational/ business strategy
Ownership	Personnel department	HR department-driven, with line clients	Line manager-driven, strategy, HR department supporting and advising	Line-championed with HR as change catalysts

The above thought suggests a parallel review of:

- The businesses we are in (or want to be in) and their competitive positionings and prospects
- Our distinctive human capabilities, which can achieve a distinctive competitive advantage.

We now turn to our research findings on HR strategy, and will look at their implications.

A STUDY IN HR STRATEGY

Research within a major UK bank and a major UK insurance company is used here to explore the possibilities of linking corporate and HR strategy much further. Interviews were conducted with a number of senior operational managers and human resource managers in 'Bank 1' and 'Insurance Company 2'. The technique used during data collection and analysis was that of 'critical incidents'. This helped managers to focus on whether and how HR strategy (and the links to corporate strategy) might have added to (or avoided detracting from) organizational effectiveness and performance. These critical incidents focused on how the HR strategy either added a significant amount of economic value to the strategy, or destroyed it through specific events.

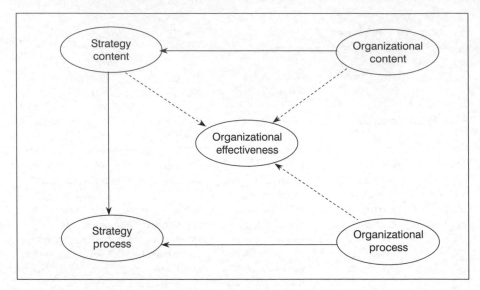

Figure 2.1
Links between competitive and organizational strategies

Categories of linkages between corporate and HR strategies

Figure 2.1 illustrates the linkages apparent in Bank 1 and Insurance Company 2.

It shows that the competitive and organizational strategies are very closely linked, as it is the organization strategy that enables the company to compete, both now and in the future. Both of these factors then contribute to defining the ongoing organizational process. In addition, the process of developing the business strategy in itself would improve organizational effectiveness. Organizational processes (for example, change management and management development) might provide support both to the strategy process and by improving organizational effectiveness.

The 'so what?' from this is that organizational (or 'HR') strategy plays a key role in both the business strategy development process and other processes, generally and proactively.

Strategy content

'Strategy content' (see Figure 2.1) shows how external change might shape the formulation of more fluid and emergent business strategies. Also at work are the polar forms of deliberate strategy in the guise of differentiation and cost leadership. Organizational strategy is a central input into both differentiation strategy (through superior service and product innovation) and cost management via flatter structures.

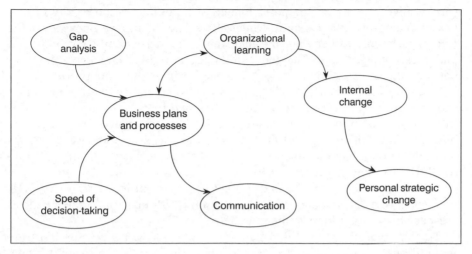

Figure 2.2
Business strategy and organizational processes

The 'so what?' from this is that 'organizational strategy' (sometimes called 'HR strategy') is absolutely central to competitive strategy, whatever generic form it takes, and is not something that comes at the rear.

Strategy process

Figure 2.2 shows both the 'harder' processes (business plans, etc.) and the 'softer' processes (organizational learning, internal change and communication at work) as an aligned system (Senge, 1990).

The 'so what?' from this insight is that without organizational strategy, business strategy is likely to be hard, sterile, and unimaginative.

Organizational process

The main issues that emerged from the research were of the linkage between mission and values, and HR management processes. There was a great concern for consistency of treatment of staff in terms of career and developmental treatment, and also in reward and recognition of performance.

The 'so-what?' from this insight is that without organizational strategy, things like 'mission and values' will sit as ornaments within corporate strategy, and will not really add value through changing actual behaviour.

Organizational context

A few very important and 'softer' issue areas emerged here. These included the style through which power is managed in the organization, and its positive (or negative) impact on the performance of its human resources. A further key ingredient was the extent to which HR-related issues were owned by the HR department rather than by line management (or jointly by both) – a major issue flagged up in Chapter 1. In addition, we found important linkages between the organizational context and the business planning process.

The 'so-what?' from these insights is that the relative success of organizational strategy is very likely to be determined by the extent to which it is well positioned/appropriately aimed/perceived as genuinely value-added and relevant within the top levels of the organization. These factors were perhaps more influential than the inherent quality of thinking within the organization (of 'HR') strategy itself.

In conclusion, Figures 2.1 and 2.2 confirm our earlier findings that HR strategy is very much a part of an open system with many interdependencies – especially with business strategy issues.

To put some flesh on and colour into these ideas, let us now illustrate them through a financial services case study. The quotations provide the data, with commentary following, by issue area.

Some of the most important areas of existing or potential linkage from the data collected included:

- Deliberate versus emergent strategy (see earlier Theme three)
- Differentiation versus cost leadership
- HR's role in business planning
- The ownership of HR strategies.

Bank 1 is one of the top ten UK banks, and Insurance Company 2 is one of the top five UK insurance companies.

A study of financial services

Deliberate versus emergent strategy

When asked about HR strategy, a very senior Bank 1 line manager responded with feelings of ambiguity:

> Although I have deliberately not tried to find out, I have to say that I cannot remember seeing a piece of paper which sets out Bank 1's Human Resources strategy. And that's not to say that there isn't a strategy.

The apparent degree of ambiguity surrounding Bank 1's emergent strategy may have inhibited some HR activities, and thus diluted their economic value. According to an HR manager:

> In this environment you could say things but not be able to make them actually happen. I think that our lack of strategy affected a lot of people's ability to do things. Yes, it did affect our ability to get things done in HR.

A surprise was the response to the question 'does this matter [that the HR strategy is emergent and not explicit]?'. A senior Bank 1 line manager vigorously replied (in a very strong tone):

> Yes, I do, I really do think so.

At Insurance Company 2, the HR manager compared the setting up of First Direct with Insurance Company 2's own relocation of a major centre to another part of the country (as a critical incident):

> ... when Insurance Company 2 moved its operations function to location X, I said don't move people from Y to X, which I thought was a big mistake – taking a century's established culture and just plonking it down in X and kidding yourself that it was a greenfield site. Sure enough, two or three years on, the danger now is that we have a Y mentality lingering around in some parts of X, which I don't think is as healthy as if we had a totally X-based culture.

He hinted strongly that an appropriately deliberate strategy, with more explicit and rigorous choices, could have been a more effective approach for his own company, and could have reduced its costs.

In summary, in both organizations our sample of managers saw a largely emergent HR strategy as being in place. They also saw a number of 'disbenefits' from having an emergent strategy in terms of lack of attention to HR issues during strategic decision-making. The implications of this are that having an emergent HR strategy does seem significantly to undermine organizational effectiveness, and thus value creation, especially as the potential resource-based competitive advantages are not being captured.

A further practical implication here is that a primarily emergent HR strategy greatly undermines the corporate strategy and also dilutes its value, and is therefore best avoided.

Differentiation versus cost leadership

At Bank 1, one HR manager drew very clear linkages between differentiation strategy, marketing and brand strategy, and people values and behaviour. People values and behaviour also underpin competitive advantage, and create the necessary alignment to create economic value:

> I think that the two (brand and HR strategy) go hand in hand. If you regard HR strategy as in part about values, about how people interact, then certainly you are now talking about it being very clearly tied up with the brand, certainly in a service industry.

Although much conventional thinking in strategic management views HR strategy as a follow-on from competitive or marketing strategy, rather than *vice versa*, an alternative and reversed view was put forward at Bank 1 by an HR manager (in his first statement):

> I am not sure, it is a bit chicken and egg (re. the links between corporate strategy and HR strategy). In terms of our culture and the skills of our staff, this leads us to a take a certain positioning in the market. The fact that we are taking that positioning has implications for the way we operate in the HR side.

Here, culture is seen as potentially the basis for designing a competitive strategy, rather than *vice versa*.

The possible importance of differentiation strategy was then weighed by the Bank 1 line manager:

> This business is not about the price of the product, it is about the quality of what we do. You can't differentiate in financial services industries in the same way as you can in the motor industry, by building in features. The cost parameters will stop you.

Differentiation and customer service were obviously very important influences on HR strategic issues. However, cost management (even if falling short of a situation of full 'cost leadership') plays an equally important, but sometimes opposing, role. At Bank 1, cost management was linked to the need to simplify the business and to the skills that underpinned this:

> This business is actually simple. The skills are not of an exceptional order.

Another line of thought was put forward by Bank 1's senior line manager, who believed that cost management and differentiation were in tension with one another:

> I think we have some schizophrenia here. We would see ourselves as being differentiated. Our Chief Executive might see us as cost leaders. He has a very strong bottom line focus. That can set up some tensions, and will do. I think that there is a need for both, it is not necessarily so destructive to have them simultaneously.

[Interestingly, one of the authors then had a mortgage with that bank, which proved itself on its differentiated sales approach in its front office. When redeeming the mortgage, the letter that came through from the low-cost bank office located in some obscure and probably lower-cost part of the UK stated: 'There is a £1000 early payment penalty'. This was accompanied by a page of misspelt, unintelligible financial gobbledegook that the author – a Chartered Accountant – could not understand. The result: the author would never again use the bank. So, is it really possible to segment your HR support according to a given differentiation/cost leadership strategy? Well, there must be some doubts . . .].

There was also a long and detailed discussion on cost ratios with one of Bank 1's HR managers. An obsession with the short term to the detriment of longer-term value creation may actually undermine economic value creation, and this was linked to HR issues as follows:

> I think there is a feeling at the moment about driving our operating costs down. We are seeing our operating costs ratios stay static. The way in which we are diversifying may alter the comparisons of our ratios. One of our objectives is to be a low-cost provider in the markets in which we operate. Not the lowest cost. But I am not sure whether they specify who we are targeted to be lower than.

This is interesting thought from several points of view. First, Bank 1's pursuit of a differentiation strategy was based on brand, customer service and quality people, but supporting skills and values seemed to be in tension, with an increasing drive for cost management. This might well eventually undermine its corporate brand value. This drive to reduce cost was not targeted at cost leadership as such (and from Michael Porter we appreciate that a differentiation strategy should be supported by good cost management). This conflict may then ultimately result in a confused HR strategy as it gets pulled in polar directions.

The bigger point from this discussion is that facilitators of HR/organizational strategy development should question and challenge the logic, completeness and consistency of the corporate/business strategy, rather than simply accept this as a given.

At Insurance Company 2, the Head of Corporate Development identified cost management and leadership versus differentiation as issues, if not as polar choices:

> The bulk of our costs is actually people cost. It isn't really easy to just define our organization as if it were an 'efficient and economic' machine. It is not just about lowering our costs and trying to follow a cost leadership strategy. At the same time we have to differentiate, and we need to do this via our people. We must always be trying to differentiate ourselves from some of these players. What we don't want to see is a 'slash and burn' approach to attacking our cost base. We can achieve a lot simply by better management, to achieve the savings we need.

At no point, however, did any of the Insurance Company 2 managers suggest that costs (and HR-related costs as a subset) needed to be competitively targeted. At both Bank 1 and Insurance Company 2 there seemed to be emergent pressures and programmes to cut costs, but these costs processes did not appear to be integrated with an overall strategy for organizational change. Neither were there explicit trade-offs between benefits and costs (organizational effectiveness).

Furthermore, no discussion of the merits of in-sourcing versus out-sourcing took place. There may be arguments for in-sourcing those aspects of the business (and people) value chain that add disproportionate value (or what we might call the 'motivator' factors). Aspects that are more routine, and need to be managed at a lower cost, are frequently those that deliver value to standards, which are taken for granted by the customer. These what might be called 'hygiene' factors could, it may be argued, become possible candidates for outsourcing. Where out-sourcing decisions do not think through the long-run effects on distinctive organization value and cost management, this too might destroy economic value.

Differentiation and cost leadership strategies thus pose major dilemmas for both competitive strategy *and* HR strategy (as we will see in the Marks and Spencer case study in Chapter 5). By pursuing both differentiation and cost leadership strategies simultaneously, with little clarification and coordination, and without particular focus on key areas of the value chain, service organizations run real risks of a self-cancelling strategy. This is another reason why HR strategy may have in the past (in many organizations) played only a weak contribution in adding to organizational effectiveness and to economic value.

A key practical implication of this is that tensions between differentiation and cost leadership strategies do need to be resolved to prevent HR strategy confusion.

HR's role in business planning

The question recurs, what is driving what in the planning process? Is it the business strategy/plans, or is it HR plans? At Bank 1:

> I think that the decisions will be driven off the business strategy, but the options and the opportunities for the business strategy, will be conditioned by what has happened on the HR side, and what the organization can accept.

Similarly, in terms of creating formal business cases (which provide an opportunity to target economic value):

> They [the HR issues] would be put there if the business managers put them . . .. But we have a process called the strategic planning process which is due to start next Monday. They tend to be driven by product and/or distribution . . .. The appraisal panel [for business cases] would be unlikely to pick up HR issues.

At Insurance Company 2, the definition of the boundary between business and HR strategies was somewhat ambiguous, as suggested by the Head of Corporate Development:

> You asked about what is or isn't HR strategy. There do seem to be some

grey areas, for instance changing how we do things in some areas is seen as really a part of the business strategy, not the HR strategy.

This would seem to be a rather obvious area of linkage or integration between HR strategy and business strategy.

'Simplicity' is also perceived to be very much a desirable quality of any HR strategy at Insurance Company 2. A manager suggested that:

> Human Resources strategy doesn't have to be particularly complicated, it doesn't require a bureaucracy. What we now need is not just an understanding of the HR tools but how to get the benefits of them. I don't think the HR strategy should be rocket science, it should be fairly easy to understand, something that a particular person (a line manager) could relate to. I don't think that the HR function has done itself any favours by trying to overcomplicate things.

It is easy to see how HR issues can be de-emphasized in importance by senior line managers partly because they are seen as being on a kind of strategic pedestal by HR. Also, where HR strategy becomes fuzzy and too general, this will tend to dilute its economic value.

The senior line manager at Insurance 2 rejected the notion of a stand-along HR strategy as follows:

> We don't believe that it should be [put in a separate plan]. We believe that it is an integral part of the plan, and not separate. If you are doing succession planning and other things then that is a separate issue, but we're saying that our Human Resources side of it and the change that we need to take on board, that is at a different level.

In addition, the Bank 1 line manager suggested that whether HR strategy exists separately from other areas of functional strategy is also seen as debatable:

> I suppose that if we compare HR strategy with IT strategy as a stand-alone, then it doesn't make sense [to have a separate HR strategy] – in IT you have lots of different things which are interdependent [with the business strategy]. For example, if you look at unsecured lending, we were doing some things which could use people elsewhere – for instance in mortgage lending.

This was closely paralleled at Insurance Company 2:

> To develop an HR strategy within each part of the business separately based on what they see should be part of it . . ., well, that is the wrong way around in terms of how the business actually operates.

The Insurance Company 2 line manager was also aware that by not confronting the downsides of HR having an emergent strategy, this might pose some very major pitfalls:

> But the fact of the matter is, it absolutely does matter. It is having a clear idea of what part of the organization, of what sort of plan you want to have. That should be clearly about the actions, also the people that deliver them, and the skills that they need, and if you don't have that, then that is where you fall over.

In summary, there does not seem to be a strong case at all for decoupling HR strategy (or separating it out) from business strategy. This is because of the increasing interdependency between operations, people, and competition and marketing strategy in many industries, as exemplified here through financial services. By separating it out it is likely to be seen as being (a) more peripheral; (b) less well integrated with other initiatives, and (c) actually implemented by only part of the organization – the HR function – thus diluting its potential economic value and its follow-through.

The key practical implications of this are that:

- There should not be a separate HR-strategy planning document; it should be a central theme within the business strategy.
- HR issues should then be grouped into an Appendix, perhaps along the lines of the detailed format contained in Chapter 1. This document should be an extract of and fleshed-out version of the organizational issues and breakthroughs already contained within the business strategy.

So whilst in Chapter 1 we gave you a possible format for an HR strategy as a stand-alone output, ideally this is a memorandum to give HR a focus, and should be interwoven with the business plan. We would like to flag this up as a non-obvious and highly relevant conclusion.

The ownership of HR strategies

Returning to the dilemma of stand-alone versus weaved-in HR strategy (our earlier Theme six, which impacts on Theme five – turbulence), HR managers in Insurance Company 2 commented:

> So is the HR strategy stand-alone, or is it weaved in? It is a separate meeting just to discuss it but do I call it stand-alone?

In Bank 1, a perceived constraint was that of the strategic planning department (paradoxically). This is perhaps because this department is seen as the home of 'strategy' and thus it may potentially crowd out HR's involvement. According to a senior line manager:

> I think it might be something possibly to do with the structure, because we do have the corporate planning area which tends to be the area from where the strategic things come, there is no wish, no perceived need to put HR into that environment. Therefore HR strategy is not thought through.

At Bank 1, we heard from the same manager that:

Planning tends to go with the pragmatic things, acquisitions, distribution, it would tend not to be things that are supportive of those main strategies with the exception of IT. We have not got to the point where we should go with HR. We spend a lot of time working on it [i.e. HR] but I still don't think we are very clear what our strategy is.

Discussing this at greater length, the above quotations from Bank 1 suggest that the very name 'Human Resource' tends to locate HR as being a 'personnel concern' in both organizations. Where personnel is not particularly influential, this tends to marginalize HR strategy. Also, where the department 'Corporate Planning' has come into being, this department may tend to have its principal (if not exclusive) focus on competitive strategy and financial planning. Softer, strategic issues like HR may then fall down a gap between departments. This may be appreciated where corporate strategy is seen as an exclusively top team affair, rather than involving senior management.

Coupled with the ambiguity of the role of line managers in operational HR/personnel issues, it is hardly surprising that no real forum for HR strategy debate exists in this and many other organizations. This is particularly the case as business planning processes are largely (financial) numbers-driven – for instance at Bank 1. In summary, a further 'strategy trap' for HR strategy is for it to be seen to be owned by HR or the personnel department. Also, where a strategic planning department exists, it does need to have sufficient skills (and inclination) to analyse the organizational issues surrounding strategy implementation.

Implications drawn from the financial services case study

From the case study, we can now suggest that:

1. Where corporate strategy is particularly emergent, then HR strategy is also likely to be emergent (see Theme three, above). For example, at Bank 1 the senior manager felt he could not evolve a deliberate HR strategy because of ambiguity at a corporate strategy level.

2. Where HR strategy is emergent, there is likely to be inadequate management of the interdependencies between HR programmes to provide the necessary (but not necessarily sufficient) conditions for improving organizational effectiveness (Themes one, two and three). Here we can distinguish between emergent strategy *content* and emergent strategy *process*. Even where there is a deliberate HR strategy (content-wise), if the ongoing process is highly emergent and relatively unguided, it is very likely to find itself rooted in the organizational structure in a most haphazard way – thus neutralizing its effectiveness.

3. Where HR strategy is highly emergent:
- HR as a source of competitive advantage may not be given the attention it deserves by senior management (it did not appear prominent in the strategic planning processes of either Bank 1 or Insurance Company 2). Although this is not a particularly surprising finding, it does underline the need to reposition HR strategy in terms of (a) what it is called; (b) where it is found in the planning outputs; (c) how it is evolved within the process; (d) who it owns it and facilitates it, and (e) how explicitly it is targeted to generate economic value.
- Differentiation and cost leadership may sometimes be pursued, in effect, simultaneously. (See again the cost material from Bank 1 and Insurance 2.) However, this may result in HR policies or decisions that are in tension or conflict, and may also result in considerable confusion in managing the value chain, ultimately destroying value at a micro-level. Organization and people (formerly HR) strategy could play a significant role here in addressing in- versus out-sourcing decisions – if this analysis is closely linked to competitive strategy.
- Brand strategy may easily become decoupled from plans to develop staff's behaviour, values and skills (again, see Bank 1). This can produce significant economic value dilution and destruction as the entire resource base becomes mal-aligned in achieving an overall brand strategy through differentiation *and* financial effect through cost cutting.
- Business plans may be destitute of thinking on softer issues, such as people's implementation capability (see Theme four). Their implementation may then be partial and uneven, diluting or destroying their economic value.

Within (3) above, the second and third points are perhaps the most interesting. Where corporate strategies are emergent or where they go in apparently opposing directions, then HR strategy faces the dilemma of either seeking to accommodate those tensions or to question the basis of corporate (and competitive) strategy. However, this can also be read the other way. If HR strategy is emergent, then there may well be little steer from it as a creative force on *corporate* strategy. If we follow the argument that *implementation* is very frequently what lets corporate strategy down, then perhaps companies are well advised to *begin* the business strategy development process with at least some thinking about HR strategy, instead of starting off with product/market and competitive positioning. Sometimes they might even *start* with an HR/organizational strategy, and then look for possible competitive strategies that would be 'naturals' for the organization.

The absence of a clear and deliberate HR strategy linked to corporate strategy (and thus the 'people gap') may therefore have a negative impact on organizational effectiveness and economic value. This may occur through inattention to crucial HR issues, or through wasted effort on poorly implemented HR management (HRM).

In the absence of a robust (and largely deliberate) HR strategy clearly linked with corporate strategy, HRM programmes may therefore easily lack direction, clarity, coherence and the necessary critical mass to add real economic value, especially where there is a high element of emergence in HR strategy. In conclusion, therefore, a deliberate HR strategy is very much to be preferred to an emergent approach to HR strategy – certainly based on the experience within these two financial services organizations.

Implications for theory and practice

Figure 2.3 shows how a much closer integration of HR strategy with business strategy might look.

This framework highlights that, as HR strategy elements are so interdependent with operational initiatives and the people resource are only one part of the operational mix, it makes less and less sense to extract the pure HR element separately (see earlier Theme two). *Ergo*, it is best to position it as organization and people strategy (or more simply, organizational strategy), as being the internal counterpart of outward-focusing competitive strategy.

The practical benefits of redefining HR strategy in organizational strategy terms appear to be as follows:

- HR strategy will be seen less as being the prime concern of HR practitioners, helping dissolve the line management/HR barrier
- A joint organization and people (HR) strategy can be more nearly dovetailed into both competitive strategy and business plans

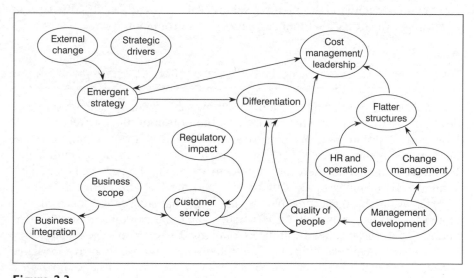

Figure 2.3
Business and HR strategies in financial services

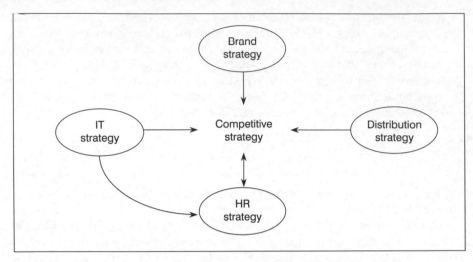

Figure 2.4
HR strategy and its fit with functional strategies in financial services

- Any 'hard' initiatives (like business process re-engineering) can be more easily integrated with HR initiatives (see earlier Theme four)
- It should become a lot easier to evaluate the business and (broad) financial effects of HR programmes because they would no longer be seen as stand-alones, thus helping to create value-based strategies targeted at economic value.

HR strategy should therefore be seen as the flipside to competitive strategy. To complete the picture, Figure 2.4 shows the fit to other areas of strategy, regarding the financial services environment.

Back to the links between corporate strategy and HR strategy

The existing HR strategy literature emphasizes an analytical approach to developing HR strategy. This is based on the notion of 'fit': between the HR base and corporate and business strategy. However, this 'fit' implies close integration of thinking on these two dimensions – yet in both Bank 1 and Insurance Company 2 there did not seem to be any longer-term, genuinely strategic HR planning process that supported the HR end of this linkage.

From what the managers told us, the idea that a very formal, analytical model that focuses primarily on HR issues would be workable appears rather doubtful. For instance, at Insurance Company 2 it seemed very unlikely that formal HR strategic planning of a comprehensive nature would prove workable because of its highly emergent corporate strategy. However, this does not necessarily rule out the possibility of an 'issues-based' process of strategic thinking about HR being viable even where the corporate strategy is still somewhat ambiguous. Here, an issues-based process would focus on maybe five to ten (maximum) more critical areas of economic leverage through HR.

 ## CONCLUSIONS FROM THE FINANCIAL SERVICES RESEARCH

The linkages between corporate and HR strategies are clearly much more complex than suggested by the earlier HR literature, making notions of linking these through 'strategic fit' now seem rather naive and simplistic. However, we have seen that HR strategy (or other HR strategy) *could* nevertheless potentially play a major and proactive role in corporate strategy formulation even at the corporate level (and not merely, or primarily, during implementation).

We also found that the internal alignment and internal consistency of HR or HR strategy was of paramount importance, otherwise organizational effectiveness could be substantially impaired. There were a number of specific critical incidents that highlighted the importance of *interdependencies* in actually harvesting the economic value from improved organizational performance.

Doubt was thus cast on the *raison d'être* for a discrete HR strategy. There did seem to be very major disadvantages and drawbacks in keeping corporate and HR strategy as separate entities. Furthermore, there appeared to be a strong case for establishing an 'organization and people' function in organizations, rather than purely HR (providing, of course, that there is not merely a relabelling of the existing HR function). The HR role would be essentially one of HR strategy facilitation, together with joint coordination with line management of specific HR strategic programmes, such as succession planning and management development. This would also help move away from the potentially unsavoury connotations of the acronym HR (sometimes cynically referred to by managers as 'Human Remains' or, by one anonymous commentator, as 'Human Racehorse Department', hell-bent on producing theoretical super-beings).

Now that we have explored our framework for linking HR strategy with corporate strategy, Chapter 3 applies this to the case of Dyson Appliances. This brings home the importance of these lessons on the interdependencies and potential integration of HR strategy and corporate/business strategy.

CHECKLISTS

1. To what extent have you got a well-articulated and robust deliberate corporate/business strategy to link HR strategy to?
2. Might new corporate/business strategy ideas be generated by starting with your distinctive organizational competencies, or what would be a

most 'natural' strategy for you, rather than generating HR strategy from competitive strategy?

3. Is your competitive strategy internally consistent (e.g. are there opposing – and strong – themes of differentiation and cost leadership simultaneously)? Does this make it hard to formulate a coherent HR strategy?

4. How does HR strategy support brand strategy?

5. How might future changes in distribution strategies in the industry impact on HR strategy?

6. What key behaviours are implied by the businesses critical success factors (to compete effectively), and to what extent can you influence these via HR strategy?

7. How does the HR strategy support and enhance the company's service strategy?

8. Has the company really got the competencies to deliver any new (external) competitive strategies, and to do this very well?

9. Will product/market extensions make the company's organization simply too complex, pushing up costs disproportionately?

10. What have you called your HR strategy, and are there any better/more digestible ways of positioning it (e.g. as 'people' or 'organizational' strategy)?

CHAPTER 3

Linking HR and corporate strategy: Dyson Appliances

■ INTRODUCTION

This shorter and more concrete chapter follows on very closely from Chapter 2. In it we trace the development of Dyson Appliances' corporate/business strategy from the early 1990s to the early 2000s, together with the organization and people strategies and success factors. We argue that by using our framework for linking, this identifies major issues for James Dyson – some he is already addressing, and some that perhaps he may not yet be addressing fully. Our core mission is referred to throughout as 'HR strategy', as this is still the most conventional term currently in use.

Dyson's innovative breakthrough in the carpet-cleaning industry underlines the proactive role of organizational skills and mind-set in generating and sustaining value-based growth. This remarkable story also poses some major organizational dilemmas for the future, which we wait to see whether James Dyson and his team can effectively address.

In the mid-1990s, James Dyson, founding Chairman of Dyson Appliances, decided to take on other (entrenched) players in the domestic carpet-cleaning industry, and with a rather different proposition. He decided to discard the assumption that such devices needed a bag. Dyson decided that, far from adding value for the customer, the bag was actually an unnecessary cost and a bother to replace. Even more radically, Dyson contended that the bag itself actually reduced the effective power (and thus the performance) of the carpet cleaner. Dyson's new product – a distinctively designed yellow, expensive, and of course bagless floor cleaner – gained market leadership in the UK carpet-cleaning market, within around just two years from start-up.

James Dyson invented and patented a device that enabled his cleaners to do without a bag by using a very fast-circling vortex of air. The dust was drawn up into a Perspex tube or cylinder, where it was dropped. Periodically the user would empty out this cylinder without producing a small dust storm, as usually happens with a bag.

Dyson's over-arching corporate goal between 1994 and 1997 appears to have been 'to beat Hoover'. By 1996, Dyson had established himself as market leader in the UK. This was accomplished through a number of 'hard' and 'soft' competitive advantages, illustrated in Table 3.1.

Table 3.1
'Hard' and 'soft' advantages of Dyson cleaners

Hard – competitive strategy	Soft – HR strategy
Patented product	Innovative design process
Superior technology	Innovative marketing
Superior performance	Internal responsiveness
New production site	Young, flexible organization

The results of this strategy were spectacular. In a short time Dyson had achieved a UK market lead. In 2½ years Dyson had moved from employing fewer than 20 people to employing 300, and had a turnover of around £100 million in 1996. By 2000, he had 1500 employees in the UK and an estimated turnover nearing £250 million. In this rapid growth period, Dyson's return on sales was a staggering 20 per cent – most unusual for a manufacturing company.

During the early expansion period, Dyson's HR strategy was partly deliberate and partly emergent. Whilst Dyson deliberately set out to reinvent very young engineers, untainted by mind-sets from larger organizations, he also recruited (through need) commercial managers from a variety of larger (and often rather political) fast-moving consumer goods (FMCG) environments. Anecdotal input from suppliers to Dyson and former employees suggested that this generated a good deal of internal rivalry within management, especially in the late 1990s and early 2000s. This gave it the 'feel' of a more mature organization.

SUSTAINING COMPETITIVE SUCCESS

The critical areas that appeared to drive the value of this initial competitive strategy were:

- Customers' perceptions of the superior value of the Dyson product and their willingness to pay a premium
- The company's ability to satisfy premium customer expectations throughout all of its product and service delivery
- Competitors' inability to compete head-on with Dyson or to evolve an alternative and more effective strategy
- Dyson's ability to harvest a good proportion of his product's premium price through its retail channels

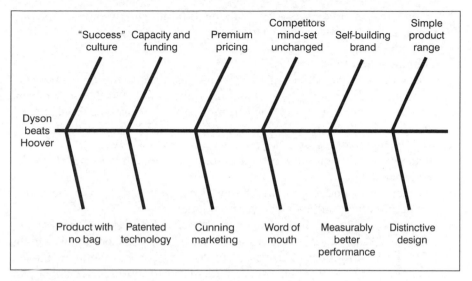

Figure 3.1
Wishbone analysis

- The company's ability to gain cost economies through scale and simplicity of the product range
- The Dyson organization's potential to create sustainable and value-focused innovation, and to avoid the well-documented problems of growing an organization at this speed.

Figure 3.1 represents this through wishbone analysis. To use wishbone analysis, you begin at the left-hand side with your vision/overall objective, and this is then supported by the alignment factors to the right. (These are the necessary and sufficient conditions of success, and need to include one area in which you have low and one in which you have high control and influence.)

Wishbone analysis is a technique for scoping an HR strategy, and also for organizational scenario development (of a positive HR scenario).

Dyson's initial market entry in 1994–1995 saw a rapid development and expansion phase for his organization. This was followed in 1996–2000 by rapid exploitation of the products, primarily in the UK. This called for some kind of review and reflection around 2001–2002, perhaps leading to subsequent adjustment of both competitive and HR strategy.

By 2002, Dyson claimed to have 31 per cent of the UK market in volume terms (and in competitive and organizational terms 50 per cent by value), and UK sales of £251 million (source – *Daily Mail*, 6 February 2002). Taking as read the assumption that one of the key areas for thinking about HR strategy is actually external market and competitive change, the following possible/probable shifts can be identified over 1997–2002:

■ Patents that might expire or be challenged (although Dyson won its long-running court battle against Hoover's 'single cyclone', these are still in the shops)

■ Cunning marketing might be imitated

■ The word-of-mouth effect might become less strong, the Dyson product being in part fashion-dependent and not quite as novel at the present time

■ Customers might query its 'measurably better performance', which it is very hard to measure objectively (in 2001, the *Daily Mail* had several double-page features of customers 'for and against' Dyson')

■ Its design style might have been imitated (as indeed it was, by Electrolux in particular)

■ Competitors' mindsets might change (and *did*) – for example, many competitors now sell a single-cyclone model

■ Most importantly, premium pricing might come under pressure from discounting (from 2000 onwards price pressure from electrical appliance retailers in this increasingly competitive and mature market did become far more intense, resulting in prices dropping between an estimated 10 and 15 per cent in a year, although volumes were still growing by a similar percentage)

■ Volume growth might actually reverse in the UK, as a result of market saturation and/or economic slowdown (whilst that has not happened yet, it might well do so soon).

Potential changes over both periods can be drawn out by using a 'From–to' (FT) analysis, which is a key HR strategy implementation technique. This is shown in Table 3.2.

Table 3.2 suggests perhaps even greater challenges for Dyson than those he needed to manage between his early start-up phase and seizing a dominant UK position in the mid-1990s.

Table 3.2
'From-to' analysis of competitive strategy at Dyson Appliances, 1994–2004

	From 1994–1999	To 2000–2004
Pricing	High price premium	Modest price premium
Competition	Low/medium rivalry	High rivalry
Market growth	Very high	Low
Product performance	Very good	Still good (relatively)
Number of products	Small (two)	Medium (six)
Market focus	Carpet cleaners	Other household products, too
Geographic markets	UK focus	UK and other markets – especially the USA (announced in autumn 2002)
Geographic sourcing	UK	UK and Far East
Cost base	Medium/high	Towards world class
Size	£100m turnover	£250–400 million turnover (more if the US launch succeeds)

FROM COMPETITIVE STRATEGY TO HR STRATEGY

When Dyson initially founded his business, it was much easier to design and implement a high quality organization than at later and possibly more mature phases of development. Dyson was able to put his own personal values into the organization by, for instance:

- Insisting that all new recruits actually built (and subsequently used) their own Dysons when they joined, thus giving them a very close identification with the organization (a 'cunning' HR programme but hard to sustain; with a growing organization you need to keep pace with the new recruits, as doing this 3–6 months in would perhaps be less effective).
- Insisting on healthier food (salads, baguettes etc.) being served in the staff canteen instead of conventional British stodge. Although initially reluctant to convert, staff subsequently became enthused with this healthier food.
- Knowing all of his staff personally by managing by walking about, and thus being intimate with all aspects of the business and its organizational issues. Obviously this was just possible with a staff of 100, it was difficult with 200, very difficult with 300, and mission impossible with 500–1500.

However, with maturity such early and useful initiatives and programmes would inevitably both tire and be insufficient to generate continued organizational energy. In addition, Dyson would have to face the additional difficulties of:

- Having more a complex and multi-layered managerial structure as the company grew and became more complex and diversified
- Recruiting and retaining not just the right quantity of staff but also the right quality (his UK base at Malmesbury might perhaps not be the best location to attract and retain high-calibre and young staff at every level; it boasts an Indian restaurant, a few pubs, and relatively little else).
- Dealing with shifts in organizational style as the organization developed. Inevitably it might become more occupied with budgets, with management processes, and in dealing with problems caused by earlier phases of growth and the additional workload from new innovations.

Therefore, Dyson was to face challenge number one – repositioning his organizational advantage. However, on top of this Dyson had a second challenge to face. As we have already seen, by 2000/2001 Dyson faced mounting external changes that can best be summarized best as a short-term from–to analysis as in Table 3.3.

Table 3.3 suggests that even by early 2000 some radical rethinking of Dyson's cost structure was needed, having a major impact on Dyson's HR strategy too.

Table 3.3
From-to analysis of external changes at Dyson Appliances, 1995–1999

Shifts	From (1995/1996)	To (1998/1999)
Competitive structure	Dyson dominant/ no new entrants	Challenge by Dyson look-alikes/ new entrants
Distribution channels	Low bargaining power	Medium/high bargaining power
UK market penetration	Low	High
Fashion	Very fashionable	Declining novelty (somewhat)
Pricing	High margin by all players	Discounting by some players and low-cost single-cyclone machines

In addition, there were a number of other signs (visible outside Dyson) that the company might well need to review how it was organized/managed. This highlights that it is possible to intuit a good part of a company's HR strategy simply by observation of, for example, its products and advertising, or of press commentary:

■ At Christmas 1999, in John Lewis, the authors spotted that the more expensive Dyson model had two big filters that needed to be replaced each year at a cost of £40. The warning was clear – instead of 'Say goodbye to the Bag', we were now seeing a switch towards 'Say hello to the Filters' – a worrying apparent shift in the mind-set. Fortunately, this move was quickly reversed in 2000. *This suggested that Dyson's innovation drive was being misdirected, and that its managers' commercial skills/judgement could be improved.*

■ On the very same visit, two customers were sold a Miele instead of a Dyson by John Lewis (following the discovery of the £40-a-year filter replacement costs). The John Lewis' sales assistant said to the customers: 'Miele is our best-selling line'. This was notable, as John Lewis stores were an early fan of Dyson and were instrumental in helping him to launch the machine in the UK. *This suggested that its account management skills could be enhanced.*

■ Around 1998/1999, Dyson's advertisements seemed to focus increasingly on the technology edge almost to the exclusion of reference to any real customer benefits – suggesting perhaps too great an internal focus on technology over and above marketing. *This suggested its marketing skills could be sharpened.*

■ In 1999, British newspapers carried stories of the pending launch of a robotic Dyson, which would sell for £2500. Whilst in the longer term a robotic machine would seem attractive to many people, its pricing seemed to be less than commercial. This was in contrast to Dyson's original product launch, which was at a good but not unrealistic premium. Had Dyson's urge to be technologically innovative become too dominant here? *This suggested a need to upgrade its strategic thinking skills.*

■ The Dyson contra-rotator washing machine was launched in 2001 at a price of between £1000–£2000, which again seemed high relative to competition in a well-served market. This was presumably driven by Dyson's desire for innovative technology, and may not have been well thought through strategically and commercially. Again, was Dyson's technological thrust getting the better of his commercial astuteness? (The jury is still out in this one.) *This again suggests improvements in strategic thinking/commercial skills.*

The above observations (outside Dyson) also suggest that just possibly Dyson's organizational mind-set was becoming more like those of other mature organizations, as we suggested earlier. *Was it thus in need of a culture change programme of some form?*

In terms of putting economic value on HR strategy, the impact of the contra-rotator washing machine and the robotic Dyson could well have been:

- To absorb many millions of pounds of unproductive investment
- To have created unnecessary organizational complexity, slowing the organization down and displacing other, better opportunities, with millions of pounds of profit
- To have diluted Dyson's brand strength with products that proved to be far less successful than the original Dyson models.

With hindsight, what might Dyson have paid to have avoided these areas of economic value dilution and destruction (potentially £10 million–£20 million)?

On top of this, Dyson would inevitably have issues surrounding leadership and management – it is always difficult when an owner/entrepreneur manages a business throughout different phases of corporate growth. More typically, around this stage we might see James Dyson changing his role (for instance becoming Non-Executive Chairman). Even Stelios at Easygroup decided to step down as Chairman of Easyjet in May 2002, to provide a more robust basis for future growth and development.

Table 3.4 provides a summary of the potential issues facing Dyson as of 2001, first from strategic issues to organizational issues, and then to HR strategy breakthroughs (this follows the logic of Chapter 2).

Notice that in this analysis:

- There is not just a focus on cost reduction, but also on innovation in customer value (*vis-à-vis* both customers and distribution channels). For example, one possible initiative that might be suggested would be not just to get new Dyson staff to build a Dyson (a current HR practice), but also to get them to sell it and to review the satisfaction with its use and with its entire service over its lifetime (from a 'cunning plan/ to a 'stunning plan'). And what could this be worth, in terms of economic value? Possibly hundreds of thousands of pounds worth of cost savings per annum through better decision-making (everyone in the organization

Table 3.4
Potential issues facing Dyson Appliances, 2001

Strategic issues	Organizational issues	HR strategic breakthroughs
Maturity of UK market/price war?	Cost innovation	Cost management training/processes
Marketing/product development strategy	Decision-making process/skills	Strategic/commercial skills
Increasing competition	Customer value innovation	Initiatives to get close to the customer
	Restructuring and sourcing from other suppliers	Redundancies/redeployment Rebuilding morale in Malmesbury
International opportunity/ challenge	International sales division	Hiring staff for its expansion
Labour market skill shortages	Internal shortages for expansion	Cunning recruitment strategy
Brand positioning	Better brand management	Recruitment
Responsiveness to change	Mind-set and capabilities	James Dyson's role change and new management skills Culture change programme and initiatives Career development, salary package, etc.

would then be intimate with product problems throughout each appliance's lifecycle, and would wish to eradicate these difficulties).

■ 'Structure change' is not just seen in isolation from culture shift. Also, were major redundancies in Malmesbury being contemplated, as this would require a significant rebuilding of morale? (This actually occurred.)

■ Whilst there were (as of 2001) significant shortages at all levels of skills for Dyson, this would clearly be mitigated (except at senior management level) by a major downsizing of operations in Malmesbury.

In February 2002 Dyson announced that the manufacture of Dyson cyclonic carpet cleaners would cease in Malmesbury and would be transferred to the Far East, with the loss of 800 jobs. The Dyson washing machine 'would continue to be produced in Malmesbury'.

James Dyson was quoted (*Daily Mail*, 6 February 2002) as saying that Far East production made it 30 per cent cheaper to make a cleaner there than in the UK. Some key strategic HR (and related) questions for Dyson at this juncture might be:

1. Was this shift not foreseeable at an earlier stage of Dyson's evolution – possibly in 1999/2000, when competition intensified, or even sooner (using competitive scenario techniques/and knowledge of how other industries have matured in the past)? If this had been foreseen using strategic think-

ing (see Chapter 12), the value would have been in the order of millions of pounds.

2. If his statement is true, then this is a huge different in costs, and so why did Dyson not consider overseas operations much sooner – by thinking ahead? And does this suggest a need for breakthrough in the organiza- tion's strategic thinking skills?

3. Have Dyson's aggressive attempts at product innovation/diversification with the robotic Dyson and the Dyson washing machine distracted him from more fundamental issues surrounding his core operations? And has this led to his pursuing this diversification over and above potentially more attractive geographic expansion internationally (until 2002)?

4. Has Dyson thought through the impact of overseas manufacture on the quality of the product and of Dyson's brand? And what HR changes will be needed to support these shifts?

5. What level of capability and role will be needed from Dyson's HR depart- ment to support these massive changes?

6. How would Dyson now attract top-class skills management skills to the organization of the right calibre and mind-set?

7. How can decision-making and power be shared with his senior managers so that Dyson's transition to an entrepreneurial/and professional organ- ization (as opposed to a primarily entrepreneurial one) be achieved?

8. Were Dyson to contemplate any new strategies, how would these be organized? (For example, if Dyson decided upon an alliance internation- ally with say Electrolux or Panasonic, how would this be managed?) Or if Dyson were to further his innovational product development, perhaps this could be done as a new nursery unit called The Dyson Centre for Innovation, perhaps with involvement from companies like Virgin, Easygroup and venture capitalists?

Looking to the future, we can now summarize some of the organization and people strategy shifts and breakthroughs resourced by Dyson in the

Table 3.5
Changes required in HR strategy at Dyson Appliances, 1994–2005

Competitive strategy	HR strategy		HR breakthrough
	1994–1999	2000–2004	
Pricing and competition and market growth	Dominant mind-set	Lean and hungry mind-set	Culture change
Product performance	Technology focus	Customer benefit focus	Organization change/new skills in design
Number of products/ new markets, international, size change	Simple structure led by James Dyson	Divisional/matrix with professional CEO	Organization change/new management team and international
Geographical sourcing /cost base	UK manufacture	Global manufacturing	International managers recruited

future (see Table 3.5). These from–to scenarios can now be linked to the changes required in organization and people strategy in 1994–2002, and 2002–2005 (again following the logic of Chapter 2).

In Table 3.5 we can trace the linkages between competitive and HR strategy by identifying the shifts in emphasis in Dyson's differentiation strategy, a large reduction in costs (to cope with price pressure), and a more complex set of businesses – entailing a new organization structure and style. Future shifts would entail a big change in James Dyson's own role and – the very hard part – the establishment of a professional and entrepreneurial top team to carry forward his vision and values. (Besides defining what you are going to change in HR strategy, you also need to define what you are *not* going to change.)

KEY LESSONS

The key lessons for HR strategy from the Dyson case study are that:

- The organizational mind-set can provide the spark for innovative strategic thinking, but it can also (in maturity) be the biggest brake on strategic development, and the costs of this are quite tangible, and potentially quantifiable
- The organizational mind-set is likely to push a company around down a non-optimal route for strategic development (the Dyson robotic or washing machine?)
- HR strategy (or organization and people strategy) has a very big role in helping shape that mind-set, and in helping to put in place the attitudes, skills and processes to support the brand, international expansion, and customer-based innovation
- HR strategy has a major role in any cost reduction/major operational change
- HR strategy needs to have a focus on organizational process as well as skills (e.g. strategic planning, financial appraisal, resource allocation, and product development processes)
- Skills shortages should be a major focus for HR strategy – this is tied up with a variety of HR strategic initiatives involving recruitment strategies, reward and recognition, career development, company values and style, and management processes
- Ultimately, HR strategy needs to grapple with very difficult appointment/succession/transition issues regarding very senior management positions
- Unless HR strategy plays an effective and incisive role in all of these areas, then strategic drift can easily intensify and accelerate – leading to potential ultimate competitive and financial failure.

Case postscript

In late 2002, Dyson's profits fell from £22.5 million to £11.5 million 'largely due to higher production and administrative expenses' (*Mail on Sunday*, 20 November 2002). Was this the beginning of difficult times for Dyson, especially as (in the summer of 2002) he announced he was going to enter the USA (thus creating a war on two fronts)?

CHECKLISTS

1. What external competitive changes are affecting your own market
   - Now
   - In the future?
2. What implications are there from these issues regarding your future organization, and what HR strategic breakthroughs do these suggest?
3. How does your organizational mind-set influence key decisions and ways of operating and thinking, and how does this need to change or develop?
4. What 'cunning plans' might be created for:
   - Organizational design
   - Leadership
   - Recruitment and retention
   - Motivation and identification with company goals
   - Organizational creativity
   - Organizational cost reduction?
5. What economic value might be created (or value destruction avoided) by pursuing these HR strategic breakthroughs (relative to not pursuing theory or just doing minimalistic actions)?

CHAPTER 4

Organizational scenarios

■ INTRODUCTION

In this chapter we will survey how organizational scenarios can be useful in developing HR strategy. Organizational scenarios involve storytelling about the future. This is a perhaps more difficult process than strategic analysis, as it involves a degree of creativity, imagination and synthesis, and is thus not a particularly deductive, linear process.

■ THE ROLE OF STORY-TELLING

Scenarios have been popular for many years (particularly with Shell managers and planners), but for many the notion of scenario development appears difficult and time-consuming, and is one of uncertain benefit. It is perhaps ironic that the most effective tool for dealing with uncertainty is rarely used because managers are so uncertain as to how to use it and of what value it will be. In fact, scenario development can occur rapidly and add disproportionate value relative to effort.

The key questions that are addressed here are:

1. What are scenarios?
2. How can scenarios help?
3. How can scenarios be developed – and quickly?

Scenarios are:

■ Internally consistent views of the future that focus on discontinuity and change (not on continuity), and also involve exploring how the under-lying systems in the business environment may generate change
■ Views of how the competitive players (existing and new) might behave.

Scenarios are not static and comprehensive views of the future. They are in many ways more like a video film – of necessity selective, but containing a dynamic storyline. Scenarios thus contain a series of views (pictures) of the future. This is fruitfully presented as a series of pictures, not as a single one. There is also a storyline that enables these pictures to hang together.

The story can be run (again like a video film) forward or backward. By replaying the story you can work backwards from a particular scenario to see what events might bring about a particular outcome (these events are called 'transitional events').

Just as strategy is frequently defined as a pattern in a stream of (past and current) decisions, so a scenario is a pattern of future events, and of the interaction between customers, competitors and other key players in the industry.

Next, although many managers understand change they are frequently bemused by the idea of 'discontinuity'. Discontinuity simply means a major break between past and future. Discontinuity can occur imperceptibly (for example, just as a train may be switched from one line to another), or it can happen abruptly and with a big jolt (or, even in its most extreme form, through derailment).

Finally, scenarios are not about creating abstract pictures (this is not modern art). As in cartoons, scenarios show players in the market doing specific things and behaving in specific ways.

Scenarios are not therefore an excuse to make broad or vague generalizations: as they are pictures, they have a clarity about them that will enable recognition. Managers need to know which world they are entering into, and the resolution therefore has to be sharp, not fuzzy. In Ansoff's terms (1965), they are ways of picking up, amplifying and interpreting weak signals in the environment.

Scenarios, like all pictures, will thus have a foreground and a background, some features of central interest, and others that are more peripheral.

By now it should have become evident what scenarios are *not*. Scenarios are not:

- Mere forecasts
- Projections from past trends
- Fixed or rigid world views
- Complete in all details
- Static.

When doing scenario analysis for the first time with a management team, it is imperative to make these distinctions – particularly, to avoid the rabbit warren of projections and forecasts.

Scenarios can help in a number of ways. Scenario planning at Shell is principally known for its very 'big picture' analysis, particularly for global or industry-broad scenarios, or for country-specific scenarios. In addition, managers can perform issue-specific scenarios (for example, the impact of regulating/environmental pressure), or scenarios specific to a particular strategic decision.

THE SCENARIO-GENERATING PROCESS

Some time ago a major company wanted to explore how to set about accelerating scenario development. The company had used scenarios to a limited

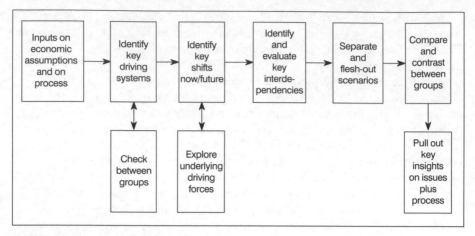

Figure 4.1
A scenario-generation process

extent in the past, but had found them to be slow and arduous to create. The challenge set was this: how could a small number of scenarios be created for a key market in under a day?

A small (but hand-picked) team was assembled, which included the representatives, technical experts and planning staff, and an external consultant whose task was to design and facilitate the process, not to give expert input on scenario content. (Note that it is in fact useful to have two small teams working in parallel on the scenario, with core common assumptions but with deliberate divergence at the later stages of the process.) Once the issue had been defined, a number of key questions aimed at probing views of the future were defined. These were supported by the process in Figure 4.1.

This begins by setting the broad background to the scenario. Just because it is looking at a scenario of the future, it doesn't mean that all assumptions are left open.

Next, the key driving systems impacting on the environment are identified. For instance, for the do-it-yourself UK retail market in the late 1990s the following were identified:

- Changes in social and demographic lifestyles (e.g. the breakdown of the 'nuclear' family)
- The impact of the housing market
- Changes in leisure patterns
- The pattern of rivalry in the marketplace (for example, the grocery chain Sainsbury bought the out-of-town DIY retailer, Texas, in the UK).

A number of systems in the external environment interact with each other here. This interaction is fluid and has key clusters of influences – particularly those regarding the housing market and the economy, family leisure patterns, and also competitive rivalry.

Here is a quick run-through of the scenario storyline, which was written in 1995 for the period 1995–2000:

- There is a Labour government and slightly higher taxes, with these eroding the incomes of income-rich people but not specifically of DIY fanatics
- Reducing unemployment, making it hard to get tradespeople to do things at a reasonable price in the home
- The (now) dominant player, as it happens Sainsbury's, therefore begins to make very good profits out of DIY, especially as no new sites can be opened (due to planning restrictions)
- Profitability per outlet goes up.

Once this analysis has been performed, it is then possible to identify those variables that are likely to be particularly unstable (annotated as a green 'U') and high impact (annotated as a red 'I'). Variables that are either or both U and I may then suggest some possible key shifts between 'new' and 'future'.

The next phase is to identify the biggest and most sensitive areas of interdependency. This helps identify these clusters of variables (and thus the shifts in 'from–to') that, once begun, could have an unstoppable momentum.

In order to separate and flesh-out specific scenarios, it is useful to turn once again to the uncertainty grid. This enables the identification of the one or more assumptions that are both extremely uncertain and very important. This assumption (the 'danger zone') normally suggests a specific scenario route.

(A practical issue is the need to make sure that each scenario group works together as a coherent team to define and then evaluate each assumption and its positioning. Frequently managers are tempted to delegate the positioning of each assumption to different individuals, who then work independently. This may lead to confusion over both what the assumption really means and why it has been positioned in a certain way. It is often faster and more effective to work together as a small team rather than to do fragmented individual work.)

Once the route has been chosen, fleshing out the various scenarios involves reviewing the key interdependencies and the potential major shifts, and then creating a storyline about how the scenario could actually come about. This storyline would entail considering things like the following:

- What will the industry (or niche or organization) really look like?
- How will the key players behave?
- What transitional events might bring this scenario about?

A most useful technique is to role-play competitors and how they might behave in the storyline of the scenario (and, for that matter, other key players like major customers, suppliers or the regulator). This helps to inject more life and dynamism into the scenario picture.

Once a small number of scenarios have been developed, they should be then exposed to cross-testing by the two teams. This will help to:

■ Reveal why particular assumptions were thought to be most important and most uncertain (and, conversely, those that are thought to be less important and most certain)
■ Draw out the implications for strategy, and for the critical success factors
■ Begin to bring out the financial implications of the scenario
■ Bring line managers and planners together to create scenarios
■ Examine key shifts in your views of the world
■ Ensure that these feed directly into planning/decision-making processes
■ Avoid too many views of the future (preferably keep to two)
■ Manage concerns that 'we will never get the right (precise) answer' – scenarios are not about doing forecasts
■ Use a few analysis tools, avoid lots of detailed data input, and free the mind to be creative
■ Refine and revisit scenarios, especially where new signals are detected in the business environment.

ORGANIZATIONAL SCENARIOS – TECHNIQUES

This section covers:

■ Uncertainty grids
■ The uncertainty tunnel and uncertainty-over-time curve.

Uncertainty grids

One way of testing the external and internal assumptions underpinning a strategy is by using a qualitative uncertainty–importance grid (see Figure 4.2, derived from Mitroff and Linstone, 1993). Using this grid, managers can plot the key assumptions driving the value of any strategic decision. These can be external and internal, soft and hard assumptions.

Having selected a sub-set of assumptions, these are now prioritized by using the grid (which can be a flip-chart, a whiteboard, or a piece of paper). Once assumptions have been carefully and skilfully defined, it is possible to debate the relative importance and uncertainty of these various assumptions (using a flip-chart, the assumptions can be easily moved around using 'post-it' notes).

These assumptions are defined in terms of 'the future world being OK'. For example, if we were using it to understand the uncertainties of getting to a meeting in London on time, an assumption would be defined as 'the trains will run on time' rather than 'the trains will not run on time'.

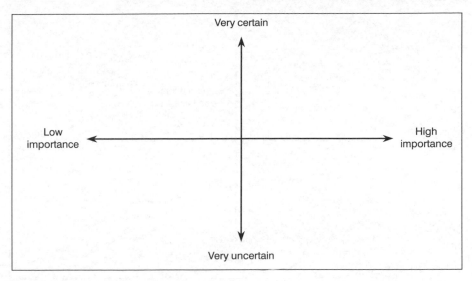

Figure 4.2
The uncertainty–importance grid

A frequent mistake (when first using the grid) is to have some assumptions defined positively and some negatively. This makes it impossible to judge the overall downsides to a strategy. An example of this would be 'Kings Cross Station might be closed' (a negative assumption), and 'there will be no London Underground strike that day' (a positive assumption).

At the beginning of the investment appraisal, key assumptions are likely to be mapped in the due north and northeast quadrants. Upon testing, it is quite common to find one or more assumptions moving over to the danger zone in the southeast.

Figure 4.3 relates to a new product launch. The extra sales volume from existing customers is very important, but is also considered relatively certain. Sales to new customers are considerably more uncertain (but also very important), as is shown in the southeast of the grid. Product launch costs are somewhat less important and are also reasonably certain (shown just slightly northwest of the centre of the grid).

Interestingly, a more fundamental assumption – implicit in managers' minds but brought out by discussion of the grid – is that competitors will not imitate with a better product in year two. In Figure 4.3, this assumption is shown as beginning life just east of the product launch costs assumption (relatively certain and less important), but actually heading southeast.

The uncertainty grid is very helpful for targeting data collection. This should be aimed at learning more about those assumptions that are most important, more uncertain, or both, and noting those bits of data that are just easier to collect.

The uncertainty grid is often misunderstood by managers for a number of reasons (Figure 4.4):

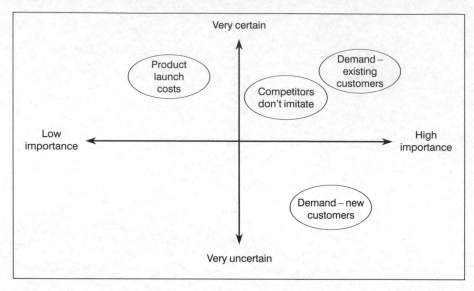

Figure 4.3
Completed uncertainty–importance grid (example)

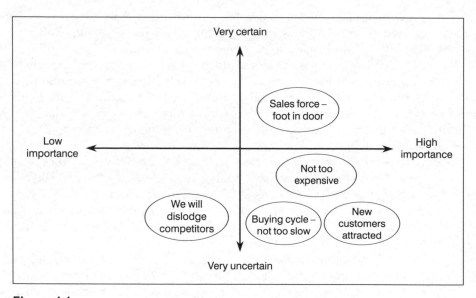

Figure 4.4
The uncertainty–importance grid analysed

■ Their mind-set is one of putting on the grid what they will actually do to achieve the strategy. Whilst it is perfectly possible to use the grid in this way, when conducting preliminary strategic analysis this is inappropriate and premature.

- Managers are not used to thinking explicitly about their assumptions, as these are taken for granted.
- Managers find it very hard to think about, let alone creatively to imagine, the future.
- Sometimes managers want to put probabilities on the grid, rather than leave it as qualitative – especially if they come from a more technical background. However, the point of the grid is to think through (unquantified) degrees of uncertainty rather than to focus on more easy-to-quantify risks.

The uncertainty grid can be used before an HR strategy decision, during its implementation, or at post-review. Indeed it is perhaps at its most powerful when tracking live implementation of a strategy. Here, assumptions that were implicit previously often crystallize in a startling and unexpected way as being both most important and most uncertain.

The key benefits of the uncertainty grid are that:

- It helps to identify the vulnerable points and blind spots in a strategy
- It helps managers to focus on the future, rather than on the present
- Its simple format allows it to be used at a very intuitive level, so that paper representation is not really essential.

Its disbenefits are that:

- It is somewhat counter the mind-set of many managers, who need to practise it a couple of times to make it work
- Managers are sometimes unsure as to what level of analysis it should be used at.

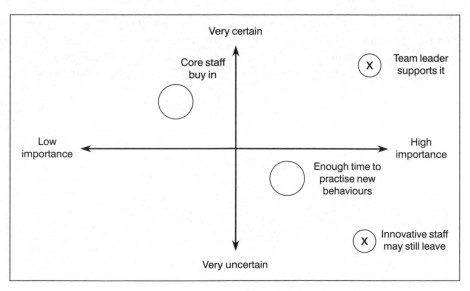

Figure 4.5
A mini uncertainty–importance grid – culture shift

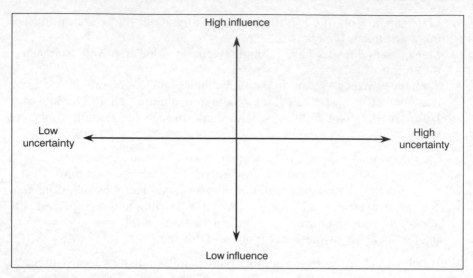

Figure 4.6
Uncertainty–influence analysis

To help with the latter point, it can be useful to do a micro-level uncertainty grid and then break down one of the assumptions using a separate and more detailed uncertainty grid. For example, in Figure 4.5 we break down the assumptions that underpin a shift associated with team-building.

It is really helpful here to make the assumptions as specific as possible, as the effect of being specific is to shift the assumption on the grid – often on both axes.

Finally, asking the question 'What is the one big thing we have missed?' can be extremely helpful in covering blind spots.

As associated technique is the uncertainty–influence grid, shown in Figure 4.6. Here the horizontal axis is low uncertainty versus high uncertainty, and

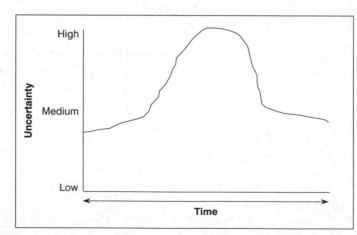

Figure 4.7
Uncertainty-over-
time curve

the vertical axis is high influence versus low influence. Again we plot the key assumptions on the grid assuming that the world is going well.

The uncertainty tunnel and uncertainty-over-time curve

Uncertainty is dynamic, and Figure 4.7 helps us to understand the phases of scenario development, its speed and impact. It also maps the way in which uncertainty changes over time. On the vertical axis there is the degree of uncertainty – whether it is low, medium or high. The horizontal axis is the time dimension. Figure 4.7 is an example of how uncertainty might increase and then actually decrease significantly once the impact of change in a market has worked its way through. An example of this would be a global economic turnaround during which there is initially general confusion generally. This culminates in a financial crisis, exhibiting great turbulence and uncertainty. Subsequently the major world economies stabilize and consolidate, and uncertainty reduces.

This curve can be plotted either for the total uncertainty of a particular strategy, or for that of a particular assumption. In order to place some prioritization on a particular assumption, we can then map its importance over time using Figure 4.8.

These subsidiary techniques can help support the scenario storyline, which we discussed earlier.

The benefits of scenario development are that:

- Scenarios can help us to 'see around corners', and thus to cope with uncertainty
- They make managers more sensitive to and alert to changes in their external and internal environments
- They get managers to 'think future' in a way that conventional planning often does not
- They encourage us to think about how we can create a desired future.

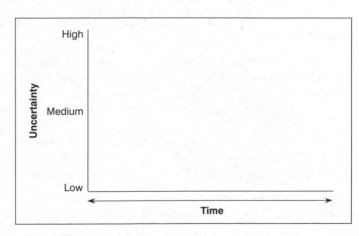

Figure 4.8
Plotting an importance-over-time curve

Scenarios are linked to other tools as follows:

- With wishbone analysis, they help to construct a desired future (see Chapter 3)
- With attractiveness–implementation difficulty (AID) analysis, force field analysis and stakeholder analysis, they help in imagining internal futures (see Chapter 6)
- With fishbone analysis (see Chapter 6), they can help to identify events that lead to negative scenarios (see Chapter 6).

APPLICATIONS TO HR STRATEGY

Scenarios can be applied to a variety of issues in HR strategy. First, they are applicable to organizational restructuring, to foretell stories of the future where the restructuring undergoes a smooth transitional path versus ones where it is highly disruptive. Second, they are relevant to identifying the future competency shifts – what will be needed to deal with future organizational challenges (this can be accompanied by a 'from–to' analysis; see Chapter 6). Third, they can be used in conjunction with HR succession and development planning (as in our Amersham Pharmaceuticals case study in Chapter 9).

Besides these higher-level organizational issues, scenarios can also be used for implementation of specific HR strategy projects, for example:

- Performance management systems
- Interventions to reduce stress
- Team-building
- Training programmes
- Off-site workshops
- Appraisal interviews
- Senior management appointments
- Rolling out company values
- Acquisition integration, etc.

At an even more micro-level, scenarios can be helpful for a particular individual – for example in:

- Foreseeing how a particular relationship might develop between the individual and another member of staff in the organization (for example, the boss, a colleague, or a subordinate)
- The individual's career strategy, and how it is likely to develop within the organization
- How a specific role might develop for that individual
- The possible lead-up events to an individual being made redundant (so that he or she can spot the warning signs early on).

Obviously, the formal tools that we have already outlined (like systems thinking, the uncertainty tunnel, the uncertainty-importance grid) are very

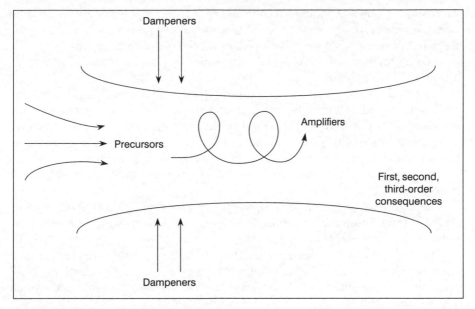

Figure 4.9
The uncertainty tunnel

helpful in providing a stimulus to thinking about the future (Figure 4.9). However, the most important thing to remember is to 'think future' – that is, set your mental clock at some future date, rather than on 'now'.

ORGANIZATIONAL SCENARIOS – EXAMPLES

In order to practise scenarios, let us first look at this imaginary everyday example of a couple's problems in dealing with an organization with uneven capability.

Homesick Homes

A couple moved into a brand new deluxe home in the south east of England. The five-bedroom executive home was a one-off speciality design nestling in undulating wooded countryside just ten minutes drive from the rich commuter belt, with a fast train service to central London. Home to both some of the wealthiest estate agents in the country and also reputed to have one of the highest rates of millionaires per square mile, this location is a most exclusive and desirable commuter spot.

The area attracted a niche property development company, called 'Homesick Homes', which opportunistically developed some one-off sites. (It was called 'Homesick Homes' to indicate that as soon as you went away from home for more than a day or so, you would feel intensively homesick.) Its website boasted of exclusive, personally tailored developments, implying that it was a highly successful builder of niche homes with a reputation for personalized service and care.

Homesick Homes was a small building firm with a small number of core staff, and relied extensively on subcontractors. The property market was overheated at the time and it was very difficult indeed to resource quality subcontractors to do quality work. Homesick Homes found it difficult to attract and retain core staff, especially site project managers, partly due to its haphazard management style and lack of quality management processes.

The company had been in business just a few years, and this was part of its early foray into an area adjacent to its home county, with its head office being some distance away.

The company was funded by outside investors. As this transaction had been held up, there was a lot of pressure on the couple to complete by 30 June in order (according to Homesick) 'to avoid paying extra interest' (which seemed odd, and was queried by the couple).

It was mid-2002, at the height of a housing boom, and the couple's housing transaction had been bogged down by a sluggish buyer and their building society. Not sure that the deal would actually go through, Homesick Homes redeployed its resources on other properties so the couple's house was almost, but not quite, finished off.

At last the couple were ready to exchange, and as this was an entirely new house the couple dispensed with any thought of a full structural survey. They assumed that anything newly built to a high specification by an established builder with NHBC certification must be OK.

Just before exchange of contracts, they met with Sandy Quickbuild, its Sales Director. Sandy oozed with charm and, waving an NHBC booklet (which detailed the protection against building problems for 10 years), explained how the couple had complete come-back if anything went wrong.

Sandy explained the procedure:

On the day before completion, if you saw the property you would think 'how on earth will they finish this off in time?' But we will send a crack team of finishers and cleaners in, who will buzz around for several hours. At the end of it you will not believe the result.

(Apparently at 1 am on the day of completion the house's very large drive was still occupied by six cars – the team still had not finished!)

He continued:

But what I would ask you is to wait for quite a few weeks and to come up with *just one snagging list* so that we can organize things rather than to-ing and fro-ing.

Exercise 1

What scenario(s) can you relate about the world not going right for the couple – particularly in terms of how Homesick Homes might behave if things were not to go as the couple expected?

You might wish to consider (on the uncertainty–importance grid) such things as:

- Homesick Homes is able to get adequate staff to finish the job
- Homesick Homes is true to its work
- Homesick will not go bust.

This seemed to the couple to be quite a sensible arrangement. They were sensible people who were quite relaxed at that point, and agreed.

Following completion, the couple moved into their wonderful new home. Quite a few things were not as they would have liked or expected, and they drew up a list of 50 'snagging' items.

Later that week, they were asked by Sandy Quickbuild what kind of gate they wanted fitting to the front of their house. Apparently the builders had fitted a tailored gate to the sister property, which they had just completed.

The couple were passing this second property that night and stopped to have a look at the gate. As they had 5 minutes to spare, they knocked on the door to say 'hello', and to introduce themselves as the (still) proud owners of a similar property. The new owners appeared at the door and said they had had some 'major problems' with the house. These major problems included:

- Kitchen units not properly fitted: these flew out of their fittings (of their own volition)
- An expensive conservatory that had caused endless problems
- Windows cracking (which subsequently had to be replaced – throughout the entire house!)
- The drive had to be completely relaid.

The couple decided that it was necessary to get a full structural survey on their own house. A local surveyor came round 24 hours later and found another 100 snagging items – including several important concerns that raised NHBC compliance issues. They confronted Sandy Quickbuild at a meeting. Initially he seemed cooperative, but with hindsight this appeared to have been a front. This resulted in the couple insisting on dealing instead with Homesick's Construction Director, Ronald Land.

Again, Ronald appeared to be cooperative initially, but when it actually came to rectifying the problems he seemed to get slower and slower, and became increasingly elusive. They contacted Homesick's MD, who was continually on holiday, but promised to 'turn over a new leaf', saying that his staff had been instructed to do whatever was necessary to fix their problems.

Ronald Land left the remedial work in the hands of Rick Pram, who appeared to be the troubleshooter drafted in to deal with a number of Homesick's properties that appeared to have gone pear-shaped.

Exercise 2

What was behind Homesick's malaise organizationally? Were these symptoms a reflection of a deeper syndrome of organizational drift or decay? Was it a sustainable business, and would the couple ever get their snagging list (including more fundamental defects) fixed?

The couple then drew up a number of organizational scenarios for Homesick:

- Scenario A: Homesick Homes gets its act together, the MD returns from holiday, but the company makes slow progress.
- Scenario B: the couple 'go nuclear', getting the local press around, writing to the planning authorities, making an NHBC complaint, and threatening to sue the builder. This produces action.
- Scenario C: this is the same as scenario B but the builder procrastinates, dragging the whole process out by 6 months, and even then some things aren't fixed.
- Scenario D: this is the same as scenario B, but the builder goes bust in the meantime.
- Scenario E: the end of Homesick Homes.

Scenario storytelling: the end of Homesick Homes

The Directors of Homesick Homes and the site manager, Rick Pram, collude with each other to pretend to fix the lot, but always delay delivery. They are so inundated by complaints that they spread resources evenly between their various irate customers, making their remedial work ineffective.

Rick Pram leaves the company for a six-month trip to Australia before important works are done. Several house owners sue the company. Homesick Homes cannot finish any new builds (or start them) because of their quality problems. Cash flow deteriorates, and the builders go bust in mid-February 2003. The couple have to employ a local odd-job man to finish the snagging list, with major structural items to be done (eventually – by March 2003) through the NHBC.

The Directors of Homesick start a new company (with their wives as Directors), called Phoenix Developments, in 2003, and appear on *Watchdog*, the consumer television programme in mid-2003.

Case postscript – Homesick Homes

The competencies needed by Homesick Homes in order to compete success-fully in their exclusive niche markets are illustrated in Table 4.1.

Notice that this organization *was* focused on some of the more crucial competencies, to build its constructions in the first place. This suggests that much of the malaise was due to its embarking on too ambitious a growth strategy whilst not resourcing itself well enough organizationally. However, the inevitable prognosis was that unless Homesick began to deal effectively with its backlog of at least four defectively finished properties, it would not be free of distractions to work on new ones competently. Either its customers or its suppliers (or both) would sue the company – perhaps in concert – and it would go bust.

Table 4.1
Competencies required by Homesick Homes

Competencies	Score out of 10 (10 = excellent, 1 = very poor)
Marketing/charm	6
Site identification	7
Basic construction	7
Tailoring	4
Finishing	0
Snagging resolution	1
Project management	1
Customer service (after sales)	2
Commercial skills	3
Organization (generally)	2
Total (out of 100)	33 (a very bad fail)

Perhaps Homesick Homes could have been taken over by a bigger builder? But this begs the question as to what value could be extracted by another organization, given its frailties.

This has given a very tangible account of storytelling, and we will now move on to a case study concerning BT.

Case study: organizational scenarios at BT

Around 1996, a small team from BT met to evolve some scenarios of BT's future. Armed with the uncertainty grid, the uncertainty tunnel and stakeholder analysis, they set about creating some challenging views of BT's organizational future – with a 3- to 5-year time horizon. This was against the assumed context of exist-ing competitive challenges – greater competition and price pressure, regulatory influences, and rapid technology change and globalization.

BT had at the time just gone through some major downsizing. It was said that between one Friday to the following Monday, BT shed over 10 000 staff – without loss of business continuity. So whilst further major downsizing was not out of the question, any major rethinking of BT's organizational size seemed somewhat far-fetched.

However, the team set out to challenge this thinking. This was done through a combination of:

- Taking the time horizons further out into the future than 12–18 months
- Challenging assumptions about the necessary scale and complexity of BT
- Using 'zero-based' thinking (or building up from a very low resource base).

The assumptions about the future made were that:

- Price pressures would continue, to sustain volume/market share
- There would be possible further efficiency savings, through automation, technology advance and changes in working practices
- The present top management would remain in place for the foreseeable future.

This collective set of assumptions did prove to be an easy foundation for the scenario development. In particular, it was questioned as to whether the assumption that the present top management would remain in place for the foreseeable future posed too much of a constraint for the organization to rethink its internal size fundamentally.

The team then decided to relax this assumption and try to describe a world in which, 2 years out in the future, there was a different leadership at BT – one that was prepared to bite the bullet on major organizational change.

The organizational storyline that then emerged – of a more radical overhaul of BT's organization with further technology investment and simplified processes – then began to hang together as a self-consistent scenario. Indeed, radical insights about what BT might look like in the future quickly emerged.

However, what was still missing was the link between the present and that particular organizational future. The team needed to assume some transitional event, and this was:

There will be a major change in leadership within BT at CEO level.

Only in that context could BT begin to contemplate the radical organizational overhaul that appeared to be dictated by its future competitive environment. Following discussion of the *exante* factors (the 'precursors') that could bring such a transitional event about (both external and internal), it was decided that this was conditional on the appointment of a new leader. (The team was effectively using the 'uncertainty tunnel', as in Figure 4.9).

The next major variable was, who would be appointed? The team drew up a profile for the new leader based on the competencies needed to lead and transform BT. The profile they came up with was of someone:

- With CEO experience in an adjacent industry (probably computing)
- With a successful track record of managing an organization through strategic change

■ With highly developed strategic vision and commercial competencies.

The 'amplifiers' of this change were to be internal pressures for change and external pressure from financial and competitive markets. The 'dampeners' were BT's traditional culture and the existing incumbent's agenda to stay on.

Using the 'uncertainty tunnel' concept, the team then talked through a possible storyline of the potential consequences of this new appointment. The first-order consequences of this appointment were that BT's management would be in a state of insecurity and some turmoil during the first 6 months.

The second-order consequences were that, following questioning of the strategy and of BT's plans by the new Chief Executive, tighter targets would be set, and the first moves to break down the organization into more market-focused business units would occur.

The third-order consequences were that BT would indicate a new corporate strategy – perhaps floating-off some of its business units, making new acquisitions, etc.

From 1996 to 2000, these storylines seemed to be remarkably close to real events within BT. Indeed, the resemblance between reality and the storyline verged on the uncanny. Sir Derek Benfield behaved on cue, following almost an identical pattern of behaviour and action – so much so that in 2000 one of the team's former facilitators had a sense of *déjà vu* when watching some business news on television and hearing BT's top management's words. So this scenario was 'accurate', even though that is never the intent of a scenario.

The organizational scenario described above did not extend into Phase 4, the effects of BT's strategy changes/business restructuring. Indeed, it would have been very interesting to bring into the storyline for 2000–2002 a knock-on scenario of over-investment into generation mobile telecommunications, and of pan-European acquisitions not working out.

However, the scenario *did* reveal:

■ That the event stream to focus on was that of changes in top leadership within BT.

■ That the influence of behavioural factors on BT's strategic decision-making process and thus on BT's future was considerable.

■ The importance of judging lags between cause and effect in the stream of scenario events – and how quickly these effects might crystallize.

■ The importance of stakeholder analysis (and of the 'out-of-body' experiences) in driving any internal transitional events (see Chapter 6). This event might lead to an in-depth analysis of the agendas of a very small number of stakeholders.

■ The close interdependence of both external (and competitive) and internal (and organizational) factors in defining the storyline.

PLANNING AND IMPLEMENTING A SCENARIO WORKSHOP

The following are important requirements in running an HR strategy scenario workshop:

- Set approximate timeframes
- Understand the precursors – internal and external
- Use the uncertainty–importance grid to test assumptions
- Work backwards from the future, describing the transitional events
- Sometimes work forwards, using the uncertainty tunnel
- Split the participants up into two groups
- Set some key questions and structure the debate.

Scenarios are an essential tool in the HR strategy consultant's arsenal. They require an element of creativity and fun, and this means using your imagination freely.

CHAPTER 5

HR strategy and competitive strategy at Marks & Spencer

INTRODUCTION

This case on Marks & Spencer (M&S) presents us with considerable organizational challenges – many of them being central to HR strategy. When a company as successful as Marks & Spencer appears to lose its way, then it is far from obvious as to the most appropriate strategy to adopt. It is all too easy to try to manage incrementally within the current mind-set; alternatively, in desperation, strategies may sometimes be adopted that, although innovative, merely plunge the company into even deeper crisis. In this case study we will ask you to help to evolve HR strategies to turn M&S (as at 2001/2002) around.

When writing an earlier case study on M&S in 1994, the use of strategic thinking techniques flushed out some disturbing strategic patterns (Grundy, 1995). These highlighted that M&S was competitively weak outside the UK, and was in great danger of complacency in its UK heartland. The completed case was shown to a strategy professor at another business school, who made the following comment:

It is a very good case. But I cannot help feeling that you have depicted M&S rather optimistically, and you could have been more critical.

Interestingly, its author felt that what had actually been written could be seen (if anything) as being highly critical. It seemed odd that the case could be construed as being 'too positive'. For some years afterwards, when running strategy seminars and discussing M&S, its author would suddenly duck down, pretending to have spotted an M&S sniper on the roof opposite, out to get him. This was, of course, until the troubles at M&S burst into the open in the late 1990s.

There are several lessons from this earlier case:

1. It is often possible to 'see around corners' – to be able to anticipate a change in fortune of a major and successful company

2. When some very real doubts emerge, it is easy to dismiss them or tone them down rather than calling a spade a spade

3. When companies experience a major drop in their performance the seeds have frequently been sown earlier – in some cases, many years previously.

To illustrate the latter point, when an external consultant was asked to facilitate an HR strategy initiative in the form of a seminar on innovation for M&S managers a decade ago, some of the rigidities in the M&S culture were already exposed as a source of difficulty. The workshop was not a success for a number of reasons, not least because it was counter the M&S culture at the time.

A major stakeholder in the programme (who subsequently became a member of the M&S Main Board and was eventually deposed in the late 1990s) even suggested to the consultant during the workshop:

> I told you [before] that this wouldn't work. This [programme] is all about Managing Change, and we have already tried that. It doesn't really work here.

Subsequently the consultant happened to bump into an ex-senior HR manager of M&S and told him this story, to which he replied:

> Well, I could have told you such a programme could never work at M&S. You just walked into a trap with no escape route.

Like many ill thought through and non-aligned deliberate HR strategies, this initiative floundered because it was not well-positioned, was not well-timed, and was not supported by parallel HR initiatives to generate real economic value.

Let us now return to the main part of our case study, which will allow you to practise your role as a strategic HR consultant.

BUSINESS POSITION MID-1990s

In 1994, Marks & Spencer plc was a very large, successful business, with a turnover of £6.5 billion and profits before tax of £851 million. Fourteen million customers shopped at M&S each week.

M&S must have been exposed to many opportunities over the past 10 to 20 years that would have provided strategic temptation, but had, by and large, chosen to build on its core competencies rather than to develop new ones.

Where M&S came unstuck – i.e. in parts of its international development and in acquisition – was where it had stepped outside its (then) core capability, without developing or bringing in new competencies. These setbacks may well also have prevented M&S from fully capitalizing on other avenues for strategic development nearer to home – for example, into other service industries in the UK and elsewhere.

M&S's core business is focused on high street retailing, and core products are clothing for all the family. This 'general' business (then) contributed nearly £3.8 billion of turnover. By 1994 it had also built a very successful niche food business, which at this stage provided a surprising £2.6 billion of turnover (40 per cent of the group). In the 1990s M&S successfully diversified into personal financial services (although this business still remains relatively small compared with the core). Growth has been primarily of an organic nature, and overseas ventures (acquisitive and organic) have met with variable success. The most successful ventures appear to have been organic, and have involved partnership with local companies from whom M&S have been able to learn.

M&S's gross profit divided by turnover (or its 'gross margin') had increased from 32.8 per cent in 1990 to 35.1 per cent in 1994, with no decreases year-on-year during the severe UK recession in the early 1990s. This was a truly impressive achievement on the surface, and represented a very hard act to follow. So how could M&S sustain this stretching performance into the late 1990s, continuing to add more economic value? And how could it create a winning organization to do this? This was a huge challenge.

M&S's annual report and accounts did not, unfortunately, give a breakdown of operating profit by type of trading activity – indeed M&S is not (legally) obliged to provide this. However, it is safe to conjecture that the 20 per cent of business activities (by number of activities) that formed over 80 per cent of profit generation were (as an approximation):

- Men's and women's clothing
- The food business.

These businesses were built on organizational competencies, including:

- Its merchandising skills
- Its product sourcing skills or product innovation.

This left home furnishings, children's wear, men's and women's shoes, financial services and other products as generating around 20 per cent of profit. Also, over 80 (in fact 87) per cent of activities were then located in a single country – the UK. Increasingly, M&S was beginning to source from non-UK suppliers, having overcome its earlier hesitation. This sourcing outside the UK had mixed success: whilst reducing costs, the quality was sometimes uneven.

Over the period 1990–1994, M&S profits grew and grew from £305 million to £873 million, with turnover up just 17 per cent (from £5.6 billion to £6.5 billion). Its accounts showed a remarkable stability in the mix of its corporate businesses over a four-year period.

However, its first-half interim results for the 1994 year end highlighted a sluggish growth in food sales (at 3.9 per cent) relative to general business (which posted an impressive 8.9 per cent growth). This perhaps highlighted the tougher competitive constraints impacting on its UK food business, and also limited innovation – a reflection of an underlying cautious mind-set, which was soon to be attacked by its more thrusting and innovative new rival, Tesco. It also indicated why M&S might have been tempted into a major push for growth outside the UK, and underlined the need to grow its international competencies.

The main driver of increased profit growth over the 10 years from 1985 to 1994 was the improvement in operating margin, up from 9.4 per cent of turnover to 13.0 per cent. This kind of improvement could come in a number of forms – higher prices, fewer or lower discounts, supplier productivity improvements, M&S holding supplier prices down, a reduction in service levels, or delaying refurbishments. Some of that improvement came through M&S exercising its very strong bargaining position *vis-à-vis* suppliers (but if that was the case, then did M&S have much further scope to squeeze suppliers or otherwise improve margins?).

In this case, the issue of reducing service levels was a critical one for HR strategy.

RECIPES FOR SUCCESS – AND COMPETENCIES

M&S's success depended upon a philosophy of value for money, quality, and service. It had built an extremely strong brand that had an appeal to a large proportion of the 'middle market' in the UK, who had high brand loyalty (M&S claimed to have 35 per cent of the British market for women's underwear, and its Marble Arch store was reputed to sell 19 000 pairs of women's knickers per day). According to *The Times* (10 December 1994), one Arab customer arrived at the till with a rack of nightdresses, only to be told by the attentive M&S saleswoman that they were all in different sizes; he replied that so were his wives.

In terms of its competitive strategy, M&S was very selective in having quality locations and relatively simple product ranges. It was also selective regarding the things it did not do – for example, it did not then take other's people's credit cards, it avoided high fashion, etc. It was also justifiably famous for insisting on the absolute best from its suppliers – a distinctive competence. According to one City of London investment analyst, speaking on Channel 4:

> Being a supplier to Marks & Spencer is a source of unprecedented pressure, and some might say is interference from a customer in those businesses. If you are producing markets which are good enough to Marks, at a price which is acceptable to Marks, and the other conditions of being a Marks & Spencer supplier are satisfied, then being a supplier to Marks & Spencer is very, very profitable.

Whilst reducing/limiting staff numbers reduced short-term costs, it actually reduced revenues in the medium and longer term. We doubt whether any business case within M&S to reduce costs took these longer-term revenue losses into effect, and believe that its HR strategy was (then) driven by headcount/cost reduction, rather than through (economic) value-based thinking of the kind outlined in Chapter 2.

The tough M&S culture

When facilitating a session with M&S many years ago, one of the authors gained first hand experience of the aggressive personality traits of its merchandisers. One of this group, a senior wine buyer, wanted to buy a round of drinks from the bar in a hotel in Beaconsfield, UK. Although the group had been consuming quantities of champagne during a syndicate exercise somewhere near a duck pond, they were still thirsty.

The barman appeared to have disappeared – presumably to go to the loo or to have a cigarette. The senior wine buyer waited about 30 seconds, then vaulted over the bar, took the group's order, and collected the money. Later on one of the authors spotted the barman being fired by the manager.

The key competencies that M&S relied upon to achieve its impressive improvements were:

- Its merchandising skills
- Its store disciplines
- Innovations in food (and equally in financial services)
- The obsession with simplicity (in 1996 M&S turned down using the strategic project management process – adopted instead by Tesco and still in use as at 2002 – as being 'just too complex for us in 1996'; see Grundy and Brown, 2002a).

In the mid-1980s M&S began to lose ground to new competitors (such as Next), which targeted M&S and offered quality clothes with just that bit more fashion. This attack was good for M&S, which for a period regained much of the initiative.

Internationally M&S had also had a variable track record overseas, and had suffered a number of disappointments both in North America (e.g. in Canada, where M&S traded for 22 years) and in Europe. Like many companies that have developed very strong market penetration of a single country, M&S had found it hard to adapt its strategic and growth recipes to quite new and different business environments owing to its organizational mind-set and management mix. For example, in Spain it was said that while local people liked M&S underwear, etc., they found that the original clothes offered were 'ugly'. This invited the question as to whether M&S's merchandising in Spain was originally driven by a tailoring of the UK offering, rather than by working backwards from local tastes (again illustrating the value-destroying properties of a company's mind-set).

Indeed, in a 1994 Channel 4 television programme on M&S, the scenes in the Valencian store suggested that the merchandising strategy in its non-UK countries was built on the UK formula. It was as if M&S was aiming to convert non-Britons to the M&S (British) formula. This might not necessarily be a bad thing – chains like MacDonalds have created and imposed an international but US-based formula – but the M&S formula, especially in clothing, was likely to be heavily impacted by localized culture.

In 1994 one of the authors visited M&S to discuss organizational development. Going up the stairs, he asked: 'I was just wondering, is M&S's international competence(s) a key issue?'. The reply was: 'How did you know that? Are you psychic? I am just meeting a Major Board Director this afternoon to discuss precisely that'. Whatever one thinks of this international development strategy, there is no doubt that M&S was seeking to exploit those opportunities in a big, albeit sometimes cautious, way. (This example also illustrates how it is often possible to intuit HR strategy issues of an organization from the outside.)

In fact M&S at that time intended to double its selling space in continental Europe over the next few years, with Germany and Italy (in addition to France and Spain) on the agenda. (The first German stores were announced in March 1995.)

According to Sir Richard Greenbury, the then Chairman, speaking on Channel 4 in 1994:

> There isn't a retailer, a big one, in the world today that can probably say that he is going to stay in his home-based economy, and just do well there. I mean all the great retailers are having to face the facts that they have yet to take their skills abroad, one way or another.

But did M&S really appreciate what it meant to become a global retailer in terms of its organizational competencies? It is questionable whether it ever benchmarked itself externally for international retailing skills.

Perhaps M&S was now much better placed to understand how to exploit its talents internationally than during its earlier experimental efforts. Maybe recruiting more staff of other nationalities (especially in senior roles) would have helped to adapt the M&S philosophy to other environments. This may seem to be a minor issue at first sight, but could in the longer term be major, as it would likely shape the mind-set of management profoundly.

M&S's brand was very much supported by its reputation for value for money and also for customer service (and its supporting culture), although a lot of this appears to be a reflection of its once-upon-a-time innovation returns policy. Around these core advantages were clustered M&S's skills in developing very close supplier linkages, and its innovation. According to one City of London investment analyst, speaking on Channel 4:

> Marks has styled itself the manufacturer without factories . . .. They probably do have the closest relationship with suppliers of any UK retailer.

Organizational competencies can be double-edged, and whilst self-confidence should be a strength, equally it can turn out to be a weakness. This was subsequently highlighted at M&S. These competencies were ones that could potentially evaporate quickly. One analyst at the time reflected on this:

> I think they are a very self-confident company, and provided that they remain self-confident and not complacent I don't think that that's a problem. But I think that retailing is a notoriously fickle business. You have to keep on reinventing it and reinventing it year after year, season after season. You have to make sure that your clothes are fashionable, that the styles and colour are what people actually want.

Some felt that even then M&S had become too rigid as an organization. Sir Richard Greenbury, its then Chairman, espoused the dilemmas of maintaining discipline versus encouraging individual spontaneity:

> You must have discipline. You can't have everybody doing their own thing. And big businesses do become bureaucratic and they do become inflexible. But the day that they become so bureaucratic and inflexible that the free thinker, the maverick, the entrepreneur, the fellow or the woman who doesn't do it the conventional way ... those people must be given an opportunity to express their talents.

But did he really mean it? One brave joiner from another retailer (a department store) took another view:

> People just don't say anything. No one will speak against the Chair, because they say it shouldn't be done. You can just see people's faces changing [when you say critical things]. People just don't believe you, when you say something bad about Marks & Spencer, so you just don't bother.

This apparently limited capacity to listen and learn at the very top became a key driver of M&S's later downfall, culminating in Boardroom disarray.

M&S also then had some organizational areas of disadvantage. First, M&S perhaps had an over-cautious approach to managing its strategic development (at least in terms of organic development in the UK – except for financial services), and its culture generally; Secondly, its apparent lack of flexibility (for example in refusing to take non-M&S credit or debit cards) limited its capacity to respond to the competition. Thirdly, its UK-centred mind-set hampered its international development, perhaps seriously.

Regarding its organizational rigidity, let us note the comments of another analyst, speaking on Channel 4 in 1994:

> They [M&S] will certainly tend to be dismissive of criticism from outside. When you think about it, when a company is incredibly successful and Marks & Spencer has been, and still is, then your starting base has got to

be, that what anyone outside is saying is potentially wrong, and that they know the best way to do things. They have been doing it like that for 20, 30, 40, 50 years and it works for them.

Again, one of the central issues of HR strategy is invariably the organization's mind-set, and how this needs to adapt and be proactive in the face of change.

One of the most distinctive elements of this culture was the attention to microscopic detail at the most senior levels. On a Channel 4 television programme in 1994, Sir Richard Greenbury, Chairman, interjected at the start of a meeting to discuss current M&S foods to point out that:

I had the potato and leek [soup] last night and it has got lots of cream in it and it has got no potato in it. You know, if you have potato and leek then I like it to have a sort of powerful taste and it was, it was rich, it was too liquid, it just didn't gel with me.

As a result of this input, in a later scene the food group merchandisers were seen taking notes of his comments as if they were about to change the formula – suggesting that organizational challenge was not the strongest competence in M&S at the time, except top-down from the Chairman.

Yes, this intervention was an example of M&S's great strength ('Retail is Detail'). But how could this level of detailed intervention be possible in the future if M&S were ever successful in generating up to a quarter, a half, or even more sales outside the UK? Could M&S truly become a substantial and successful international retailer with this apparently high degree of centralized, top-down direction and control in its merchandising?

This was an example of a value-destroying incident. The meeting (attended by a dozen or so top M&S executives, including its Chairman, probably cost several thousand pounds. Its output – to make the soup much stronger tasting and lingering on the breath – led to reduced sales, destroying shareholder value.

Also, the issue of M&S's (then) refusal to take other credit or debit cards might have been seen as justified in terms of the virtue of strategic choice – saying 'no' to a costly strategy. This one-time strategic decision had become an integral part of the M&S mind-set. However, the costs of excluding (or reducing) the business of many customers lacking M&S charge cards were considerable, if unquantified. Some customers maybe found it difficult or perhaps too inconvenient to acquire M&S cards (for example, tourists). It has not always been the case that, on seeing a Visa, Access or American Express card, M&S have said 'I am afraid that we can't take that particular card, but if you would like to complete an application we may be able to issue you with your M&S card in about 5–10 minutes at customer services, where we have an on-line approval system.' M&S later addressed this issue if a frustrated customer asked the right question, and although this is now M&S's typical response, a credit card was previously seen as a threat.

Again, the history of M&S's attitude to non-M&S cards was symptomatic of a twin organizational strength and weakness. As one analyst, speaking on Channel 4, put it:

> You are looking at a company which essentially you have to characterize as a 'family dynasty', everyone is schooled in the history and in the traditions. I think the disadvantage of this kind of culture is that it can make it inward looking, it can perhaps breed a kind of arrogance.

Turning to M&S's international business, although its brand strength had power and it still had a clear market and product focus, it did not necessarily originally have a complete fit with local cultures. Also, although M&S still had a strong supplier base, this was offset by significant difficulties of logistics and attendant higher costs internationally. It was only in the late 1990s that M&S was able to lift European sales, and this success was achieved by exporting its 'outstanding value campaign' from the UK, and thus reducing its prices and its margins significantly. Probably the perceived need to obtain early(ish) profits from overseas (part of its financial mind-set) led M&S to pursue a strategy that only partially worked.

Harder still to remove was M&S's UK-centred culture. According to their Chairman, Sir Richard Greenbury (again speaking on Channel 4 in 1994) these attitudes were changing:

> One of the most exciting things amongst young people joining the business today is they think internationally. They are going to have to deal with a much more competitive, much more demanding trading climate. They are going to have to deal with customers who are not short of choice, or product at any price, of any quality, anywhere in the world. The consumer today is not just king, the consumer today is dictator.

Sir Richard Greenbury's statement perhaps reflects more a vision of the future rather than a reality at M&S. Its core management echelons were then staffed substantially by British managers.

In summary, we see that M&S strategic development and financial performance are very closely bound up with and induced by its HR strategy and implicit HR policies.

RECENT EXTERNAL POSITION 1997–2002

From the previous section, it is clear that M&S had an impressively strong bundle of multiple and reinforcing sources of competitive advantage and underlying competencies during the period of 1990–1996, but it had become somewhat bureaucratic and rigid. It was also not particularly receptive to change, and did not seem to have developed new competencies to keep up with or stay ahead of competitors and new(ish) entrants.

By around 1997, M&S's business portfolio was of varying competitive strength (depending whether it was clothing, food, other items and financial services, UK or international). Although M&S had some impressive product lines, particularly women's lingerie and its niche foods business, this benefit was offset by a number of strategically and (probably) financially less interesting business areas.

Financial services also represented a potentially attractive opportunity to M&S. The particular strengths that M&S brought to this arena were its brand awareness (if tarnished in recent times), its reputation for quality and (at the same time) value for money, and its focus on a narrower product line.

Financial Services had developed as a relatively separate business unit. Its Head, Keith Oates, used this success as a springboard for his later pre-emptive strike to run M&S.

With hindsight, it would appear that M&S did not really have the skills to become a more innovative business or, if it had, people were not allowed to express themselves fully in the organization of the time. Indeed in the 1990s the best and most innovative staff often left, but it was much, much harder to get really good incoming talent to join, and even harder to get them to stay. Again, the organizational mind-set made this very difficult.

M&S did not, in about 1997, change its strategic direction fundamentally, other than to change the design focus of its clothes in an attempt to become more fashionable. During the period 1997–1999, a number of external market shifts (effectively external performance brakes) crystallized, making it even more imperative for M&S to move with (and maybe even ahead of) the times in terms of leadership, culture, mind-set and innovation:

■ Despite continued economic recovery, consumers became more discerning. Where they were asked to pay a premium, they appeared to want a brand – and that brand was (at least in the young and middle-age groups) not M&S.

■ Because of an increase in the sales of mobile telephones, computers (including access to the Internet) and overseas holidays (through cheap flights), a squeeze was put on the retail sector generally. M&S proved to be not well placed to withstand this.

■ Competition for upmarket foods increased significantly – for example, Tesco's 'Finest' lines was a direct copy of M&S, and was set up with some staff poached from M&S.

■ M&S's international expansion (perhaps predictably) faltered, with a U-turn on investment in territories such as Germany.

■ New entrants to the UK retail market, like Gap and Matalan, began to take a greater share of the younger market, pushing M&S up the age range – where it was under increasing attack from Next and Debenhams.

■ The fashion cycle was accelerating so that the two-seasons-a-year merchandising process at M&S became unwieldy and obsolescent. The mind-set at M&S was that the two-season process was OK, but it clearly was not – making M&S even more vulnerable.

However, instead of performing a radical overhaul of its skills and style of working within its HR strategy, M&S carried on working and thinking in more or less the same way.

Meanwhile, M&S continued to pursue its international expansion plans whilst its UK position came under increasing attack, and eventually came very unstuck. This was reflected in M&S's results over 1997–2000 (see Table 5.1).

Table 5.1
M&S Financial Performance 1997–2000 (from Annual Report and Accounts, 2000)

Turnover (£ million)	2000	1999	1998	1997
General	4629	4765	4811	4602
Foods	3201	3110	3157	3024
Financial services	365	350	275	216
	8195	8225	8243	7842
Operating profits	471	512	1103	1022
Earnings per share (pence)	13.2	15.0	28.7	26.2

M&S did make some major changes to its strategy in the period 1998–2000. It decided partially to abandon its dependency on its traditional brand, St Michael. Ambitious plans to develop more exciting merchandising ideas came from its 'Autograph' range. Trialled in the more prestigious stores, the plan was to get well-known designers to design expensive, upmarket clothes to be sold in a separately demarcated section of M&S. (This strategy met with only partial success, and by 2001 signals were given that M&S was to rethink it.) This plan would have necessitated recruiting new merchandising staff, who might think differently; however, the results of this strategy makes it appear that this did not happen.

Its previous chairman, Sir Richard Greenbury, eventually retired under much internal and external pressure from the Board. Sir Richard had overseen M&S's success in the early-mid 1990s, but now admitted (*Money Programme*, 2000) that its financial success was at least partially due to its past cost-cutting. In that same television programme, many suggested that in order to make service levels look rosy for Sir Richard, extra staff were deployed on the days when he was to make a formal visit – presumably to ward off fears of criticism. This must have been instigated by line management, HR, or both, and appears to have been the response to a culture of fear within M&S.

This cost-cutting resulted in service erosion (the absence of an integrated HR/competitive strategy perhaps meant that M&S was misguided by an inappropriate and self-defeating cost-reduction strategy). With hindsight, it was admitted by Sir Richard Greenbury that, given the investment in greater service by players like Tesco, this strategy might have been unwise.

Following considerable boardroom acrimony, Sir Richard was replaced by a successful European retailer, Luc Vandevelde. Vandevelde's original aim was to turn around M&S within 2 years, which, given the scale of its problems as identified in this case study (which has evolved over the years) and others, seemed hopeful to say the least. For even more fundamental than its weakening external position was its hierarchical bureaucracy, its politics, its fear culture and, some would say, its antiquated mind-set.

M&S was then getting desperate to be even more innovative. Its advertising campaign (on TV and on billboards) then featured a 'normal-sized' and attractive lady taking her clothes off to celebrate her size 14 body, and was aimed to appeal to Ms and Mrs Average UK. Unfortunately, Ms and Mrs Average UK did not want to identify with that image, so the campaign backfired. Like the Autograph range this initiative seemed to spring out of tactical desperation rather than strategic thought. Again, it is doubtful that the HR strategy (at that point) demanded the injection of new blood.

M&S tried to enliven its underwear range by joint ventures with Agent Provocateur, appearing to push very aggressively into more adventurous and sensual markets. This again (unsurprisingly) proved unsuccessful, and the M&S standalone lingerie shop pilot was halted. M&S was at that stage similar to the Ancient Egyptians getting bored of papyrus ships and building their first airliner – but out of reeds(!)

M&S sought to fill its gap in HR competencies by recruiting George Davies (ex-Next) to form an alliance to create a new sub-brand, called Per Una, which appears to have been a sales success. However, George Davies' arrival signifies that M&S had a major gap in its competencies – in fashion and design. Furthermore, the penalties of this success were to be (a) profit sharing with George Davies; (b) possible cannibalization of M&S mainstream products, and (c) vulnerability to following out with George Davies, and dependency upon his competence. Davies had once vowed never to avoid a major row with them over the years, and there was an even greater chance that he would get bored and want to move on. His irritation at M&S attitudes was tangible during a television documentary shown at the time. M&S's mind-set on customer returns and on not giving staff fashion shoes to keep sales was like a brick wall. Was this part of a sustainable and cunning HR strategy?

By 1999, M&S's dividend per share was only just covered by current earnings, whereas in previous years (in the mid-1990s) it was twice covered by earnings. In 2000, its profits after tax and after exceptional items were £258.7 million compared with a £258.6 million dividend, leaving a surplus of just £0.1 million.

At one shareholders' meeting, one angry shareholder and customer brandished an M&S bra, claiming that it was so fundamentally unexciting that it was no wonder that customers were alienated. Whilst M&S still has an enviably well-known brand and deep customer loyalty in some market segments, there is no question that its brand has been significantly tarnished by that stage. Somewhere and somehow its buyers (major value destroyers) in M&S appear to have lost the plot.

■ STRATEGIC CHANGE 1999–2002

The half-year results to September 1999 then revealed that M&S had made a number of changes, aimed at influencing both internal and external performance drivers.

Its long-standing Chairman left the Board, and a number of other top-level management changes were made. A number of television documentaries at the time suggested that Sir Richard had been somewhat autocratic – based on sources inside M&S. His exit followed a boardroom battle, which involved Keith Oates (then a senior director) making a pre-emptive strike for the chief executive's role whilst Sir Richard was away on holiday. Keith Oates was then forced to resign by the non-executives. (Apparently the struggle for succession was a major distraction for the Board.) Interestingly, well before this M&S's non-executives had suggested Richard Greenbury might not be a suitable Chairman as he was not really a strategic thinker (Bevan, 2001). Apparently in the early 1990s one non-executive director prophetically suggested that Greenbury would probably be its best ever Chief Executive but its worst Chairman. This, we presume was 'emergent HR strategy', which in the end proved to be extremely value-destroying.

A marketing director was then appointed (for the first time), and was recruited from outside, to try to introduce new blood and new thinking. A 'big name' was not recruited, and the M&S share price tell slightly soon afterwards (this is an interesting example of how HR strategy can sometimes have an immediate impact on share price). Apparently in 1990 the word 'marketing' was a 'no–no' in M&S. At the same time, one of the authors was asked by M&S to Tipp-Ex® the word 'consultants' on his letterhead, as M&S was allergic to seeking outside advisory help. Whilst not suggesting that consultants are always or even often a good thing, this kind of 'critical incident' does seem to suggest a peculiarly dangerous cultural introversion.

In its marketing and promotion, M&S began to advertise more aggressively and to introduce more aggressive promotions, signalling a major change in mind-set. It also changed its credit card policy, allowing stores to accept credit cards for the first time in its history. This occurred by spring 2000.

However, by late 2000/early 2001 M&S appeared to be in ever-deeper trouble. According to the *Financial Times* (24 January 2001), Christmas trading had decreased and, in the 16 weeks to January, group sales were down 3.1 per cent (down 5.1 per cent on a comparable store basis). Clothing, footwear and gifts were down by a staggering 9.3 per cent. On the plus side, there was an improvement of 2.9 per cent in food. The 25 new concept stores were only 4 per cent ahead, despite refitting expenditure of £60 million.

Mr Vandevelde, M&S's new Executive Chairman, had given himself 2 years to turn the store around, but time appeared to be running out. One analyst, Tony Shirt of Credit Suisse First Boston, said at that time:

which indicated general neglect and a lack of attention. The external visitors found that:

- The store was a rabbit warren, which, given M&S's poor signage, it was hard to navigate around.
- Its 'look' appeared old-fashioned, and attempts to brighten it up with a couple of TV screens showing videos seemed to create an even worse, patchy effect.
- Merchandising was not well displayed, with piles of unsold clothes (presumably left over from the sale) cluttering up the stores.
- With one or two exceptions (more healthy convenience foods), M&S's food range appeared almost identical to that offered 10 years ago. M&S's foods seemed to have been stuck in a kind of time warp.
- There was a tiny office bar situated at the back of foods in the basement (not the best place to generate footfall), and this was unattended. Spaces were there for three clocks showing the times in London, Los Angeles and Singapore; the Singapore clock was missing and the Los Angeles clock time was wrong. What had happened to M&S's famed organizational attention to detail and discipline?

If aliens had visited this store (after being briefed on how successful M&S had been throughout 1975–1995) they would have had a real surprise, if not a shock. What had gone wrong? Was M&S actually being run by humans with retailing skills, or maybe by some other (enemy) aliens from another star system?

At another visit of managers to M&S's Moorgate store in July 2002, things had not changed fundamentally. The managers found that:

- The store was very hard to navigate, with minimal signage and minimal service levels. Despite the managers walking around the store in groups of six taking notes, the few M&S staff around appeared to be oblivious to anything unusual.
- Again, there was little real change in the foods offering.

Drawing the helicopter view from this analysis, it would not have taken 700 pages of a strategy consultant's report by LEK strategy consultants (which was rumoured to have been presented to M&S top management in 2000) to have realized that:

M&S strategy still needs still to be fundamentally rethought

---

and

Incremental tinkering with that strategy is not going to work

---

and

Does it yet have a robust HR strategy to pull all this together?

FUTURE STRATEGY

Given M&S's malaise, it appeared extremely unlikely that the company would ever get back to the profitability levels that it enjoyed prior to 1998 unless there was even more radical rethinking. Were the company to be truly run for shareholder value, then M&S might be up for unbundling, for instance through:

- Full disposal (in 2000 it was rumoured that Tesco might have been interested in acquiring M&S, but wisely this move never materialized – it would have been a major distraction for Tesco, and there would have been massive cultural misfit and huge integration difficulties).
- Partial disposal of, for example, M&S foods, either to another retailer or to be floated off as a separate plc (thus recapturing its shareholder value, which had become lost within M&S). Interestingly, in mid-2002 M&S announced the expansion into smaller stand-alone food stores, an idea that had come up on public strategic thinking courses repeatedly during 1994–1996, seven years earlier!
- Disposal or flotation of M&S financial services (again with an immediate boost to shareholder value), and more innovation, including a chain of M&S Financial Cafés – with deluxe coffee at 50p a time and the opportunity to browse products. Interestingly, one of the authors came up with this idea only to find that Abbey National was doing something not entirely dissimilar on a pilot basis, but from a position of less strength.
- Unbundling the general business into core M&S lines and new venture mini retailers (set up as alliances with former staff as entrepreneurs, or with other ex retailers with flair) to make M&S a more exciting place to be, and in place of more mundane items like shoes, furnishings, menswear etc.

It is not believed that M&S has thought through such radical options, principally because of its mind-set and culture. And such options would have demanded considerable thought about M&S desired future competency set – what would be required (minimalistically) for this to offer future competitive edge?

However, even if we were to set aside radical thinking about business scope and strategy, there is plenty to reflect on simply in terms of its potential strategic HR breakthroughs.

HR STRATEGIC BREAKTHROUGHS

In this section we ask you to exercise your mind on the topic of a viable future HR strategy for M&S. To achieve this we ask you to sketch out the key competencies that M&S would need in the future to survive and succeed, and the HR

Table 5.3
M&S competitive and HR strategies

Strategic challenge	Organizational competence(s)	HR strategic breakthroughs	Value added	('High', 'medium' or 'low')
Intensified competition – clothing				
Intensified competition – food				
Store design/layout				
Service				
Faster design cycles				
Cost management				
Property portfolio management				
Alliances				
Challenging mind-sets				
Hiring (and keeping) superior managers				
Investor relations				
Better quality general management				

strategic initiatives that would support this, using Table 5.3. (Having followed the Dyson case study in Chapter 3, you should be well equipped to have a go at this.)

Exercise: M&S strategic challenges 2002–2005

Complete a number of lines in Table 5.3, beginning with M&S's strategic challenges for 2002–2005.

Once you have completed it, go to the end of the chapter for suggestions.

CONCLUSION

The M&S case study is a fascinating account showing just how interwoven competitive strategy and HR strategy actually are. Looking back over the past decade, HR constraints appear to have been a fundamental cause of strategic drift and competitive decline at M&S – probably even more important than actions by competitors/new rivals.

Unlike Tesco, which had a major management clearout in 1993/1994, M&S persisted with the mind-set that appeared to have worked in the past. Whilst Tesco overtook Sainsbury's in market share and even M&S in profit – and with a much lower percentage of margin on sales – M&S chose to starve its stores of service, investment and innovation. The root causes of these problems all seem to go back to its leadership, and to its conservatism – the very conservatism that made it so successful in the future (see Bevan, 2001, for an absolutely fascinating and longer account of the story).

Had we travelled back in time to, say, 1993, and helped M&S to look at some organizational futures, this cataclysmic fall from grace could well have been anticipated – and as a quite detailed storyline.

Certainly when one of the authors' worked there in 1990 (and some bruises are still recovering), it seemed like an organization (even then) beginning to move out of sync with the times. Often the seeds of self-destruction are built into the organizational fabric, even when a company is appearing to be doing very well indeed financially – and for its shareholders. However, longer-term shareholder value has its ultimate roots in superior organizational competencies, which have key influences on value and cost drivers (see Chapter 6). It is precisely these future superior competencies that HR strategy should be trying to create.

Finally, the detailed step-by-step process of analysing competitive challenges and organizational competencies, supporting HR strategic breakthroughs, and diagnosing economic value added that we saw in our final exercise, coupled with some scenario development (see Chapter 4) can go a long way towards evolving a value-added set of HR strategies. In addition, we should always remember to work the analysis the other way around – that is, look at the set of natural (existing and potential) organizational competencies that we might have available in the future, and *then* set about identifying the new competitive strategies that they suggest.

Having looked thoroughly at the HR strategy context, it is now time to move on to Part II to look at developing and evaluating an HR strategy, and implementing and project managing it.

Suggestions for exercise

A list of potential HR initiatives that are candidates for HR strategic breakthroughs (see column two of Table 5.3) at M&S could include (value shown in brackets):

- A culture change programme (high)
- Downsizing Head Office (high)
- Relocating Head Office (medium)
- Restructuring Head Office (e.g. creating a more autonomous foods division) (high)
- Alliance(s) with other retailers (maybe starting a new venture/s) (low)
- Outsourcing M&S's property function (low)
- Further reduction of central management (medium)
- Organizational development prior to a management buy-out (MBO) of M&S's financial services division (medium)
- Making George Davies an offer he could not refuse – to be M&S Chief Executive (medium)
- Poaching top retailers (e.g. from Tesco or elsewhere) (medium)
- Offering rewards to top managers based not on shorter-term profit improvement, but on a balance of indicators that reflect M&S longer-term value drivers (low)

- Joint management development with other companies (to open up the M&S culture/mind-set) (low)
- Secondments of high-potential staff to other companies/industries (low)
- A recognition/rewards scheme for staff, for superior service (medium)
- A staff innovation scheme (coming up with creative ideas) – e.g. for store design/new products/ better service (medium)
- Developing the HR function to add more value through organizational interventions/learning (low).

Table 5.4 provides an example.

Table 5.4
M&S competitive and HR strategies – example

Strategic challenge	Organizational competence(s)	HR strategic breakthroughs	Value added
Better quality general management	Strategic thinking	A strategic thinking process	Better (positive) strategic decisions – delivering economic profit
		Strategic workshops on real-time M&S issues (with external facilitation)	Inappropriate (negative) strategic decisions avoided
		Strategic thinking skills – management development (as input to the above)	Improved communication (less costs of confusion – an intangible)
		Performance management – to reflect the quality of strategic thinking on the job	Faster change and implementation internally
		Succession and career development – based on input through assessment of strategic thinking competencies amongst senior staff	New competitor moves spotted/anticipated
			Superior project management, giving better results for less time and cost

PART 2

HR strategy process

overall implementation difficulty, and who are the key stakeholders (at a high level)?

2. *Options* – and the cunning plan: what cunning options are available for implementing the HR breakthrough?

3. *Planning*: for these strategic HR options, how attractive are they versus how difficult to implement? What key activities are needed, and with what resources?

4. *Implementation*: is implementation proving effective, and if not, why not? What new implementation forces and stakeholders have come into play, and how might these be handled? Do the original objectives need revisiting, and are these more easily met by other strategies? If so, what are the costs of refocusing efforts?

5. *Learning and control*: is the implementation of the HR strategy on track in terms of its intended competitive, financial, operational and organizational effects? Did you achieve what you set out to achieve? If not, what were the factors you might have controlled, or attempted to influence, but didn't? Or do you need to revisit and change your recipes for developing strategies for growth (or for their implementation)? Finally, were the implementation difficulties much greater than envisaged, and if so, why?

To summarize which strategic thinking techniques are appropriate in managing each stage of the implementation process, consider Table 6.1.

Table 6.1
Strategic thinking techniques for each stage of the implementation process

Diagnosis	Options	Planning	Implementation	Learning and control
Performance drivers	Strategic option grid	Wishbone analysis*	Force field analysis	Fishbone analysis
Fishbone analysis	Uncertainty–importance grid*	Uncertainty–importance grid*	Difficulty over time	Wishbone analysis
Performance drivers	AID analysis	Value and cost drivers	Stakeholder and agenda analysis	Performance drivers
From–to (FT) analysis	Stakeholder analysis	How–how analysis	Stakeholder influence analysis	From–to (FT) analysis
Motivator hygiene factors		AID analysis	Influence analysis	Force field analysis
Force field and stakeholder analysis		Value-over-time curve		
		Force field and stakeholder analysis		

*Already covered in earlier Chapters

Exercise: diagnosing implementation

For a past area of implementation in which you have been involved, answer the following questions:

1. What were the strengths and weaknesses of each phase of the HR strategy implementation process, particularly:
   - Diagnosis
   - Cunning options
   - Planning
   - Implementation
   - Learning and control?
2. What dos and don'ts can you distil for the future? Look at some tools for diagnosis, for creating cunning options, for planning, implementation, and learning and control.

IMPLEMENTATION TECHNIQUES AND TOOLS

Performance driver analysis

Performance driver analysis helps to diagnose organizational performance, either externally or internally (or both). A second way of analysing business and financial performance is to identify the key performance drivers using a tailored version of force field analysis (see later in this chapter). Performance drivers are drawn here as upward arrows, and brakes are shown as downward

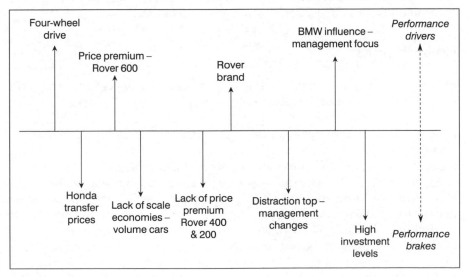

Figure 6.1
Performance drivers – Rover

arrows. Figure 6.1 illustrates this with reference to the perceived perform-ance drivers of Rover cars, based on external data synthesized around late 1995.

Although this method does not purport to be an exact picture of Rover's performance drivers, it does yield some important concerns about the medium-term attractiveness of BMW's acquisition of Rover, even if there were longer-term opportunities beyond this analysis.

Performance driver analysis can be used for:

- Analysing an organizational performance
- Understanding a team's performance
- Analysing an individual's performance.

It is especially helpful in turnaround situations.

In many ways performance driver analysis is more incisive than SWOT analysis, as it focuses on those factors that have an impact on economic value generation in a business. This gets us away from the 'nice-to-haves', which often cloud the 'strengths' of SWOT analysis. Also, with the vector format the performance drivers are automatically prioritized.

The key benefits of performance driver analysis are that:

- The 'so-what?' drops out much more readily than in a SWOT analysis
- It is already prioritized
- It gives a better feel of the overall business context before addressing a specific organizational problem or bottleneck (so that we do not simply respond reactively to a problem)
- It makes judgements on performance less of a personal issue.

The performance drivers are, in effect, scored according to their import-ance multiplied by their relative strength or weakness.

Fishbone analysis

Fishbone analysis is a very quick and easy way of going behind the more immediate definition of the HR problem or opportunity. For instance, Figure 6.2 illustrates why strategy is frequently not well implemented. This can be done for a variety of reasons, or underlying root causes – including, for example, having too abstract a strategic vision, not fully thinking through implementation, or having too many unprioritized projects.

Figure 6.3 gives us an example of a rather spectacular diagnosis. This is taken from an ITV series called *The Complainers*, which was shown in the mid-1990s. In *The Complainers*, an entrepreneur is depicted in daily activity supervising his staff. There have been some rather major errors in the business, which places advertisements for companies – sometimes getting these very wrong. In this real-life documentary, the entrepreneur/manager is very angry at the start, and his anger mounts as his staff appear to be unable to cope with his verbal pressure and criticisms. He increasingly loses the plot

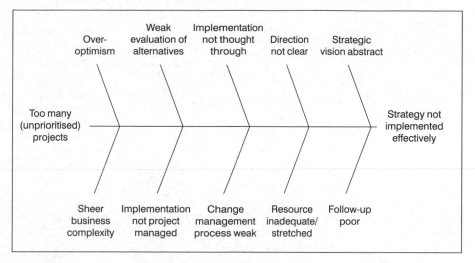

Figure 6.2
Fishbone analysis

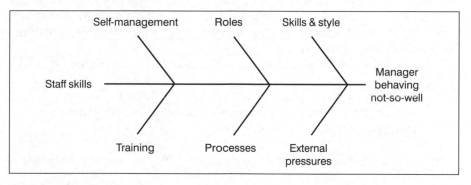

Figure 6.3
Manager behaving not-so-well

and eventually appears to lift the office table in the air, propelling it in the general direction of an employee – after the latter has been fired.

Figure 6.3 suggests that the underlying causes of this extreme behaviour are to be found in:

- His management skills (perhaps he has had little, or no, management skills training)
- His role in the business (which appears to be too dominant)
- His self-management capability (he appears to be unable to manage his frustration – he appears red at the start going on a radiant purple towards the end)
- His organizational skills (in terms of project management, delegation, coaching, interpersonal skills etc.).

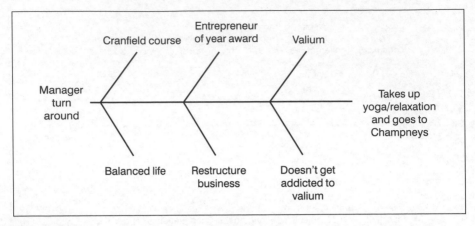

Figure 6.4
Wishbone analysis – manager behaving not-so-well

Moving on, we now look at how we can create a vision for development, turning to wishbone analysis. This begins with the vision to the left-hand side of the picture, while to the right hand-side we plot all the alignment factors (see Figure 6.4). These are the necessary and sufficient conditions of creating (and sustaining) the vision.

For the entrepreneurial manager, we see a possible developmental vision as being:

To have developed to such an extent that he gets the South Coast Entrepreneur of the Year Award.

In order to deliver and sustain this vision, alignment factors might be:

- To go on the Cranfield School of Management's Entrepreneurs Programme
- To undergo an intensive programme of management coaching
- To take valium for 6 months
- To not get hooked on valium (or some other drug)
- To get a clearer balanced life (work is not a battle, let alone all-out war; if you think that, why not join the SAS if they will have you?)
- To restructure the organization
- To take up yoga and meditation
- To go to Champneys health resort once a month.

Obviously, when dealing with an individual who is in a turnaround situation, there may be a very real issue about whether these alignment factors *will ever be in alignment.*

There are some important guidelines for using fishbone analysis. The do's are:

- Identify the symptom of the cause and position it over towards the right-hand side. Where there are a number of possible symptoms, you might need to analyse several problems (and thus draw up several fishbones). Or, you may need to summarize a number of issues into a single, over-arching fishbone.
- Make sure that the root causes are the real root causes (or at least quite close to being root causes). If you can ask the question 'why?', then you are still at the level of a symptom.
- Use your common sense to understand at what point you should cease going back up the causal chain. Thus 'lack of leadership skills' for most purposes is a satisfactory root cause, rather than going back to 'the Board appointed the wrong leader' or 'there were no really suitable candidates'. (You do not need to go back to the dawn of time to scope and diagnose a problem.)

The don'ts are:

- Don't worry about whether the fishbone causes should go vertically or downwards; there is no special priority in where they are positioned and they are all equivalent. Most fishbones are more complete if they are drawn up in a creative flow rather than in some prestructured manner. If you do want to prioritize the fishbones, write the root causes on 'Post-its' and then move them around, perhaps in order of priority of difficulty, or degree of influence, or their attractiveness.
- Don't clutter up the analysis with sub-bones off a main fishbone on the same sheet of paper. This produces a visually complex, messy, and hard to interpret picture. Where appropriate, do the analysis of a particular mini-fishbone for a particular cause on a separate page.
- Don't forget to consider the external causes as well as the internal root causes, and also the tangible versus the less tangible causes of the original symptom.

One of the major objections to fishbone analysis is that it is merely a list – so what other value does it add? (This is an objection sometimes raised by those who appear inherently sceptical of the value of strategic thinking tools.) Our main responses to this view are that:

1. The fishbone itself is a powerful device for mapping causality of organizational issues, and is not therefore just a brainstorm – it repeatedly asks the 'why–why?' question, picking up more and more of the causal system of the problem. This generates more ideas than a simple list because:
   - The 'why–why?' question stimulates further thinking about root causes – either at a deeper level or more laterally (and into other areas of the organization)
   - Each fishbone can usually be traced back to its sub-fishbones (with a list each point is usually the end of the analysis, and thus is not analysed in greater depth)

■ Subsequently each fishbone can be prioritized using, for example, the attractiveness–implementation difficulty (AID) analysis or the import-ance–influence analysis (see our explanation later in this chapter). This effect can be powerfully shown as an overlay of two acetates, one on top of the other, the first acetate being the fishbone and the second one on top being its prioritization. The fishbone can be explained first before moving on to its prioritization.

2. The fishbone is a visual device, making it easier to communicate (especially to top managers) and generally much more interesting than a list.

3. With a list the symptom tends not to stand out from the root causes. Also, a common tendency (without using a fishbone) is to talk around general issues rather than real causes.

Having used fishbone analysis for nearly 10 years to diagnose strategic issues, we realized that a number of generic factors were at work. These factors interact as a system, which we now call the 'root cause system'. The ten main generic systems that appear to be at work are:

1. The competitive environment
2. Operations (internal)
3. The wider environment
4. The customer
5. Resource availability
6. Decision-making
7. Politics
8. Culture and style
9. Structure and skills
10. Financial imperatives and pressures.

Figure 6.5 plots the main interdependencies of these systems. By creating a variety of fishbones for quite different issues, it is quite usual to find a small number of themes coming up over and over again. Often these are inter-related. We suggest that you use this picture to stimulate thinking about the possible root causes, or as a quick check on their completeness.

The BP case study provides a most interesting example of root cause systems at work.

Case study: root cause systems of culture change at BP, 1989–2001

At BP in the late 1980s there was an increasing sense of organizational drift. Decision-making was perceived to be slow, the culture and style of the organ-ization was highly bureaucratic, and it was felt that there was perhaps too much in the way of internal politics. Resources were not always well allocated across the Group, as it (then) used accounting-based (financial) measures for its business plans and for control, whilst cash-flow analysis was used in isolation for longer-term decisions. This created some confusion in strategic priorities.

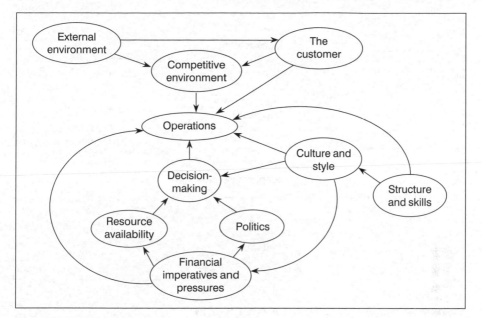

Figure 6.5
Root cause systems (generic)

BP was able to operate in this way and still succeed largely because of an absence of fierce competition, generally favourable oil prices, and its strong cash flow from its rich North Sea and Alaskan oilfields. (One example of its paternalistic culture was BP's canteen lunch. This was once said to be 'the best five-pence lunch in the City' – BP introduced identity cards partially, it was believed, to keep out unwelcome students. Many staff then spent their lunch-time savings on a few lunch-time pints, not helping with decision-making speed but maybe dampening organizational politics.)

Quite clearly BP's malaise was due to complacent culture, and it was for that very reason that in 1989 the new Chairman, Bob Horton, instigated BP's 1990 'culture change' project. In parallel with that initiative there were considerable structure changes, investment in management skills and asset changes, divestment, and cost reduction in operations. Financial plans and targets became value-based – that is, based on cash-flow generation (BP was one of the first exponents of value-based management; Grundy, 1992). BP then made a number of shrewd and successful acquisitions, propelling it (some would say) to its current position as the world's Number Two oil company.

Figure 6.6 plots the key root cause systems at work within BP's strategic change 1989–2001. These capture the interdependencies between the key root causes, and highlight those that are organizational in nature – and call out for HR strategic breakthroughs.

The BP case fishbone analysis exposes some major management dilemmas. Where there are some underlying problems, such as culture and style,

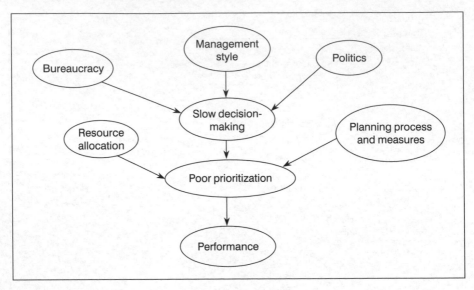

Figure 6.6
BP strategic change 1989–2001 – root cause systems

or leadership, then do you attempt to deal with them as a separate programme or initiative, or do you attempt to manage around them, minimizing their effect?

The answer to this tough question depends to a large extent on the situation. Where there is a real determination to tackle these issues from the top – and an ability actually to deal with implementation difficulties or barriers on the way – then there is hope in tackling them directly. Where this is not the case, it may be better to work bottom-up on individual issues until the time is right to take the bigger ones on.

In the words of the HR Director of a water company undergoing strategic change, when speaking to some senior managers who were asked to champion change:

What we want you to be like is like the Vietcong: resourceful, innovative, sometimes patient and hidden, but always ready to dart out and fight when and where you can actually win. You will prepare for the grand battle – but later.

Here we see the HR Director not wanting to confront the biggest issues head-on yet, but beginning to introduce change – by stealth.

Even where it is entirely appropriate to tackle a big change challenge head-on, it is still worthwhile breaking it down into specific breakthrough projects. For example, in the mid-1990s the supermarket chain Tesco was simultaneously hit by the effects of prolonged recession, government restrictions on new out-of-town supermarket expansion, and a price war triggered by new entrants.

Of a number of breakthrough areas, one in particular – culture – was chosen for a new focus. Initially it was unclear as to how to tackle this and what was likely to come out of it. This breakthrough became a process of transformation into practical projects to improve operational performance, which would in time improve culture. These included:

- Tesco's superior customer services, through 'one-in-front' (if a queue of more than one customer built up, where possible further check-outs would be opened)
- Service training for front-line store staff
- Investment in management training (often with a behavioural focus)
- Simplification of processes at Head Office (making the retail head office interface easier to deal with, thereby reducing the sense of there being 'two cultures').

Sometimes, however, fishbone analysis can actually inhibit creative thinking by reinforcing the 'it's a problem' mind-set. A more creative approach is to see each problem as an opportunity – a chance to get additional value out of the situation, and in cunning ways.

At a practical level, the key benefits of fishbone analysis are that it:

- Helps to diagnose a problem in much greater depth, assisting in scoping strategic issues much more effectively
- Usually goes halfway (at least) towards suggesting solutions
- Reduces the tendency for managers to talk about the same issues over and over again – just using different words creates greater confusion and slows progress significantly
- Communicates the scope and the key reasons for the problem in a politically neutral way – this is an essential technique for managing upwards
- Allows you to go freely up and down levels of analysis without getting irretrievably lost down any rabbit holes of microscopic diagnosis.

Its potential dis-benefits are that:

- It can reinforce the 'it's a problem' mind-set
- Managers do tend to restrict themselves to solving the causes of the problem with fishbone analysis, rather than examining where they might be (the 'cunning plan')
- Unless a fishbone is prioritized (which we will see later), it only takes you a limited way forward.

Finally, it is useful to highlight that fishbone analysis can be of considerable help in structuring organizational problems. Generally several problems hide inside each other, but are interrelated. This invites splitting them out in a way where they are still linked. We call this 'piranha analysis', to highlight the fact that whilst smaller problems can appear to be more manageable, they can actually be deadly and ferocious.

Figure 6.7 gives an excellent example of this, using a relationship problem as its focus. Relationship problems are endemic in complex, changing

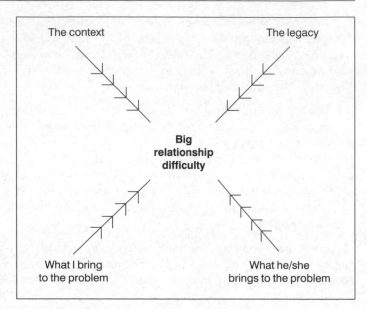

Figure 6.7
Piranha analysis

organizations, and strategic thinking is a vital tool in helping to deal with them. Typical relationship difficulties occur with your boss, with a subordinate, or with a close rival.

Figure 6.7 splits into four piranha problem areas:

1. What do you bring to it yourself?
2. What do others bring to it?
3. The current organizational context
4. The past organizational legacy.

This problem structure forces you into assessing what you brought to the situation. Besides helping you become more objective, it also focuses on something that you ought to have much more influence over – yourself!

The 'context' should generate some thinking about what is currently going on around the relationship – for example, restructuring, performance pressures, inconsistent organizational priorities. The 'legacy' can in some situations be very important, as it helps with understanding how the problem might have developed and how this might have been (at least partially) caused by past organizational mistakes.

Having used the piranha, it is not unusual to witness a partial or even a complete turnaround of a relationship, especially if it has been shared openly between both sides. (It is also very helpful here to use the wishbone analysis seen in Chapter 3 in the James Dyson case to create a vision for a much better working relationship and the alignment factors for it to go right.)

Let us now leave fishbone analysis by reflecting on what one manager said of it:

Unless you pull a problem up by its roots, like a weed it always grows back.

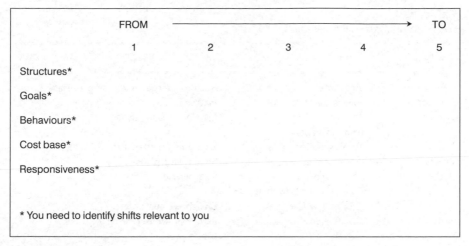

Figure 6.8
From–to analysis

From–to analysis

From–to (FT) analysis helps to scope the extent of the strategic project that you are working on, but in terms of its breadth and its degree of stretch. It is another useful tool for scoping the extent of implementation, especially for organizational change or for operational development. Where a development project has a significant impact on 'how we do things around here' or the 'paradigm' (see Grundy, 1993), then it is essential that at least a rudimentary FT analysis is conducted.

The 'paradigm' embraces a raft of organizational processes, some of which are 'hard' and tangible and some of which are 'soft' and intangible (see Figure 6.8 for a generic FT analysis).

For example, managers within Prudential Life Administration used FT analysis based specifically on the paradigm to scope their organizational change project. This helped them to get their minds around the 'soft' as well as the 'hard' factors (see Table 6.2).

This kind of analysis can also be used to monitor the progress of a project – perhaps using a score of 1–5, with 1 being the 'From' and perhaps 5 being the 'To'. (In some situations, however, we might well be starting off with better than a 1, as we could already have made some progress towards our goals, prior to embarking on the project. Equally, we might not wish to go all out for a 5, as a 4 or even 3 score might be more realistic and acceptable, depending upon the situation.)

The Prudential example of FT analysis is very much a more 'gourmet' approach. We see a semi-structured approach being used to generate the key shifts that the strategic project is aimed at delivering. A simplified approach is quickly to brainstorm the froms and tos in a way much more specific to a

Table 6.2
From–to analysis – Prudential

Paradigm	From	To
Power	Restricted	Resides at the lowest appropriate level
Structure	Hierarchical	Flatter
Controls	Instinctive and 'seat of pants'	Measured objectives
Routines	Retrospective-looking	Live and forward look
Rituals	Loose plans	Structured plans
Myths	'The Mighty Pru' 'Life Administration is OK'	Real world
Stories	Our job well done	Delighted customers
Symbols	Status hierarchy	Rewards for performance
Management style	Aloof	Open

particular project. Our main caveat here is that you really must think about the softer factors that are required to be shifted – for example, behaviours, attitudes and mind-set generally.

To perform FT analysis, you need to carry out the following steps:

1. What are you trying to shift? (the critical categories)
2. By how much are you trying to shift them? (the horizontal from and to shifts).

By now it may have become apparent to you that FT analysis is essentially an extended form of gap analysis (see our previous section). Because it breaks the gap down into a number of dimensions, it is generally more specific than gap analysis and is frequently the next step on.

The key benefits of FT analysis are that:

■ It gives a clear and more complete vision of the extent of the potential difficulty that achieving that vision may cause
■ It can be used actually to monitor strategic progress
■ It is a very useful technique for communicating what needs to be done, or for exploring the implications and for getting greater buy-in.

More specifically, it is especially helpful in presenting a business plan for an HR strategic breakthrough.

If it does have any drawbacks, these are that managers may struggle to come up with their desired categories for development and change (presumably because of a lack of clarity and ownership).

FT analysis also links into a number of other techniques, as follows:

■ It can be used to summarize changes in the external marketplace, for example by drawing, as a prelude to delivering, the key HR/organizational issues

- It can help to move from a performance driver and/or fishbone analysis to a programme of development and change
- It can help give an overview of the more detailed 'how–hows'
- It can be used prior to force field analysis and stakeholder analysis (see later in this chapter) to scope likely implementation difficulty and the level of stakeholder support.

Exercise: FT analysis

For one area of HR strategy implementation of your choice, and in particular one for which there is already an existing state of affairs that you are trying to change or shift:

1. What are the key dimensions that you are trying to shift?
2. What are the extremes of these shifts (from left to right) – i.e. where have you started from originally, and where would you like to end up ultimately?
3. Where you are actually now? (Note: this does not have to be a 1.)
4. Where do you want to be as a result of this strategic HR project? (Note: this does not have to be a 5.)
5. What specific actions or interventions might make each shift feasible?

How–how analysis

How–how analysis is useful in the detailed planning of implementation, which comes originally from project management. It is also useful for finding a way forward that might not have been considered before.

Figure 6.9 gives an example of a potential how–how analysis – a possible strategy by Dyson to recruit a new set of senior managers to take it forward into 2005 and beyond.

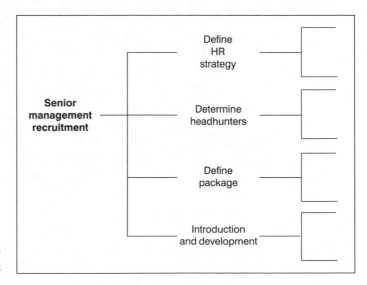

Figure 6.9
How–how analysis

While fishbone analysis works backward from the current situation to find out how and why it exists, how–how analysis works forward to see how it can be resolved in the future.

How–how analysis adds the most value when you have not really thought very hard about the detailed implementation steps that will be needed to achieve something. However, even when you have thought about this, it will be useful just to help identify the less tangible as well as the tangible aspects of HR strategy, especially:

- Positioning
- Communicating
- Influencing
- Team-building.

How–how analysis will also help to get some approximate order of the likely sequence in which things need to happen – and potential critical paths, which are likely to be soft and approximate for HR strategic breakthroughs, rather than something you can manage on Microsoft Project Manager Software.

The major benefits of how–how analysis are that it is common sense and it exposes assumptions about what actually has to happen, thus reducing blind-spots. Its key potential disadvantage is that it can tell you little more than you already know, if you have thought about something really well already.

How–how analysis links to other tools as follows:

- It may help to go from the fishbone's root causes to some potential implementation solutions
- It can help to operationalize the various shifts that have been identified in the FT analysis
- It can feed into the attractiveness–implementation difficulty (AID) analysis.

Attractiveness–implementation difficulty analysis

By looking at the relative attractiveness and its difficulty of implementation (see Figure 6.10) it is possible to begin to evaluate HR strategies at a micro-level, from a number of perspectives:

- A portfolio of strategic activities, any one of which can be undertaken, can be prioritized
- Mutually exclusive strategic activities can be prioritized
- Different options for implementing the concept can be evaluated
- The different parts or activities within an activity can be prioritized.

It is sometimes the case that parts of a possible strategy can be undertaken without doing others. For example, a competency analysis is a preliminary project to a training intervention, or could be a stand-alone project.

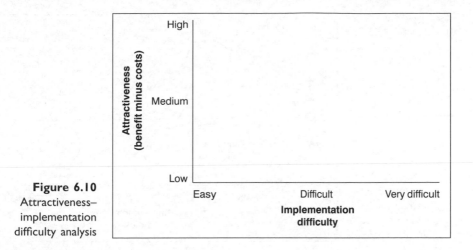

Figure 6.10
Attractiveness–
implementation
difficulty analysis

Thinking now about the vertical dimension of attractiveness, each part of a training strategy may vary in its relative benefits and in its relative cost. For example, a training project might have the following profile:

	Benefits	Costs	Attractiveness
	(B)	(C)	(B) ((C)
Pre-diagnosis	High	Medium	Medium
Pre-work	Low	Low	Low
Main programme	High	Medium	High/medium
Interim support	Medium	Low	Medium
Follow-up programme	High	Low	High
Ongoing support	High	Low	High

The attractiveness–implementation (AID) tool enables trade-offs to be achieved between strategies. The vertical dimension of the picture focuses on benefits less costs, while the horizontal dimension represents the total difficulty over time (this time being the time up until the delivery of results, and not of completion of earlier project phases). This tool enables a portfolio of possible projects to be prioritized. Figure 6.11 illustrates a hypothetical case.

In Figure 6.11, Strategy A is seen as being both very attractive and relatively easy to implement. This project is non-contentious, and will probably be given the go-ahead. Strategy C is relatively difficult – it will probably end up being zapped unless it can be reformulated to make it both a lot more attractive and easier. Strategy D presents the biggest dilemma of all. Although it appears to be very attractive, it is also very difficult to implement. Yet managers will tend to focus on the attractiveness of the project rather than its actual difficulty – and this can occur *even though* they have gone through the force field and stakeholder analysis thoroughly.

When one of the authors was using the AID tool at Hewlett Packard, this happened twice. Quite separately two 'D' type strategies were identified, and

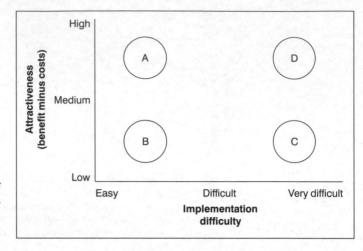

Figure 6.11
Example of
attractiveness–
implementation
difficulty analysis

as managers spent more time analysing them, commitment to action levels built up. Although neither of the projects went ahead – in their existing form – both the author and the (then) internal facilitator Stuart Reed had to be relatively strong to convince the teams that some further refinement was necessary.

Stuart Reed said at the time:

> I had gone through with them [the managers] both the implementation forces and the stakeholders. Although it did seem to be an attractive project our two organizational tools were telling us 'it is not going to happen'. I think because the managers were going through the analysis tools for the first time (and hadn't actually tried to implement it) they hadn't quite realized that it really *wasn't going to happen*.

Strategies in the northeast zone do present some interesting management dilemmas. Following up one HP school of thought, the viewpoint is that it is unlikely to be worthwhile doing these projects as, realistically, the organization will lack the commitment to drive them through. However, a second HP school of thought is that such projects merely represent a challenge for creative thinking, and as long as they are potentially very attractive it may be very fruitful to do this.

At HP another senior manager re-examined a strategic project with which one of the authors had been personally involved some 18 months earlier. This potential strategic project concerned a business process change and a restructuring. At the time, the position of this strategic project was due east on the AID grid, i.e. medium attractive and very difficult. This strategic project went into suspended animation for around 18 months. On further contact with HP we discovered that the new senior manager had solved the problem, both creatively and decisively, by out-sourcing the process rather than by internal reorganization. The project thus shifted from due east to northwest – that is, to high attractiveness, low implementation difficulty.

We uncovered a third school of thought when working with Pioneer UK, the hi-fi company. Its Japanese managing director said to us:

Perhaps we should do that project because it is difficult.

Initially we wondered whether this was perhaps an example of management heroism. On reflection, however, this philosophy fitted in well with the notion of breakthrough management, or *hoshin*. Here a breakthrough is frequently something that is both highly attractive *and* very difficult to implement. (Whilst breakthroughs do not have to be very difficult to implement – just hard for others to imitate – they frequently are.)

A particularly cunning plan is to target HR strategic breakthroughs that, whilst they are likely to be between very difficult to mission impossible for others to implement, will be easier for us. Here, mission impossible (MI) is just off the page to the east of the AID grid.

If we do decide to target HR projects that are very difficult, then, following the philosophy of breakthroughs, it is important to narrow the focus to a very small number of projects within a specific period of time. It is very unlikely that more than three can be undertaken simultaneously without distraction of organizational attention and loss of energy generally. Our experience is that in HR strategy, typically one of the biggest problems is trying to do too much. The AID analysis is an essential tool to prioritizing.

The positionings on the AID grid are likely to be relatively tentative unless tested by using other techniques. For example:

■ The 'attractiveness' of the project may require further analysis using value-driver and cost-driver analysis (ultimately this attractiveness can be financially quantified, albeit perhaps approximately)
■ The implementation difficulty can be tested using force field analysis and stakeholder analysis
■ The difficulty over time can be visualized using the difficulty-over-time curve.

A useful rule of thumb for the less experienced user of the AID grid, or for those who have not used force field and stakeholder analysis to check out their horizontal positioning, is that:

■ If you think the project is easy, it is probably difficult
■ If you think the project is difficult, it is probably very difficult
■ If you think the project is very difficult, it is probably MI even worst still MFI (work this one out – it does not refer to that high street furniture retailer!).

Another technique is to tell scenario stories about the evolution of the project over time (see the work on scenarios in Chapter 4). This may help to tease out its likely trajectory on the AID grid. For example, many projects start out with an assumed northwest position (very attractive and easy), but then zigzag south and east to the southeast (low attractiveness and very difficult).

A final point on AID analysis is that this technique can be used to prioritize each of the bones of the fishbone (or indeed the wishbone). This can be done either using a separate AID picture or (and this is neat) actually along the edges of the fishbone, as mini-AID pictures with a cross drawn of the positioning.

To summarize, AID analysis can be used:

- To prioritize strategic HR breakthroughs as a portfolio
- To evaluate the sub-components of a strategic HR breakthrough or project
- To track (in real time) an area of HR strategy implementation.

Its key benefits are that it:

- Is a quick and easy technique to use
- Is a visual way of representing and debating priorities.

Its potential dis-benefits are that:

- It can be subjective unless it is accompanied by further analysis – for example of value and cost drivers (for attractiveness) or of force fields (for implementation difficulty)
- It can just represent existing thinking on a breakthrough, rather than, more creatively, the 'cunning plan'.

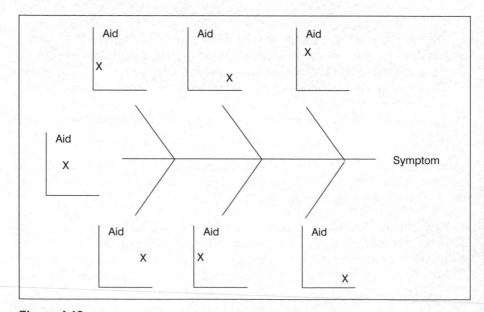

Figure 6.12
Fishbone with attractiveness–implementation difficulty analysis

AID is linked to the following other techniques in the following ways:

■ Value and cost driver (or performance driver) analyses help us to scope 'attractiveness'
■ Force field analysis helps us with 'implementation difficulty'.

The root causes on the fishbone can be prioritized individually using the attractiveness–difficulty criteria (this can be done as per the overlay of the two techniques in Figure 6.12.) Here the 'attractiveness' and 'difficulty' are concerned with resolving that particular case generally, as opposed to that of a very particular solution.

AID analysis helps us to prioritize the froms and tos of the FT analysis.

Value and cost driver analyses

Value and cost driver analyses help us to get a better steer on the 'attractiveness' of a particular strategic breakthrough (the vertical axis of the AID grid). A value driver is defined as 'anything outside or inside the business which either directly or indirectly will generate cash flows – either now or in the future'; a cost driver is defined as 'anything outside or inside the business which either directly or indirectly will generate cash outflows – either now or in the future'.

Examples of value drivers include:

■ Organizational responsiveness
■ A highly motivating leader
■ Excellent cross-functional teamwork.

Examples of cost drivers include:

■ Organizational complexity
■ Excessive and inappropriate politics
■ Bureaucratic processes and structures.

Each one of the above bullet points is then broken down into its sub-drivers, just as we did earlier for 'how–how' analysis.

Value and cost driver analyses can be used to restructure a company's cost base strategically (Grundy, 1998b), to avoid costs beings managed primarily on a short-term basis, and in isolation.

Value and cost driver analyses are essential for anyone doing a business case for HR strategy, especially before doing the financial numbers. (Imagine how wrong our numbers would have been had we not done this analysis!) Example of value and cost drivers of culture change are depicted in Figures 6.13 and 6.14.

Its key benefits are that:

■ It provides a key bridge between HR strategy and finance
■ It helps to stretch thinking laterally about less obvious areas of value and cost
■ It is highly flexible.

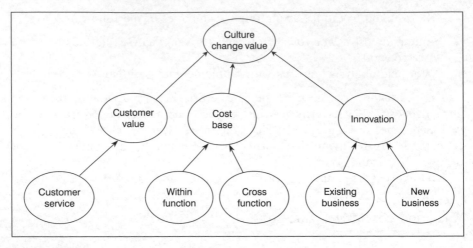

Figure 6.13
Value drivers – culture change

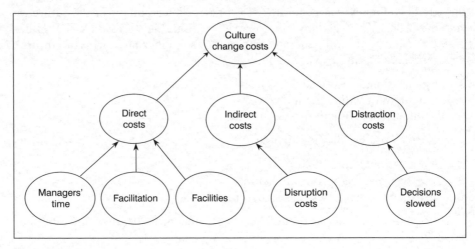

Figure 6.14
Cost drivers – culture change

The key linkages with other techniques are as follows:

- With AID analysis, to test out assumed 'attractiveness'
- With performance driver analysis, to analyse an individual performance driver in depth.

Value-over-time curves

The value-over-time curve helps us to understand when value will be delivered over time. This curve (especially if coupled with scenarios) is helpful

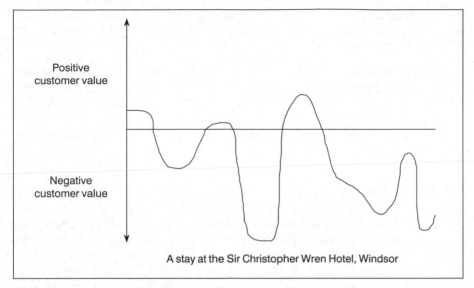

A stay at the Sir Christopher Wren Hotel, Windsor

Figure 6.15
Value-over-time curve – a stay at the Sir Christopher Wren Hotel, Windsor

not only when doing a business case for an HR project, but also for project management generally, and for monitoring the value/for corrective action. The curve can be used to track (in real time) the value added during an HR strategic meeting or workshop.

Figure 6.15 shows a value-over-time curve of service delivery by a hotel, as a more humorous illustration. (The hotel charged £220 a night, it has to be said.) The various 'value destroyed' phases were:

- On getting to the hotel, we were asked 'are you staying at the hotel?', we replied 'Yes', to be told 'well you can't park it here – you must park a quarter of a mile away at the local station' (not only inconvenient, but also exposing the car to possible theft – hardly welcoming!).
- At 12.30 pm the heavy curtains in one room collapsed, making it impossible to sleep easily with bright sodium lights outside. The hotel said 'we can't fix it until maintenance arrive at 8 pm tomorrow'. (Apparently no other rooms were available.)
- On trying to rig up artificial curtains using a number of towels, the sash window slipped and trapping and squashed my fingertip.
- In excruciating agony I went down to the front desk to complain, at which time the porter suddenly found an available room – which when we arrived at it, was more luxurious.
- Checking out of the hotel the next night (in response to this poor service), the hotel subsequently tried to charge us for both rooms (we had apparently given too little notice). This statement was ultimately retracted, under threat of 'likely' nuclear war!

■ When we tried (eventually) to leave the hotel, we couldn't because the car keys were all jumbled and our cars (now in the precious car park) were behind others whose keys could not be located.

Now although this example is a rather graphic personal experience, it does illustrate very powerfully the value-over-time curve dynamic. The same kind of thinking is equally powerful for any HR strategy project, workshop or meeting.

The value-over-time curve can be linked with value and cost drivers, also to 'AID' analysis.

Force field analysis

Force field analysis is a technique that brings to the surface the underlying forces that may pull a particular HR strategy project or programme forward, prevent its progress, or even move the change backwards. These 'forces' can be separately identified as 'enablers' or 'constraints'. However, neither set of forces can be adequately identified without first specifying the objectives of the implementation.

When managers first see force field analysis, they often read it as being some form of extended cost–benefit or 'pros and cons' analysis, which it is definitely not. Force field analysis is simply concerned with the difficulty of the journey that a strategy is likely to make throughout its implementation.

The difficulty of this journey, like that of any other journey in life, has nothing to do with the attractiveness of reaching the destination. The only sense in which it is permissible to incorporate the perceived benefits of a strategy as a force field enabler is insofar as:

■ There is actually a genuinely attractive business case for the HR strategy, and one that has turned on its key stakeholders, and/or
■ Key stakeholders are attracted by the strategy for other reasons.

The most effective way of evaluating the forces enabling or constraining the achievement of the HR strategy's objective is to draw this pictorially. This picture represents the relative strength of each individual enabling or constraining force by drawing an arrowed line whose length is in proportion to that relative strength.

A horizontal version of force field analysis is depicted in Figure 6.16. Note that in this case that, on balance, the enabling forces appear less strong than the constraining forces. It shows that although enablers had been put in place, it was nevertheless difficult to envisage implementation being a complete success. Subsequent events suggested that implementation difficulties at the company were very severe.

The example of the telecommunications company highlights one important truth about force field analysis, namely that the degree of ease of the strategic project is only in proportion to the extent of your pre-existing *cunning implementation plan.*

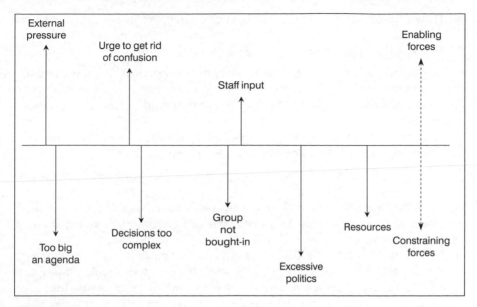

Figure 6.16
Force field analysis

Managers who have not already thought hard about the phases of difficulty and about options to get round potential hurdles (for example, push versus pull strategies), may be doomed to suffer a Very Difficult Project.

As a rule of thumb, the enablers should be outweighing the constraints by a factor of at least 1.5 to 2 overall, in accordance with the principle of military dominance. Otherwise we should be concerned and potentially worried that implementation droop will set in. Also, any stoppers really *must* be addressed, otherwise implementation really won't happen. During (and before) implementation the key implementation forces should be continually monitored to ensure that none of them threaten to 'go critical' and become a stopper.

The next issue that arises is how to evaluate the relative strength of the various forces. Two methods used successfully in the past include:

■ Scoring each force as having 'high', 'medium' or 'low' impact
■ Scoring each force numerically on a scale of 1 to 5.

Where a team may wish to change its mind (and does not wish to spoil its artwork), then by using 'Post-its' the length of the arrows can be changed.

One of the common objections to force field analysis is that the whole scoring exercise is highly subjective. This feeling normally occurs within the first 10 minutes or so of any analysis exercise. It arises usually because all managers have done is to identify that a force is an enabler or a constraint, without exploring questions including:

■ Why is it an enabler or a constraint?

▪ How important an influence is it on the change process (and at which stage)?

▪ What underlying factors does it depend upon in turn?

This highlights that any force field analysis is dependent on many assumptions, a number of which are implicit. A more successful and less subjective analysis will have brought to the surface, shared, and agreed these implicit assumptions.

A number of pitfalls need to be avoided in the use of force field analysis for managing HR strategy implementation. These include:

▪ Focusing primarily on tangible (as opposed to less tangible) implementation forces

▪ Missing out major constraints because the team wishes to paint an 'ideal' rather than a realistic picture of the change (we will return to these issues in a moment)

▪ Failing to identify a 'stopper' – that is, a change that has such a powerful impact that it is likely to stop the change in its tracks. 'Stoppers' should be drawn either as a thick black arrow or as an arrow that goes right to the bottom of the force field analysis and 'off the page'. (This assumes that you are using the vertical format for force field analysis.)

A 'stopper' can be defined as an influence that will effectively put an end to the initiative either through direct confrontation or passive resistance. There may also be cases where a specific enabling force can be made strong and prove decisive in moving the strategy forward. This kind of force may be described as an 'unblocker', and can be drawn as a very long (or thick) positive line upwards on the force field picture.

There may be instances where a negative and constraining force can be flipped over to make a positive force, and in so doing transform the picture. For instance, if an influential stakeholder (who is currently negative) can be turned around in favour of the change, this can provide a major driver in the strategic project's progress. To prioritize which force to focus on, begin with the most presently limiting (or constraining) factor. This is the first key tenet of the Theory of Constraints (Goldratt, 1990).

A useful tip is to look beyond the existing enabling forces to the context of the implementation itself. Within that context, ask yourself whether there are some latent enablers that if brought to the surface, could be used to unlock organizational energy. For example, if staff feel overburdened with work, then a restructuring that is geared not so much to *reducing cuts* but to *reducing organizational stress and strain* is likely to be most gratefully received.

Using a 'pull' strategy to get staff's ideas on future organizational processes in advance of a restructuring might flush out some really good ideas for simplification. It might also get staff on board, as they see these ideas already incorporated in the plans for the new structure.

This is the second major tenet of the Theory of Constraints – that within any really difficult situation there is buried somewhere some latent, naturally enabling force.

The key benefits of force field analysis are that it:

- Encourages you to think about the *difficulty* of an HR strategic break-through as opposed merely to attractiveness
- Helps you to focus on the context and process for its implementation, rather than its context
- Gives an early warning of 'mission impossible' HR projects.

The key dis-benefits of force field analysis are that it:

- Is sometimes too much of a snapshot of the short and medium term (however, this can be remedied by a later technique of the 'difficulty-over-time' curve)
- Can be incomplete, which might give you the misleading impression that implementation is not too difficult really (this can be availed by again asking the question, 'what is the One Big Thing we have forgotten?).

The key linkages with other techniques include the following:

- With attractiveness–implementation difficulty analysis, to test out the assumed level of difficulty
- With stakeholder analysis, to understand the context for change more deeply
- With how–how analysis, to analyse the difficulty of specific activities
- With fishbone analysis, by using fishbone analysis to ask the question for major constraining forces, 'why is this so difficult?'.

Difficulty-over-time curves

Whilst force field analysis is very good at tackling the short-and medium-term difficulties of HR strategic breakthroughs, it may not stretch managers' thinking about the longer-term dynamics of implementation.

To address this issue we need the difficulty-over-time curve (see Figure 6.17). This plots the precise degree of difficulty (easy, difficult, or very difficult) over time, and is the sister technique to the value-over-time curve (see Figure 6.15).

Sometimes implementation of HR strategic breakthroughs gets easier over time, but more commonly it gets more difficult. This can occur at all kinds of different stages, perhaps as a steady incline, or the level of difficulty could climb a little and then fall back before getting really, really difficult.

This reminds one of the authors of his experience on a roller coaster in Los Angeles. It appeared to be two roller coasters, one small and one that was quite awesome. He thought he had gone on the small one until he went over the first peak to see the Very Big One right ahead. The experience was amplified by the fact that it was very quiet and early in the day. Indeed, he and his companion were the only two people on the ride – so they couldn't get solace or company from other people's screams. They

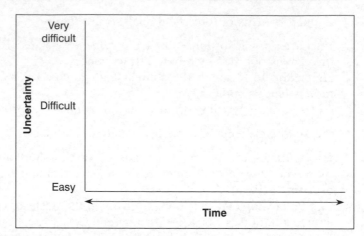

Figure 6.17
Difficulty-over-time
curve

would also probably not have been missed had they fallen out – until the bodies were found!

A roller coaster strategy of this kind can be just as bad as you are not prepared for the sudden onrush of difficulty as implementation proceeds.

The difficulty-over-time curve can be plotted either for the total difficulty of the implementation activity or project, or for just one constraining force. The difficulty-over-time curve is most helpful when creating scenario storylines for implementation.

The curve is also really useful for plotting the trajectory of a workshop or of a meeting, and is a major aid to the HR strategy facilitator.

The key benefits of the difficulty-over-time curve are that it:

■ Is dynamic, and helps to stretch our thinking about the future about an HR strategic breakthrough
■ Is easy to visualize mentally.

The difficulty-over-time curve has the following linkages to other techniques:

■ With force field analysis, it provides a visual way of thinking about the various forces through time
■ With AID analysis, it helps to think about where a strategic project might shift to
■ With stakeholder analysis, to examine how the difficulty of dealing with them is likely to change over time.

Stakeholder analysis

Stakeholder analysis is another major tool for analysing implementation (Piercey, 1989; Grundy, 2002). A stakeholder is an individual or group who has one of the following:

■ A decision-making role
■ An advisory role
■ An implementing role
■ A role as a user or as a victim.

Stakeholder analysis is performed as follows:

1. Identify who you believe the key stakeholders are at any phase of implementation.
2. Evaluate whether these stakeholders have high, medium or low influence on the issue in question. (You need to abstract this from their influence generally in the organization.)
3. Evaluate whether at the current time they are for the project, against it, or idling in 'neutral' (see Figure 6.18).

In order to estimate approximately where a stakeholder is positioned, you will need to see the world from that particular stakeholder's perspective. From experience, we have found that the best way to convey this is to ask managers to have, in effect, an OUT-OF-BODY EXPERIENCE – not quite literally, of course! This involves trying to sense not merely the surface attitudes of stakeholders to a particular issue, but also the deeper-seated emotions, focus, anxieties and even prejudices.

Later we will illustrate how a specific stakeholder's agenda can be mapped using stakeholder agenda analysis, which is another application of force field analysis.

To bring home the point that stakeholder analysis really *does* involve having the out-of-body experience, we usually go as far as showing an acetate of the two television stars of *The X-Files*, Moulder and Scully! From experience, managers who *literally* take the perspective that 'I am the stakeholder' are typically at least 50 per cent more accurate in their analysis.

The three steps listed above give a good 'first cut' of the pattern of stakeholders. The cluster of stakeholders depicted on a stakeholder grid (see

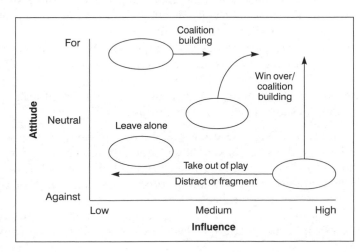

Figure 6.18
Stakeholder analysis (based on earlier versions by Piercey, 1989)

Figure 6.18) should then be assessed to see what the overall picture looks like, particularly:

- Is the HR project an easy bet? or
- Is it highlighting a long slog? or
- Or, finally, does this seem to be mission impossible?

For instance, if most of the stakeholders are clustered towards the bottom part of the stakeholder grid, then you clearly have a mission impossible on your hands (unless the stakeholders can be repositioned).

Another difficult configuration is where there are equal numbers of supporting stakeholders in, for example, the northwest of the picture (although with lesser influence), and in the southeast (but with greater influence). Once again, this means that implementation is likely to experience major difficulties.

Finally, where you have a large number of stakeholders floating in neutral in the middle of the picture, this very neutrality can present major problems due to organizational inertia.

It is a particularly useful idea to position yourself on the stakeholder grid, especially if you are the project manager. This helps you to re-examine your own position and your underlying agendas, which may be mixed.

Following your tentative, first-cut analysis, you should then move on to the next phase:

1. Can new stakeholders be brought into play to shift the balance of influence or can existing players be withdrawn in some way (or be subtly distracted)?
2. Is it possible to boost the influence of stakeholders who are currently in favour of the project?
3. Is it possible to reduce the influence of any antagonistic stakeholders?
4. Can coalitions of stakeholders in favour be achieved so as to strengthen their combined influence?
5. Can coalitions of stakeholders antagonistic to the project be prevented?
6. Can the project change itself, in appearance or in substance, and be reformulated to diffuse hostility to it?
7. Are there possibilities of 'bringing on board' any negative stakeholders by allowing them a role or incorporating one or more of their prized ideas?
8. Is the pattern of influence of stakeholders sufficiently hostile for the project to warrant its re-definition?

Once you have done the stakeholder analysis, it may well be worthwhile revisiting the force field analysis either to introduce one or more new forces, or to revise earlier views. The force field analysis will now incorporate all of the enabling and constraining forces, including some of the more political and the less tangible ones.

Often a particular stakeholder may be difficult to position, and this may be because his or her agendas are complex. It is quite common to find that it is only one specific negative agenda that has made a stakeholder into an influential antagonist.

Where there are very large numbers of stakeholders at play on a particular issue, this may invite some simplification of the implementation. For instance, the implementation project may need to be refined, perhaps even stopped and then restarted, in order to resolve an organizational mess.

In order to use stakeholder analysis effectively, you may need to set some process arrangements in place where a team project is involved. First, the analysis may be usefully performed in a 'workshop' environment so as to give the analysis a 'reflective' or 'learning' feel. This will help to integrate managers' thinking on a key strategy. It may also be useful to devise code words for key stakeholders in order to make the outputs from this change tool feel 'safe'. On several occasions managers have decided to adopt nicknames for the key players. An element of humour will help to diffuse the potential seriousness of performing stakeholder analysis.

Example: stakeholder analysis

A major financial institution was introducing some new processes that were fundamental to its operations. It decided to use the stakeholder analysis technique to identify who the key stakeholders were on the project, and where they were likely to be positioned.

The half-day workshop began by identifying the key stakeholders. No less than 31 stakeholders were defined. At the end of the exercise the question was put: 'Who is the one big stakeholder we have forgotten?' The answer was that there were actually two big stakeholders omitted:

- The customer
- The media.

The moral: unless stakeholder analysis is used in strategic thinking, your implementation could easily fall over as key players may be overlooked.

So far we have used stakeholder analysis in a relatively static manner. However, obviously key stakeholders are likely to shift over time, and early support for the project may therefore evaporate. A number of things therefore need to be anticipated, namely:

- Senior managers' support (especially from line management) is likely to be very sensitive to the perceived ongoing success of the strategic project as it evolves. Any signs of failure are likely to be accompanied by suddenly diminishing support.
- New stakeholders may enter the picture, and others might disappear.
- Certain stakeholders may increase in influence, or even decrease in influence.

■ Where the project changes its scope or focus significantly, stakeholders will change their positions.

Stakeholders' own agendas might change owing to external factors outside this particular project. For example, other projects might distract them, or result in a reprioritization of agendas and of this project in particular.

Owing to the above, it may be necessary to review stakeholder positions at least several times during the lifetime of the HR project.

For further analysis, it is possible to examine how stakeholders may change over time by plotting:

■ Their attitude over time (ranging from 'against' through to 'for')
■ Their influence over time (ranging from 'for' through to 'against').

This is depicted in Figure 6.19.

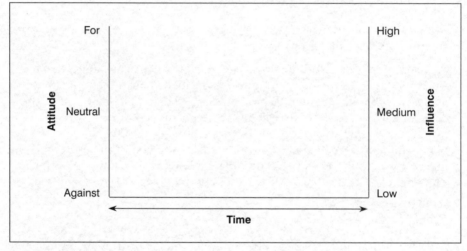

Figure 6.19
Stakeholder attitudes- and influence-over-time curves

Also, it is possible to prioritize which stakeholders to focus on by plotting:

■ *Their* level of influence on this issue, and
■ *Our* degree of influence over them.

In Figure 6.20, the two axes have been plotted. Note that it is important to try to evolve strategies for gaining more influence over those stakeholders who are most influential, and who we have currently least influence over.

One thing to watch with stakeholder analysis is that you do not make fixed and rigid assumptions about stakeholders' attitudes. Using the grid over many years leads us to believe that often managers have a pessimistic bias – assuming that certain stakeholders will be 'against'. In fact, they are often in neutral due to overload of existing agendas or to perceived resource constraints.

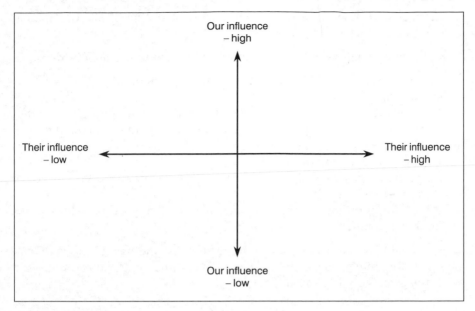

Figure 6.20
Influence over stakeholders grid

When confronted with positionings of themselves as 'against', they are often slightly surprised. The lesson here is that often many organizational agendas are actually more fluid than is perceived. This is good news for strategic thinkers who may feel there is little real chance of their ideas being actually implemented.

Stakeholder analysis is useful:

■ At the very start of the HR strategic process – even as early as the ideas stage
■ When prioritizing HR strategic breakthroughs
■ When performing detailed planning of HR strategic breakthroughs
■ During mobilization of implementation
■ Mid-way or at the latter stages of implementation
■ After implementation, to draw out the learning lessons
■ During workshops.

Stakeholder analysis is also particularly useful for focusing on communication strategy. Here it will help you to identify which stakeholders to communicate with, when, how, and with what message.

The key benefits of stakeholder analysis are that:

■ It deals effectively with the political issues associated with strategy
■ It encourages mental agility and the ability to take a variety of perspectives on an issue (through the 'out-of-body' experience) simultaneously
■ It defuses organizational politics and makes particularly sensitive issues

discussible (these issues are sometimes called 'the Zone of Uncomfortable Debate, or the ZUDE).

Stakeholder analysis is linked with the other techniques as follows:

■ Fishbone analysis can be used to ask the question, why is a particular stakeholder against?
■ How–how analysis can break down the tactical steps required to influence either a collection of stakeholders or an individual stakeholder
■ Stakeholder analysis can also be used to deal with political uncertainties through the uncertainty tunnel
■ Stakeholder agenda analysis (see next) helps to go beyond the surface of these positionings
■ AID analysis or importance–influence analysis can prioritize which stakeholders to influence

Force field analysis can help with understanding the overall difficulty and potential for influencing a stakeholder (what things make this easier, and what things make this more difficult).

Stakeholder agenda analysis

Stakeholder agenda analysis helps you to go down a level deeper – to the agenda of a specific individual – distinguishing between positive agendas (or 'turn-ons') and negative agendas (the 'turn-offs') – see Figure 6.21.

Stakeholder analysis has a very high potential for frequent, everyday use. Besides being applied at a macro-level on the bigger strategic issues, it can be used on projects, for meetings generally, and even for drafting a simple letter or e-mail, or making a telephone call.

The major benefits of stakeholder agenda analysis are that:

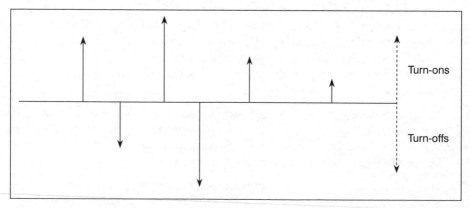

Figure 6.21
Stakeholder agenda analysis

- It can be used to help identify your own position on something and why you are in a dilemma
- It helps you to make a business case or to make a strategic presentation for an HR strategic breakthrough
- It can suggest what the deeper agendas of the organization are, so that you can target your activities in strategic thinking to the 'hotter spots' – thereby avoiding unnecessary frustration.

Stakeholder agenda analysis is linked to:

- The attractiveness–difficulty grid, in measuring how attractive is it to persuade a particular individual to shift their agendas, and how difficult this is.

Importance–influence analysis

Importance and influence analysis helps us to look at the extent to which we have control (or do not have control) over various strategic factors within the HR breakthrough (see Figure 6.22).

Most attention is often drawn to those areas over which we have most influence, and those that are most important, rather than those that are both most important *and* where we have least influence (the southeast of the importance–influence grid). Yet it is frequently possible – through creative thinking – to get at least some influence over these areas.

For example, one department at British Telecom was responsible for strategic advice (Grundy, 1998a), but when managers put its issues on the

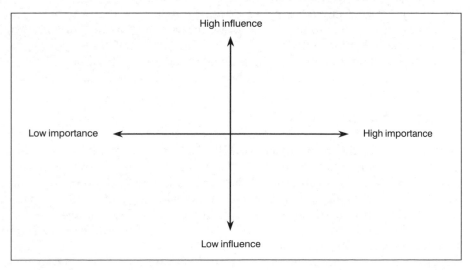

Figure 6.22
Importance–influence analysis

grid they found that most of them were indeed positioned in the southeast of it. This suggested that:

1. They needed to build their own influence over the organization
2. They needed to develop their competence so that their input on these issues was sought by many stakeholders, and naturally
3. They needed to form coalitions with other areas of the organization to deliver these activities
4. They needed to cut down what they were trying to do so that they could provide more leverage where it really mattered.

Importance–influence analysis can be used:

- As part of an HR scenario development process
- When influencing stakeholders, to determine where the pivotal points of influence might be
- To challenge your own mind-set that some things are simply beyond your control.

The key benefits of importance–influence analysis are that:

- It forces managers to think more proactively about what they can do about HR-related issues
- It helps them scan their own external and internal environment and acts as a focus for action.

The key linkages of importance–influence analysis with other techniques are:

- With performance driver analysis – again this can be prioritized for action, picking off the higher influence areas first
- With fishbone analysis, to help to prioritize which of the root causes to focus on (it is usual to begin with those that are most important and over which there is most influence)
- With stakeholder analysis, to help debate how the most important stakeholders that you have least influence over could be influenced.

Motivator–hygiene factors

Before we leave the core process of HR strategy implementation, we will cover a final tool: motivator–hygiene factor analysis, which allows us to link customer value with organizational delivery. This tool is optional, and can be used both externally and also to assess the value generation of a department, of the HR department specifically, and even the HR strategy itself.

Here the 'motivators' are the distinctive aspects of a product or service that will make it very difficult for a customer to switch to another source of supply, and will encourage repeat buyer behaviour. The 'hygiene' factors are those basic standards of delivery that are assumed, but have not been delivered well.

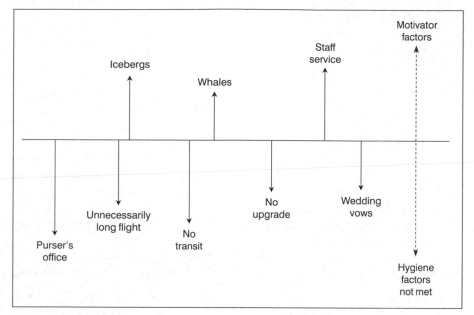

Figure 6.23
Motivator/hygiene factors on a cruise

The motivators and hygiene factors are now drawn as vector areas or lines, their relative lengths being dependent on:

■ Their degree of importance
■ The extent to which they have been delivered distinctively well (motivators) or have not been fulfilled (hygiene factors) – where hygiene factors have been met well, you do not need to draw a downward line at all.

These are illustrated in Figure 6.23 for the following case study on Windsor Cruises. This is a humorous but real story, which will provide lighter relief after we have spent a lot of time going through the toolkit in the main part of this chapter.

Case study: HR strategy at Windsor Cruises

This case study of a cruise line is based on a couple's honeymoon. The case study illustrates the good (and also, in some respects, the not so good) ways in which HR strategy was implemented by this cruise line.

The holiday in question was a 9-day cruise from Anchorage to Vancouver. Following the booking of the honeymoon, the couple were notified that instead of taking the 9-hour direct flight, they would have to fly indirect. Flights were only reserved after the holiday had been booked, although this was not communicated up-front to the customer. (Is this in accordance with Windsor Cruises vision statement, assuming there is one?) The journey, as it turned out, went as follows:

Heathrow to Washington	8 hours
Washington to Seattle	5½ hours
Seattle to Anchorage	3½ hours
Total	17 hours

The 5½-hour journey from Washington to Seattle was termed 'coach' – although the aeroplane had wings the travelling experience reminded the couple of a school bus. Imagine being trapped on Easyjet, doing three trips both ways to Amsterdam, with just one drink.

Landing in Anchorage, it appeared that Windsor Cruises had not actually booked their transit to the ship. The excuse given to them by a laid-back Windsor Cruises representative was that 'many people made their own way to the ship' – presumably Americans hunting for bears.

They were then told that rather than being a half-hour drive, it was actually *another three hours by coach*.

The couple could have embarked on a very similar cruise starting and finishing at Vancouver (with direct flights). Revisiting their schedule, this would have read:

Flight time to date	16 hours
Plus coach to Seward, Alaska	3 hours
	19 hours
Less direct flight to Vancouver (a possibility)	9 hours
Difference	10 hours

Assuming that the couple were highly-paid self-employed professionals who earned (after expenses) about £120 an hour, and that their leisure time was worth say a third of that (£40), their value destruction was 2 × 10 hours × £40 = £800.

As they had no transit booked (this was subsequently refunded), the representative forced them to pay US$110 to board the coach, which had no refreshments. One of them then managed to liberate some food from the airport café by snatching it and throwing a $10 bill at the cashier – otherwise he and his new wife would have missed the coach.

Eventually arriving exhausted for the start of their LUXURY CRUISE, the couple boarded the cruise ship the Royal Corgi to the niceties of 'Have you had a nice day?' from the staff. The couple approached the purser's desk, still remarkably calm considering their ordeal (had Windsor Cruises expected them to hitchhike or kayak to Seward?) Instead of their various problems being sorted out apologetically, the desk was unhelpful, leading to a dispute. Not only was the transit issue not (then) resolved, but their honeymoon cabin upgrade had also not happened and the cruise line had even forgotten to book their renewal of vows. This was only resolved by the end of the week, perhaps partly due to an interesting confrontation between the angry couple and the Captain, who looked at them as if they were potential terrorists and seemed unable to respond even though he had several minders with him.

At the couple's renewal of vows (performed by the Captain later that week), the Captain's face betrayed his negative feelings and only one of the honeymoon pictures taken was actually usable. Strangely, the experience of customer service regarding these particular issues was in sharp contrast to the excellent service that the cruise ship otherwise delivered. For the rest of the week the service in the 24-hour restaurant, and from all the other staff on the Royal Corgi, was absolutely impeccable.

The couple's experience is depicted graphically as a motivator–hygiene factor picture (see Figure 6.23), focusing on the distinctive turn-ons (their importance, times and how well they were delivered), the motivators, and the turn-offs, the important hygiene factors (those not met, or met badly). These hygiene factors were substantially due to uneven implementation of the cruise line's HR strategy.

So how can an organization like Windsor Cruises get the implementation of its HR strategy simultaneously so right and also wrong? Let us examine the question more deeply.

The areas of the organization that did not appear to delight the customer (and in the Captain's own words as the couple boarded the ship, 'create a perfect holiday') were:

- Its marketing/sales operation
- Its payments area
- At disembarkation (which was not well managed, as the couple had to stand around for nearly an hour for their baggage, and were then told that they couldn't just go off and get a taxi once they had collected this).

This suggests the strong possibility that there were some rather different sub-cultures at work within parts of the operation, which undermined delivery of its hygiene factors. Yet in the rest of its operations the HR deployment was immaculate, and actually quite cunning. For example, this involved:

- Sourcing staff from a myriad of countries around the globe, and obviously motivating them to an extremely high level
- Getting maximum productivity out of staff by having them work nearly every day during their contract on board (i.e. giving them very few days off)
- Having rolling contracts, so that the company had maximum control over the quality of its staff – every single member of staff was on contract, including the Captain.

Again, this example underlines the imperative of complete organizational align-ment underpinning HR strategy along the lines of the wishbone analysis tool that we saw briefly in Chapter 3.

In summary, Figure 6.23 shows the HR-related motivator–hygiene factors picture for this cruise experience. As it demonstrates, this was to be the couple's last cruise on Windsor Cruises ever, and they were to turn down an offer for £150 off their next cruise.

CONCLUSION

To summarize, the five key stages of HR strategy implementation are diagno-sis, options, planning, implementation, and learning and control. Within these stages a number of areas to remember include:

- At each stage there are a number of tools that can be used. Some tools work for different stages – so they can be used more than once.
- Performance driver analysis and fishbone analysis can be very helpful in organizational turnaround situations.
- Fishbone analysis can be used to diagnose organizational problems of considerable complexity, and can be used to uncover the systems at work between root causes.
- FT analysis will help you to explore the scope of HR strategy implementation, to determine the level of desired stretch. It will also help you to communicate it within the organization and to monitor progress towards goals.
- How–how analysis then breaks down each shift of the HR strategy within the FT analysis into manageable breakthroughs or sub-breakthroughs.
- Attractiveness–implementation difficulty analysis is needed to prioritize particular strategic HR projects.
- Force field analysis and the difficulty-over-time curve then tests out its difficulty.
- Stakeholder analysis identifies the key stakeholders, positions them, and also suggests new influencing strategies.
- Stakeholder agenda analysis enables you to go a level deeper, to explore a particular stakeholder's ambitions and anxieties about an HR issue.
- Stakeholders' attitude and influence can be plotted over time using the attitude-over-time and the influence-over-time curves.

Stakeholders can also be disaggregated into:

- Those who have the greatest influence
- Those we have greatest influence over
- Those who are least/most important (see the importance–influence grid).

Figure 6.24 shows how the various tools are interrelated.

There is a very logical rationale for the clusters and for the arrow flows, which indicate the general order in which they should be used. Also note that it would be rare to use them all in one sequence! Two or three are often sufficient, but sometimes a longer sequence is worthwhile – for example, for performance drivers we may use fishbone, AID, force field and stakeholder analyses.

Some of the most interesting linkages are:

- Performance drivers give a higher-level picture, which can identify performance brakes, which are then diagnosed individually with several fishbone analyses
- Specific performance drivers can also be diagnosed to explore their financial impact, using value and costs drivers
- The 'cunning plan' can refine the how–how analysis and deal more effectively with key uncertainties (the uncertainty grid), and has all the alignment factors (wishbone analysis) lined up

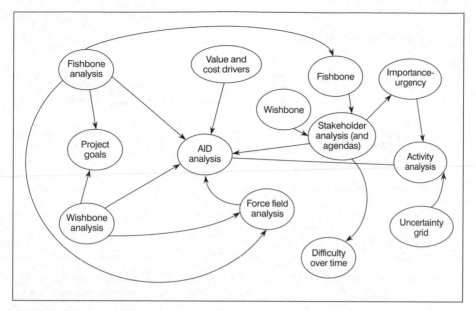

Figure 6.24
Key linkages between tools

- The fishbone analysis can be diagnosed with an 'AID' analysis overlay
- The how–how analysis can be refined, having done the force field/stakeholder analysis and the difficulty-over-time curve.

Where an issue is complex (fishbone analysis), it may be necessary to do a number of force field/stakeholder/difficulty-over-time curve analyses. These will reveal the complexity of the HR strategy, and the need to work separately on a number of mini HR strategies rather than at a more general level.

Project managing the implementation of HR strategy

INTRODUCTION

This chapter deals with the implementation process at an even more practical level. Whilst Chapter 6 gave you the core tools for diagnosing implementation, Chapter 7 is now a reminder that HR strategic breakthroughs require clear project management.

As HR staff tend to see HR strategy as a relatively abstract idea (although it is evident so far that we see it as quite tangible, and very specifically targeted at generating cases with economic value), they often do not appreciate that it is not only helpful but also essential to project manage the breakthroughs within it.

This chapter provides the remainder of your core HR consulting diagnostic techniques, complete with detailed checklists. However, before we go into these in detail, a simple but very important insight in HR strategy is that to call an HR initiative a 'project', and to think of it in that way, adds a lot of value in itself. In doing so it becomes an entity that needs a special focus in order to deliver its results. An ongoing activity, by contrast, may lack that same clarity of focus. This is really important, as many HR managers do not tend to think of what they do as a stream of projects. Defining HR strategy as a project also lends itself to targeting its economic value much more readily, too. It is therefore also worthwhile at this juncture to define that a project is:

> A series of activities which have a predetermined result, and which is to be accomplished on a particular time and cost.

The definition is best visualized by using the Project Triangle (see Figure 7.1). This suggests that if you attempt to deliver any two of the three goals of the project, the third one will tend not to be delivered. So, for example, where the result is delivered to time, the cost may be overrun. Where the result is delivered to cost, there may be time overruns. And where cost and time targets are met, the result may not be met. Equally, the result might be

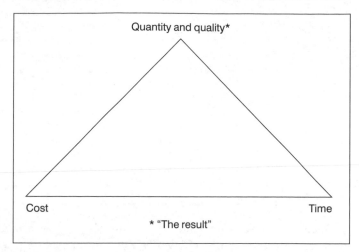

Figure 7.1
The project
triangle

delivered in terms of quantity but not quality. How many HR initiatives fail to deliver because of a lack of realism in the Project Triangle?

PROJECT MANAGEMENT TECHNIQUES

Besides how–how analysis (sometimes known as 'work breakdown'), already covered in Chapter 6, we may need to draw on some additional techniques (both old and new) from project management for HR strategy implementation.

For instance, once the major activities have been generated the next stage is to begin to think about their phasing in over time (perhaps initially with the 'difficulty-over-time curve'; see Chapter 6). This can be done in one of two ways:

1. With an HR project with relatively few interdependencies in the sequencing of activities, you can go directly to a Gantt chart – which displays activities over particular times
2. With an HR project where there are likely to be extensive interdependencies in the sequencing of activities, you might seek instead to develop an Activity Network, to identify its possible critical path.

Figure 7.2 shows a Gantt chart (named after its creator) for an organization turnaround project plotted earlier. Note that many of the activities occur in parallel with one another.

Gantt analysis is normally very easy to use. Even where there might be a complex underlying network of opportunities, it may still be worthwhile doing a quick Gantt chart to get a 'feel' for when things may need to happen by.

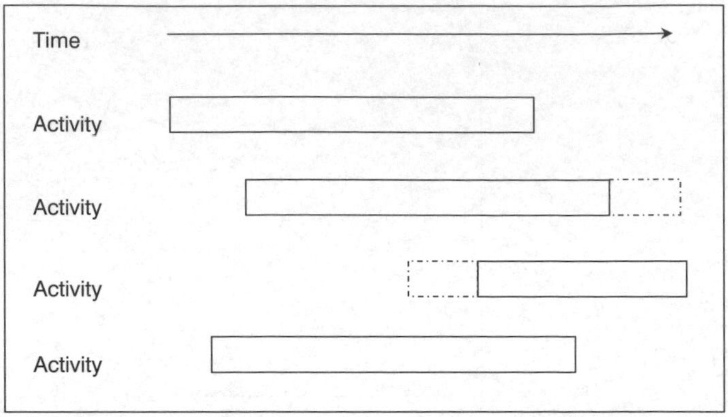

Figure 7.2
Gantt chart

Once again, we should not see Gantt analysis as a mechanistic process, for there are frequently many possible phasings of these activities. Even where there are well-trodden ways of doing particular kinds of HR projects (such as training projects), there are still often choices as to when activities can begin, and in what order.

Project management is also a way of increasing time-based competitive advantage (Stalk, 1990). In most industries it is becoming increasingly important to accelerate the implementation of strategies, and as HR strategy implementation can be slow and faltering it is crucial to be able to accelerate its implementation.

To illustrate this particular strategic breakthrough, one senior Tesco manager once said to one of the authors:

> What we are trying to achieve in 2 weeks, Tony, is what we and others used to achieve in 3 to 6 months.

This means that in timing an HR initiative into a project, you should not be trapped or pre-conditioned by previous mind-sets – as we see in example of the Metropolitan Police.

Projects, as we have already defined them, are all about achieving a pre-targeted result in a specific time and at a specific cost. It is therefore imperative to see what we can do (through Gantt chart analysis, the activity network and the critical path) to accelerate these.

A very solid rule of thumb that might help us to achieve this is:

> Try to do activities sooner than you might otherwise think of doing them.

This rule of thumb applies especially to activities that are more likely to be on the critical path, and those that are the most constraining.

Besides parallel working activities and accelerating the start of activities, it is also perhaps possible to split the activity up into at least two phases. The most obvious phases are planning and implementation. For example, even if you cannot do an activity now, you can certainly create a *plan* for doing it.

Project managing HR strategy: the Metropolitan police

Several years ago, the Metropolitan Police (which employed many tens of thousands of staff) developed an HR strategic vision. Whilst this contained the broad themes of HR strategy, there was still a perceived need to break this down to implementation plans, and ultimately into projects.

The process then adopted was:

- To take the strategic HR themes and do a how–how analysis of what steps would be needed to deliver them.
- To write the main HR strategic actions on 'Post-its', and then group them on a whiteboard. Each potential project was then clustered most closely to those others with which it had most strong interdependencies.
- These interdependencies were then drawn in so that each project could be managed not in isolation but in terms of the other changes on which it was dependent (see Figure 7.3 for an example).
- The team then asked, 'what is the one big thing that we have missed?'
- The approximate timelines for each strategic HR project were then mapped out using Gantt analysis.

Focusing on 'culture shift', the team felt that this would take quite a long time to achieve. The team's facilitator challenged this, and proposed that 'the longer we allow it to take, the longer it probably will take'. To give the Met a time-based focus, he proposed a series of rolling 100-day plans, with clear deliverables, for culture shift. The Met's commissioner really took to this idea, making the 100-day plan theme the centrepiece of his strategic change process for the Met.

Accelerating activities works up to a point, but only provided the quality of the process can be maintained. Accelerating HR projects seems therefore to behave as follows. Up to a certain point there are some very real cost savings (due to time and resources saved) as you accelerate activities. However, after that point the costs go up, sometimes quite disproportionately, as errors are made and costs are generated elsewhere or later, or because resources get in the way of each other. Another rule is: if you accelerate, then you really must simplify!

Another possibility in activity analysis is delay. Whilst this may not be an obvious strategy, sometimes it may be wise to delay an activity if there are simply too many activities happening at once. When you try to do a number of things simultaneously, efficiency quickly starts to decline. If, therefore, particular activities do not need to be done at the present time, a temporary delay may actually help to accelerate other activities disproportionately.

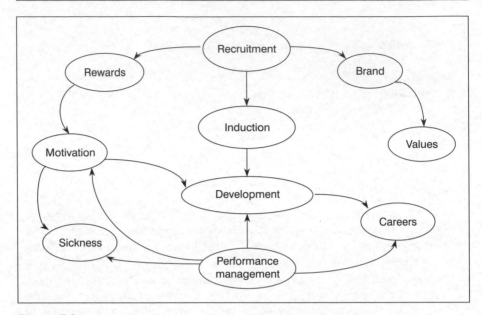

Figure 7.3
Interdependencies – HR strategy

Indeed, there is invariably a good deal more flexibility within the activity analysis of *when* things need to get done by. The major constraining factors are not so much performing the activities, but rather the availability of data, decisions being made, resources being made actually available, and sheer physical constraints. These are the factors that are most constraining for the strategic project, rather than necessarily the activities themselves.

At this point we would remind you that the techniques of force field analysis and stakeholder analysis (see Chapter 6) are initially important additional tools for project management. Also, fishbone analysis is essential for an initial diagnosis of the problem, or of 'why are we doing this project?'. Finally, attractiveness–implementation difficulty (AID) analysis will help to prioritize a number of projects, or the sub-parts of each project.

Activity analysis, the critical path analysis and uncertainty

Critical path analysis is at the very centre of traditional project management. Whilst being absolutely imperative for complex technical projects, it needs to be set in context amongst the other tools in its degree of importance when considering an HR strategic project. Whilst there is invariably a real critical path for a strategic project, this is frequently likely to crystallize during the HR project rather than before it is started (see Figure 7.4).

If you have already done an approximate Gantt chart, this will give you some strong clues to the likely structure of the network of activities of the

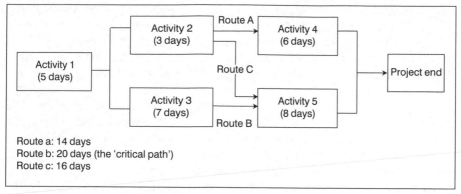

Route a: 14 days
Route b: 20 days (the 'critical path')
Route c: 16 days

Figure 7.4
Critical path

HR strategy project. Essentially, you will need to decide which activities need to be done, and in what order – so for each activity you will need to work out which activities have to have been completed already *in order for* this activity to be started. Quite quickly a chain or network of activities can be built up. One useful way of doing this is to write each activity on a 'Post-it' and then simply place these in the appropriate order on a flipchart. Then, once you have the order sorted out, draw in the arrows to represent the activity path through the activity network.

In practice, this methodology is perhaps most useful for HR projects where you are working out which stakeholders you are trying to talk to, and in which order. Where stakeholders are part of both a formal and an informal network, the order in which you go to talk to them might have a significant impact on how well you position the HR project, and on how well you win them on board.

Alternatively, the 'Post-its' can be arranged on an importance–urgency grid (see Figure 7.5), which is another classic, quick and dirty way for prioritizing activities. With this grid it is important to avoid over-focusing on the

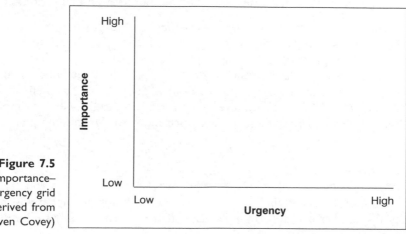

Figure 7.5
Importance–
urgency grid
(derived from
Steven Covey)

most urgent at the expense of the most important. The grid can also help you in time management – for example, spend 80 per cent of your time on the few really important projects, focusing on them all at once, and then spend the remaining 20 per cent of your time (on dedicated days or half-days) to specialize in clearing the less important projects before they become too urgent and distracting.

Using 'Post-its' is a good way of testing your assumptions about the relative order in which the key activities need to be carried out. Using this process you can often parallel work activities that might previously have been assumed to be strictly sequential, for instance (see Figure 7.4, which gives a network of activities for a business turnaround plan).

Turning now to the critical path of the project, we need to identify the sequence of activities that, if subject to any delay at all, will delay the whole project itself. This is actually what the critical path really is. So, for example, in Figure 7.4 we see from the duration of activities that path C is the critical path.

With strategic HR projects (as opposed to more technical ones), it is less obvious not only which sequence of activities is the critical path, but also how determinate this path will be. In real life the critical path will shift considerably for a strategic project, operating in an incremental and often turbulent organizational environment.

Whilst it is useful to have some view as to what the most likely critical path is for a strategic HR project, it is equally important to:

- Monitor the key uncertainties
- Identify the most constraining factors of data, decisions, resource and physical constraints
- Be aware of whether any activities can be accelerated internally, to make up for the delay
- Be aware of whether deploying additional resources (possibly through out-sourcing) can be brought in in order to accelerate key activities, or to make them more effective or better.
- Be aware of which activities frequently take longer than assumed, especially softer activities like shifting mind-set and behaviours.

This makes critical path analysis a much more flexible process for strategic projects – indeed, it becomes just as much a 'soft', intuitive process as an analytical process.

In order to assess the relative *difficulty* of specific activities, it may well be useful to draw up a mini force-field analysis. This will help to identify those activities that may require more time, more resources, or simply more thinking through (bringing us back once more to the cunning plan).

Uncertainty analysis

Moving on to uncertainty, our classic technique for managing and monitoring this is Mitroff's uncertainty grid, which we have already seen in Chapter

3 on Organizational Scenarios. The main difference here is that we are now narrowing our focus to *implementation uncertainty*, as opposed to any kind of business or organizational uncertainty generally. This grid can be used for a variety of HR strategic breakthroughs, including:

- Recruitment strategy
- Organizational restructuring
- Performance management initiatives
- Culture change initiatives
- Management development programmes
- Career development pathing.

The grid is used specifically for surfacing the assumptions underlying the particular activity within an HR project. It plots the degree of importance horizontally against degree of uncertainty vertically. Once again, 'Post-its' can be used to represent the key assumptions and then position them on the grid.

Probably the majority of your chosen assumptions will end up between the centre and the right of the grid – that is, from medium to high import-ance. This is not a problem, as long as you do capture some of the assump-tions that are of lower importance. Quite frequently these lower-importance assumptions increase in importance, either as you think harder about their implications for the activity, or just as they shift during the project.

Not only might the assumptions shift from left to right, but they are also likely to move from top to bottom as uncertainty increases. The most danger-ous assumptions are obviously in the southeast of the grid: these are of high importance *and* most uncertain. The grid helps to focus managers continu-ously on the areas where economic value might be destroyed. Figure 7.6 gives

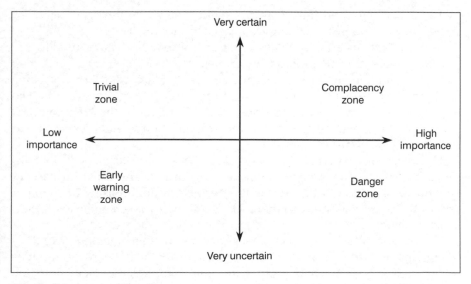

Figure 7.6
Uncertainty–importance grid

some generic descriptions for each one of the quadrants, making it more user-friendly.

As explained in Chapter 4, the usual convention in defining your assumptions is to think of the world as 'going right' – in other words, these are the assumptions that need to be fulfilled in order for project success. From experience, many managers seem to find working with assumptions like this surprisingly difficult. To some extent this appears to be due to the in-built optimism that managers have – a culture of 'before it goes wrong, our only assumption is that it will go right'. This seems to be coupled with the phenomenon once described as 'the Nietzsche syndrome' or 'the Will to Power' – that is, if it goes wrong we will just get on and fix it (Nietzsche was a famous German philosopher who focused on mental strength as a source of power).

Mitroff's grid dates back to the 1960s, when sociologists were keen on examining taken-for-granted assumptions. These taken-for-granted assumptions give a sense of a coherent social reality. Challenging assumptions can be a strenuous process and thus is not in keeping with normal management activity, which focuses principally on getting things done as opposed to *thinking* about what things *should* be done, and how (helicopter/strategic thinking).

Returning now to activity analysis, activities that have a heavy concentration of assumptions in the danger zone (or are in the southeast of the uncertainty–importance grid) are very likely to suffer:

- Delays
- Uneven delivery of results
- Additional costs
- Knock-on difficulties in other activities, or even in other projects.

The uncertainty grid thus helps to identify the really 'hot-spot' activities throughout the project, enabling us to helicopter over it.

Coupled with uncertainty analysis, scenario storytelling can be used to 'see around corners' for HR projects.

Implementation scenarios need not be purely framed in terms of being 'optimistic' or 'pessimistic', but in terms of simply 'alternative worlds'. The scenario given here concerns the implementation path of the HR project as opposed to the general canvas of the organization's wider environment (which we looked at in Chapter 4).

The uncertainty grid can thus be used to check the robustness of the critical path analysis. For example, what happens to the critical path if particularly time-sensitive activities exceed their projected durations by 20 or 30 per cent? This enables almost certain blockages to be foreseen, along with their knock-on effects.

Clearly only a foolish project manager of an HR implementation strategy would operate with no slack to accommodate for activity over-runs. It is essential, one way or another, to build some 'oxygen' or 'float' into the project. 'Float' is defined as the amount of time allowed for over-run of activities, and can be built-in either as a final activity in the HR project (that is,

Implementation scenario – culture change in a services organization

One of the authors has been involved in a major HR intervention over a period of several years in a large service organization. Begun as a management development initiative, it started to be seen more as a cultural change intervention, partly because of the manifest mind-set resistances to new thinking.

In years one and two the programme was a mixed success, so in year three the client redesigned it with the facilitator and began to run this together with the facilitator, rather than this being principally out-sourced.

Looking forward, a number of scenarios could be imagined:

- *Scenario 1*: year three's programme is a success, the programme continues, and the partnership with the facilitator continues
- *Scenario 2*: the programme is a success, but the company wishes to take over the programme fully from the facilitator with a transitional period
- *Scenario 3*: the programme has just one wobble, causing the company to take it over fully without any transition
- *Scenario 4*: the key HR managers in the client team leave, so the programme has no home and it ends
- *Scenario 5*: the key HR managers in the client team leave, but the programme continues and is taken up by its new client
- *Scenario 6*: the key HR manager leaves and someone new arrives, who changes the programme and drops the facilitator
- *Scenario 7*: the company gets taken over and the programme ends.

Looking at the above list of scenarios, the big 'so what?' is that this is a very volatile situation in the medium term. Objectively speaking, if each scenario were of equal probability, the odds of it continuing to a full year (with the facilitator) are about two in seven (scenarios 1 and 5), or 28 per cent! Postscript – Scenario 3 actually happened.

explicitly), or by particularly generous time allowances for one or more activities. Another approach is deliberately to front-load the time pressure on early-stage activities so that should slippage occur, you are still actually on schedule. Minor apparent slippage actually has the effect of stimulating concentration and effort, which, if not present at the early stages of a project, is hardly likely to be there later on.

Tighter targeting of time for activities seems to have a number of effects that are very evident when running HR strategy workshops, namely:

- Set-up time (getting started) is much reduced
- Talking around more peripheral issues is also minimized

- Managers are more likely to devise a process to get to their targeted result
- Managers will be much more conscious of time.

If instead of using a 'float' more time is deliberately allowed for a project activity, then there is the opposite result. It is incredible how wasteful managers can be if given luxurious time targets. For example, one workshop facilitator mistakenly gave a team an hour and a quarter to achieve a task, rather than 45 minutes. After about fifteen minutes, hardly anything had been accomplished – in fact, the managers kept drinking coffee for five minutes. After half-an-hour the teams had just got started, and were rambling around the issues. When the facilitator prompted them about progress, they simply turned around and said, 'well, we have 45 minutes to go'.

The moral of this is: if you give people a lot of time, then they will take it!

RESOURCE MANAGEMENT

Critical path and activity analysis leads us on naturally to the topic of resource management – for it is possible to produce a fabulous-looking project plan, but one that is also hopelessly unrealistic considering resource constraints. Imagine, for example, a situation where a number of activities have been scheduled in parallel within a certain time period. Figure 7.7 shows this in relation to the availability of resources over time. At the mid-part of the activity there is a big resource gap, which, if not fulfilled, could lead to a significant delay in the project. Indeed, the ceiling of available resources may not necessarily be flat but undulating and changing over time, depending upon:

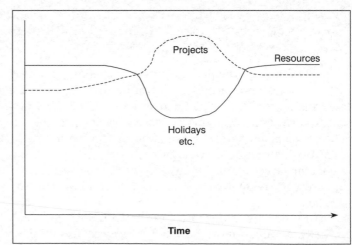

Figure 7.7
Resource
availability over
time

- Holidays, sickness and training
- New joiners or leavers
- Staff working on other projects elsewhere
- The ability to source-in extra skills from outside – either as consultants or as sub-contractors.

Here, the Gantt chart for the HR project (see Figure 7.2) gives a strong clue as to the shape of this profile.

Again, project software (with suitably injected intelligent assumptions) should flag up any resource gaps – at least in terms of the quantity (if not the quality) of skills missing. In this regard it is wise not to go for overkill in project management sophistication for HR breakthroughs. However, there can be times when this level of sophistication is appropriate – for example, during major acquisitions or mergers, in the integration phase.

We should now add a final note on activity and critical path analysis. Highly elaborate HR project plans (especially those compiled using computer software) can give the impression that everything will just happen on time. However, one of the most critical assumptions is the actual release of resources to the project on a just-in-time basis. Whether these resources come from a general pool of resources or from another specific department, it cannot simply be assumed that staff *will* be available to start on time. Even where they work on projects within the same department, they may be delayed in completing other projects. So it is important to establish check-points in the project plan to double-check that future resources will be available as and when assumed. This will not only highlight potential bottlenecks in advance, but may also help to accelerate activities in other projects so that staff can be made available.

Often the process of resource allocation will not go wonderfully smoothly. There will be real conflicts, which may not be resolved by just mere horse-trading. This problem underscores the importance of prioritizing projects effectively, and also assessing the costs of delay.

'Costs of delay' is a fundamental concept for HR project management. Costs of delay can be defined as:

The total costs, both directly and indirectly (and tangible and less tangible) of delay in a project relative to each unit of time.

Costs of delay are well understood in at least some industries, such as in oil exploration (where delay exacts penalty charges) and in major construction projects. However, other industries have yet to catch onto the importance of this concept when performing project prioritization and planning. Here, the relative costs of delay are an essential measure to enable at least some organizational politics to be dissolved.

The idea of the 'cost of delay' is an important and useful notion when getting HR (or 'organization and people') budgets agreed, for these budgets are typically set on perceptions about what can be afforded during a particular time-period. Projects that will add considerable value but cannot be squeezed in simply drop into the next budget period. However, HR initiatives usually have a short-shelf life (to deliver economic value), as they have typically been aligned to a current and perceived organizational need. Delay can thus be very costly. By actually quantifying (in an illustrative or indicative way) the cost of delay, it may well be more feasible to get top management's attention.

Also, as we argued strongly in Chapters 1 and 2 that the HR (or possibly 'organization and people' strategy) should be championed by the Chief Executive, then the impact of short-term thinking and the associated budgetary distortions should be minimized.

SKILLS OF THE HR PROJECT MANAGER

The HR project manager needs to have developed the following key skills:

- Diagnostic and problem-solving skills
- Strategic skills, to be able to think through options
- Logical reasoning
- Planning and coordination skills
- Change management skills
- Commercial (and even some basic financial) skills, to prepare an adequate business case
- Interpersonal, influencing, and political skills
- Communication skills
- Presentation skills
- Leadership skills
- Time management skills.

Looking at the above skills, they do seem much more to be concerned with general management-type ability rather than traditional personnel skills. It is sometimes found that former marketeers (or even accountants) have a more appropriate skill set for this role than perhaps traditional (and operational) personnel managers.

The above skills are not necessarily the most well developed in HR managers (or indeed in many managers!) Often HR managers are drawn to HR because of their 'softer' skills (particularly interpersonal, influencing and political skills), but they may be less skilled in the areas of planning and coordination, commercial, and strategic skills. (The issue of consulting skills is tackled further in Chapter 13.)

CHECKLISTS

Having discussed HR project management, we next look at a number of checklists for managing HR strategic projects. These checklists are split into two sections:

1. Process checklists
2. Issue checklists:

Process checklists

Our process checklist is divided into:

- Diagnosis
- Options
- Planning
- Implementation
- Learning and control.

Diagnosis

1. Where the HR strategy issue is a problem, what is the main symptom of the problem, and what are its root causes?
2. For each of its root cases:
   - How attractive is it likely to be to resolve?
   - How difficult might it be to address?
   - How is it therefore positioned on the attractiveness–implementation difficulty grid?
3. Where the HR strategy issue is an opportunity:
   - What is your vision (what do you really, really want from it)?
   - What is its potential economic value?
   - What would need to align to deliver it? (i.e. what are the necessary and sufficient conditions of achieving this vision?)
   - For each one of these alignment factors, how uncertain is it and how important is it? (uncertainty– importance grid)

Options

1. What more obvious options are available to meet or to exceed your objectives?
2. What less obvious options are available to meet or to exceed your objectives?
3. What less obvious options are available to meet or exceed these objectives (for example, arrived at by benchmarking best practice elsewhere)?
4. How attractive–difficult are these to do? (AID analysis)

Planning

1. For each HR project (or sub-project), what is your project triangle of intended results, costs and time?

2. What activities need to be conducted? (Gantt chart/critical path)
3. How important/certain is it that these will be accomplished to deliver the result, the cost, or to time? (uncertainty grid)
4. What value will be delivered over time? (value-over-time curve)
5. What will the costs be over time? (cost-over-time curve)
6. Given the investment and the speed of paybacks, does the project give a good enough return?
7. Or could it even be bettered?
8. Who will need to be involved, when and how? (stakeholder analysis)

Implementation

1. What are the most likely implementation difficulties going to be (phase-by-phase)? (force field, difficulty-over-time curves)
2. Will stakeholders continue to support? (stakeholder analysis/agenda analysis)
3. What assumptions about 'the world going right' exist implicitly, and how are these positioned on the uncertainty–importance grid?
4. If there are problems in implementation, why do these exist? (fishbone analysis)

Learning and control

1. If the project succeeded, why did this occur? (wishbone analysis)
2. If it did not succeed, why? (fishbone analysis)
3. How did it shift over time on the AID analysis grid, and why?
4. How did it cause a significant impact on business and financial performance? (performance drivers, value and cost drivers)
5. Why did some scenarios occur and others not?
6. Why did stakeholders behave differently from expected? (stakeholder analysis/agenda analysis)
7. Why did key phases become more difficult than expected? (force field analysis/difficulty-over-time curve)

Issue checklists

Dealing with more content issues (and highlighting particularly useful tools from previous chapters), let us now consider:

- Competencies
- Recruitment
- Performance management
- Rewards

- Career development
- Training
- Mentoring
- Team-building
- Innovation
- Stress management
- Work patterns
- Restructuring
- Change management
- Communication
- Benchmarking
- Decision-making processes
- Acquisitions.

(Succession planning is dealt with in Chapter 9, so no detailed checklists are given here)

Competencies

1. Why do you need to develop a 'competency framework' (i.e. what economic value might it add)? (value and cost drivers)
2. Who do you need to develop a competency framework for? (fishbone analysis)
3. What are you going to do with it once you have got it, for example in terms of:
    - Recruitment
    - Performance management
    - Career development
    - Training
    - Restructuring
    - Benchmarking?
4. Which competencies are likely to be most important? (AID grid)
5. For which competencies is there likely to be the biggest gap, now or in the future? (FT analysis or just simple gap analysis)
6. Who do you need to involve in its development? (stakeholder analysis)
7. What are you going to actually call it (e.g. competencies, skills, 'success factors' etc.)?

Recruitment

1. Where are the biggest and most important gaps, now and in the future? (FT analysis)
2. What options exist for recruitment (e.g. external versus internal sources, out-sourcing, contractors, consultants)? (AID analysis)
3. To what extent have you benchmarked the intended quality of recruits (e.g. top quality), and is this consistent with the packages being offered?

4. Do you really need these roles on a permanent basis? (AID analysis)
5. Are these roles really likely to be needed in the next two or so years, given the likelihood of restructuring or merger? (scenarios)
6. What is the economic value of recruitment likely to be? (value and cost drivers)
7. How can this economic value be maximized (e.g. by avoiding early drop-outs, training, performance management, etc.)?
8. What other things need to be put in place in order to capture its full value (e.g. induction, mentoring)? (wishbone analysis)
9. Will the packages offered upset internal strategies?
10. How is it best to socialize new staff into the company culture? (how–how analysis)
11. What criteria for recruitment should be set (for instance, to avoid just reinforcing the existing mind-set of the company)?
12. What specific competencies are you looking for?
13. Is it advisable/not advisable to use psychometric tests in recruitment?
14. To what extent will these roles change significantly (in the not-so-distant future), and what impact might this have in the future? (scenarios)
15. Are you looking just to recruit local nationals, and if so, what might be lost in the way of a more global mind-set?
16. To what extent have you thought through the further investment that will be needed in these people?
17. What are the linkages to other HR initiatives, including (for example) career developments, performance management, rewards etc.? (inter-dependency analysis)
18. Where there are difficulties in recruiting specific scarce skills, what is your 'cunning plan' for getting around this? (fishbone analysis, plus the 'cunning plan')
19. To what extent have you positioned the organization as an exciting and attractive brand that will draw high quality applicants? (this is especially relevant to sectors not necessarily seen as highly exciting, like some public sector organizations, banks, insurance companies, utilities, accounting and legal firms, etc.)

Performance management

1. Why do you wish to implement performance management, and what economic value is it likely to add?
2. What economic value might it actually destroy (for instance in terms of confusion, staff resistance, extra management time)? (value and cost drivers)
3. Do you have a sufficiently robust competency framework (or equivalent) in place? (see previous section)
4. How will it be linked to rewards systems, and will these linkages be sufficient to achieve the desired effect?

5. Have you benchmarked your proposed process against other organizations to avoid repeating their implementation errors/to produce a world-class process?
6. Are you planning to implement 360-degree feedback, and if so, have you prepared managers sufficiently to manage the special difficulties and sensitivities that are likely to arise in your specific organization? (stakeholder analysis/stakeholder agenda analysis)
7. What are the links going to be with further training/career development, and will these links ensure that appraisals do not focus primarily (if not exclusively) on short-term performance issues as opposed to longer term development?
8. How are you proposing to deal with underperformance?
9. How will you set about diagnosing under-performance/performance problems in an objective way – for example, using fishbone analysis?
10. How will you make sure that this process also focuses on performance interdependencies (for example, on team behaviour, resources availability, stress levels etc.), rather than simply seeing the individual as the behavioural unit? (wishbone analysis)
11. What ongoing links will be made to training needs analysis generally in the organization?

Rewards

1. How well is your reward system linked to performance management?
2. How well is it linked (explicitly) to economic value added?
3. How competitive is it relative to your competitors, and how well has this been benchmarked?
4. To what extent is it linked to 'softer' factors like open behaviour and communication, and to leadership and strategic thinking skills, and to innovation?
5. How has being able to cope well with stress and any particularly high workload been reflected in it?

Career development

1. Have alternative career paths been considered in any career development review? (AID analysis)
2. Are future career paths sufficiently supported by training and mentoring, etc.? (wishbone analysis)
3. Have the career development aspirations across the management population been related to future organizational needs? (scenarios)
4. How open is the discussion of future career development opportunities?

5. Do career paths allow sufficiently for development of international skills, development across functions or business boundaries, to prevent high performers getting trapped in their existing roles for too long?
6. Do career paths allow sufficient flexibility to cope with secondments, work on special projects, maternity leave, etc.?
7. How has the future likelihood of downsizing or organizational regeneration been reflected in discussions on careers? (scenarios)
8. Has the most appropriate and balanced set of future appointments been determined, given the need to bring in new blood to the organization, as well as providing a sufficient incentive to existing, internal staff?

Training

1. Have training requirements been subjected to a sufficiently rigorous process of training needs assessment? (fishbone analysis, scenarios)
2. Has this process made adequate and appropriate use of competency processes?
3. Have training needs been appropriately diagnosed (for example, with fishbone analysis)?
4. To what extent have training interventions adequately taken into account the existing mind-set, culture, and other changes in working practices (for example, performance management, rewards etc)? (wishbone analysis)
5. Do training programmes contain sufficient linkage both to on-the-job activity and further reinforcement to be fully effective (for example with the trainee's own boss)? (wishbone analysis)
6. What is the economic value of training programmes? (value and cost drivers)
7. Is adequate use being made of mentoring? If not, why not? (fishbone analysis)
8. Is there the most appropriate balance between on-the-job training, public training programmes and in-company training?
9. Has internal, in-company training been appropriately positioned in the organization?
10. Have external qualifications like MBAs (and their funding) been adequately thought through to give both incentive to the individual and economic value to the company? (AID analysis, value and cost drivers)
11. Are the right people being sent on training courses, and for the right reasons? (fishbone analysis)
12. Has the training precision been adequately benchmarked against other companies to ensure that it is 'best-in class'?

Mentoring

1. Is mentoring considered to be a 'nice-to-do' or a more fundamental way of achieving greater performance, managing role transition, and undergoing personal development?

2. What economic value added is it targeted to have? (value and cost drivers)
3. Do its recipients know what they should do, and are they prepared to put what they need to into it? (wishbone analysis)
4. Are the mentors fully aware of what they should do, and what they should put into it? (wishbone analysis)
5. Are the right people being mentored, and for the right reasons? (wishbone analysis)
6. Where senior staff feel unable to/do not want to be mentors, are they really the right people for their jobs?

Team-building

1. Why is team-building actually needed? (fishbone analysis)
2. What economic value would this add? (value and cost drivers)
3. How sustainable are the benefits likely to be? (uncertainty–importance grid)
4. What other things need to be aligned (for example, does the team have the most appropriate leader)? (wishbone)
5. Would it be useful to use some psychometrics (for example Belbin's team roles), and if so, how would this be positioned?
6. What other interventions might be needed to get full value (for example, changing team membership, simplification processes, strategic thinking/ leadership training etc.)? (wishbone)
7. How does team-building relate to organizational values?
8. How will cross-cultural issues be effectively addressed? (how–how analysis)
9. What cunning plans exist for team-building across different geographic sites?
(See also Chapter 11.)

Innovation

1. Why is the organization not perceived to be innovative? (fishbone analysis)
2. How appropriate is innovation, given the organizational unit's critical success factors?
3. What economic value is it targeted as adding? (value and cost drivers)
4. What other interdependencies does it rely upon (for example, more open communication, value statements, performance management, rewards, career development, team-building etc.)? (interdependency analysis)
5. Are there sufficient external recruits to produce a free-thinking mind-set?
6. Is there adequate training in and opportunities to develop and practise innovative thinking (through workshops etc.)? (if not, use a fishbone)

7. Do staff have sufficient thinking space to think in an innovative way? (if not, use a fishbone)
8. Does the organization have a good process for screening, evaluating and prioritizing ideas? (if not, use a fishbone)
9. Is there sufficient time, resources, and opportunity to implement innovative ideas? (if not, use a fishbone)
10. What economic value added has occurred through past and current innovation, and may potentially be added through future innovation? (value and cost drivers)
(See also Chapter 3.)

Stress management

1. Why is stress perceived to be a problem in the organization? (fishbone analysis)
2. What economic value added has been destroyed (for example by staff leaving, errors, delays, political disagreements, unfair dismissal cases etc.)? (value and cost drivers)
3. Is the current culture one where excessive stress is actually not just tolerated but is actually promoted through overly-stretching senior management behaviour?
4. Are there particular areas of the organization highly prone to stress, and why? (fishbone analysis)
5. Are there particular managers who are especially prone to causing stress, and if so, why? (fishbone analysis)
6. Have you benchmarked the level of stress with other organizations?
7. How well is stress relieved by training and/or mentoring?
8. How well (and openly) is stress dealt with within the performance management process?

Work patterns

1. Why are staff working too long? (fishbone analysis)
2. How might this overwork be avoided?
3. What economic value does it destroy?
4. Is adequate provision made for home-working, to enable staff to be more productive?
5. To what extent are staff actually discouraged from working excessive hours?
6. When staff do work excessive hours, how is this monitored and what corrective action is taken to ensure that this is temporary? (how–how analysis)
7. Do senior managers themselves practise this organizational code by not working silly hours? If not, why? (fishbone analysis)

Restructuring

1. Why is the restructuring actually needed? (fishbone analysis)
2. How sustainable is it likely to be, and to what extent is it appropriate for the future environment and competitive challenges (as opposed to merely the present)? (wishbone analysis)
3. What are its value and cost drivers? (for example, responsiveness, simplicity, and unit costs)
4. What (overall) is its likely economic value added, and what is the business case? (value and cost drivers)
5. How difficult is it likely to be to achieve this intended value? (force field analysis and difficulty-over-time-curve)
6. How well is it supported by other HR indicators, such as training, mentoring, team-building, recruitment, etc.? (wishbone analysis)
7. What are the most critical uncertainties, and how can these be managed (for example, key staff being unhappy and leaving)? (uncertainty–importance grid)
8. What scenario stories can be told about how it is a great success, how it drifts off course, and how it fails in its main objectives?

Change management

1. What do you intend to change, and why? (fishbone analysis)
2. What is the extent of the gap between where you are now and where you need to be? (FT analysis)
3. For each of the 'from–tos', how do you propose to achieve these shifts, remembering the 'soft' as well as the 'hard' factors? (how–how analysis)
4. What is its targeted economic value added? (value and cost drivers)
5. How will this economic value actually manifest itself? (consider measures, indicators)
6. How will it be project managed, by whom? (how–how analysis)
7. How will it be facilitated?
8. How will any new ideas or themes be positioned in the organization, to avoid unnecessary resistances being set up? (try to avoid unnecessary management jargon like 'paradigms', or whatever the new concept on the block is, unless you are completely committed to it and understand it fully)
9. How will the change be sustained in the longer term (e.g. what reinforcement will it need)? (wishbone analysis, scenarios)
10. Will it be adequately supported/linked to other things like recruitment, training, performance management, rewards, restructuring etc.? (interdependencies)

Communication

1. Why is communication seen as being a problem? (fishbone analysis)
2. To what extent is this a reflection of the current culture, politics and structure of the organization?
3. Have people actually been trained to communicate well?
4. Are there company guidelines on the use (and abuse) of e-mails?
5. What is the economic value currently being destroyed by not-so-good communication? (value and cost drivers)
6. Is communication performance considered explicitly enough in performance management?
7. What are the really important things in the organization that are not being communicated well, or at all, or at the right time, or to the right people?
8. Where there is a major restructuring in the organization, is the communication process actually project managed?

Decision-making processes

1. Where decision-making processes need to be improved, why is this the case? (fishbone analysis)
2. What is the economic value currently being delivered or destroyed by poor processes (for example, slow decision-making, decisions not made at all, decision-making errors, etc.)? (value and cost drivers)
3. What is the incremental economic value added by much improved decision-making?
4. How might decision-making be improved? (how–how analysis, FT analysis, or both)
5. To what extent are criteria set for decision-making (for example, using AID analysis or value-based management types of approaches)?
6. To what extent can you use decision-making workshops to improve major decision-taking (with or without facilitation)?
7. When you are implementing new bases of decision-making (like value-based management), have you thought through the changes needed in other organizational processes – e.g. culture change, mind-set change, performance management, rewards systems, etc.? (interdependencies and wishbone analysis)

Acquisitions

1. How similar is the culture (really) between the acquired and the acquiring company?
2. What is the most appropriate leadership style for the organization (given its context and the integration strategy)?
3. What leadership options exist, and which is most appropriate?

4. What are the skills (and skill gaps) of the acquired organization? (may require competency analysis – see Chapter 10)
5. How difficult is integration likely to be over time? (difficulty-over-time curve)
6. Who are the key stakeholders for any specific integration issue, and where are they positioned/how could they be influenced? (stakeholder analysis)
7. What are the key organizational uncertainties? (uncertainty–importance grid)

PUTTING A VALUE ON AN HR PROJECT

The value of a specific HR strategy can be assessed by first thinking through the extent to which the project is sufficiently stand-alone, to begin to get an intuitive feel of its incremental cash flows. Figure 7.8 provides a good set of rules of thinking about how to judge this. When there are many inter-dependencies, where these are complex and where they cannot be easily quantified, it is sometimes necessary to perform the financial appraisal at a higher level – that of the 'strategic project set' (or perhaps even one level higher still, at the HR strategy programme level).

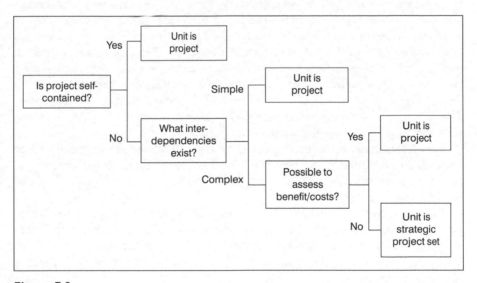

Figure 7.8
Strategic project set

STRATEGIC HR BENCHMARKING CASES

It is worth adding a quick note here on HR strategic benchmarking (our last topic). This can be a very powerful input, and is one that is typically neglected by HR managers. Why reinvent the wheel if someone else has already solved the problem, for instance in another industry where there are very strong parallels?

Strategic HR benchmarking can be performed for all of the areas listed in the HR project checklists covered earlier. It is particularly relevant to some of the more difficult processes or less tangible areas, such as leadership, change management and management development.

It is essential that senior operational and HR staff are actively involved in any visits to other organizations, otherwise the benchmarking consultant will return with most of the insights (and possibly get a few new clients!) Meanwhile the consultant's client may lose many of the insights or, even worse, not create sufficient will to implement them, as in the insurance company case study shown here.

Case study: benchmarking in a major insurance company

A major insurance company commissioned two major benchmarking projects. The first one was on the change management associated with business process re-engineering. The company's consultant introduced the team to several financial services companies, and also a major oil company. Whilst the (middle-ranking) team did guess many insights, some of these were lost because following the site visit they shot off home rather than finding a local café for an immediate debrief.

Moreover, as the benchmarking team lacked a really senior manager, there was little commitment to the radical rethink of the scope of change to processes that was needed. The result was that the company did little differently until 2 years later, when it went overboard into a massive business process re-engineering exercise, with a large firm of consultants, which proved difficult and disruptive. The benchmarking lessons from the earlier exercise were lost, and were not reflected in the subsequent change initiative later.

Some years later, the insurance company initiated a benchmarking exercise on leadership development. This time the consultant went alone to five other companies ('we are too busy' was the client's excuse for not going – or was it that the client was too embarrassed?)

The consultant again brought back some very interesting ways of developing more effective leadership programmes (using self-managed development, peer coaching etc.), but once more little changed – except for the fact that the existing leadership course proposals were given the go-ahead, with apparently relatively little change.

Having read this case study, you might be getting sceptical of HR benchmarking projects. However, this uneven success is primarily down to process inefficiencies and positioning. Whilst the Lloyds TSB case study shown here is not perfect, we can see that it did lead to major economic value being generated – albeit down the line.

Interestingly, the economic value of organizational interventions is often found much later, and proves to be 'latent' for some considerable time. This 'latent value' is often a bonus on top of the business case, but from the authors' past experiences of clients, it can sometimes be very significant indeed (especially in the area of management training).

Case study: benchmarking management development strategies at Lloyds TSB

Many years ago a consultant was asked to benchmark management development strategies at Lloyds TSB (then Lloyds Bank). The exercise was commissioned quite quickly, meaning that there was not time for visits to be done by both the benchmarking consultant and the management development head. Whilst only some of the insights that emerged were acted upon in the short term, the management development head subsequently led a major initiative to upgrade the bank's general management capability generally. He was subsequently promoted a number of times, finally becoming Group HR Director.

A useful process for benchmarking is shown in Figure 7.9, along with relevant diagnostic tools.

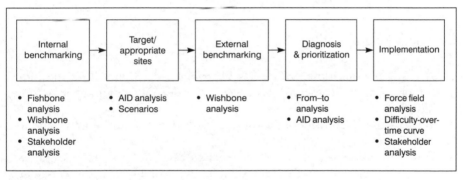

Figure 7.9
Strategic HR benchmarking – a process

Figure 7.9 highlights the following points:

■ The importance of initial benchmarking to elicit our current performance (and reasons why it may not be so good)
■ Where it is good, this can be captured through a wishbone analysis
■ Stakeholder analysis helps to identify key stakeholders with an influence, and thus helps to select who might actually participate in or sponsor the benchmarking project
■ AID analysis can help to target appropriate sites
■ Scenarios can assist in determining whether a site will be worth visiting (what might we actually get out of it?)

■ Wishbone analysis can help to identify what is going well (alternatively, performance drivers)
■ AID analysis and FT analysis can practise and scope implementation
■ The usual tools (force field analysis, etc.) can be used for implementation.

Besides the above techniques, it is essential to actually identify a small number of key questions to use for the benchmarking. These may include, for example:

1. What value do we get out of change management projects currently?
2. What are the strengths/weaknesses of our processes?
3. How do we track and review the benefits?
4. How is this positioned in the organization?
5. How well do we integrate this with other organizational processes?

Following a number of interviews internally, the same questions should be asked during the external interviews. The responses can then be compared, using a matrix approach (of questions against their responses). This should then be followed by a process of careful extraction of insights (which leads to the diagnosed prioritization phase).

Benchmarking checklists

1. Are key organizational processes benchmarked either within the industry or as a 'best-in-class' *vis-à-vis* other leading companies in other industries?
2. What is the likely economic value added of benchmarking? (value and cost drivers)
3. How will you ensure that the insights gained during benchmarking will be actually implemented? (for example, by involving senior line management actively in it)
4. How will you prioritize issues for benchmarking/for implementation? (AID analysis)
5. What will your benchmarking process be – for example, what key questions do you want it to ask? Have you benchmarked yourself internally sufficiently first, and how have you targeted benchmarking sites? (how– how analysis)

CONCLUSION

All HR strategic initiatives should be thought of, and also managed, as 'projects'. This means:

■ Defining their targeted results, cost and time
■ Targeting their economic value (and not just leaving the 'results' as an intangible)
■ Following a process for project managing them
■ Not only using some of the conventional project management techniques (like Gantt analysis, how–how analysis or work breakdown), but also drawing from the implementation techniques (like force field analysis and stakeholder analysis; see Chapter 6)
■ Using uncertainty analysis and selective scenario storytelling (for implementation) to steer the HR project to its destination
■ Defining a project manager and (where necessary) a project sponsor
■ Adapting to the role of being a project manager
■ Drawing from the HR project management checklists listed earlier.

A number of major organizations, including the Metropolitan Police, the Royal Bank of Scotland and Tesco, have incorporated much of this thinking into their management of HR strategy implementation. We encourage you to do the same, whatever the size and complexity of your company.

PART 3

HR strategy issues

CHAPTER 8

HR strategy, culture and strategic change

INTRODUCTION

HR strategy is very closely entwined with culture change. Indeed, HR strategy is one of the central vehicles for creating culture change. Before we get deeper into this issue with our fascinating case study of Champneys Health Resort, we will first take a quick look at a short case study of Tesco's culture change project some years ago.

CULTURE CHANGE AT TESCO AND BP

Case study: 'culture change' project at Tesco

Around the mid-/late 1990s, Tesco decided to consider embarking on a major culture change project to enhance its responsiveness throughout the organization. A consultant was called for discussion with senior HR staff and very senior line management. There was a great deal of enthusiasm for embarking on some culture change. However, the consultant suggested that if you looked at the actual value added by past culture change projects at major organizations, the results were somewhat patchy.

One of the main problems, he explained, was that 'culture change' was too nebulous an organizational intervention. Also, calling it 'culture change' tended to get middle-ranking managers' backs up immediately, making it very difficult – if not impossible – to get buy in (without virtually entirely changing the managers). His recommendations were to take something more tangible, whose benefits could be more clearly targeted – like 'customer service'. Having discussed this input, Tesco abandoned the 'culture change' label which incidentally had attracted a clutter of stakeholders in the project's stakeholder analysis grid (these are used extensively by Tesco).

So 'customer service' was born, which was a change programme of specific projects such as 'One-in Front' (flexible checkouts with faster queuing), behavioural training for staff, and rules of engagement for more open and effective meetings.

Looking back after the event, these combined initiatives probably helped Tesco to gain an incremental ½ per cent market share (the authors' own estimate). Tesco then had around 15 per cent market share. If that incremental turnover were of the order of, say, £500 million, the incremental profit per annum (at a margin of around 5 per cent) was approximately £25 million per annum.

The key lessons from the short case study on Tesco are as follows:

- HR strategic breakthroughs are often emergent, and then become deliberate
- Before they are rolled out, HR breakthroughs often need reformulating and simplifying (so they go through a further 'emergent' phase)
- Where they involve 'softer' issues like culture change, there is even more of a need to be specifically targeted, and as far as possible in economic value terms.

Picking up on the last point – economic value – whilst it is not an easy task even in the case of culture change, it is still possible to target the value of the change. For instance, in 1991, one year after BP had initiated its culture change 'Project 1990', a review of the economic value of culture change was aimed out. This was done by BP's Central Culture Change team, with the aid of one of the authors. Initially it was very difficult to put a meaningful value on culture change, for BP had sought to shift the 'values' of its staff, and these were truly relatively intangible and not easily linked in a specific way to financial performance. (By 'values' we mean here 'the deeply held attributes and tacit rules that influence behaviours'.)

After 3 days of reflection, the answer dropped out as follows.

Whilst it was very difficult to define and observe incremental financial performance changes through shifting organizational values (which were themselves very difficult to measure), it *might* be possible to look at *changes in behaviour*. These changes in behaviour were a consequence of shift in values.

By looking in effect at a different phase in the causal chain, it suddenly became feasible to put an economic value on culture change. The next major insight (see Figure 8.1) was that to make the valuation task easier we should focus on identifying 'critical incidents' (an idea drawn from learning theory) – moments when value breakthroughs were created. Now these were indeed relatively easy to identify and to put a value on.

Very quickly the team drew up a flipchart list of easy-to-identify 'stories' of different manifestations of newer culture, and were able to say what they were worth. Even these early stories were worth over £50 million.

One particular later story was worth even more. Apparently there had been a technical/environmental problem at one of BP's facilities. The tech-

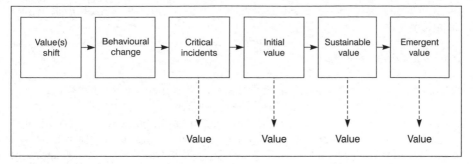

Figure 8.1
Putting a value on culture change

nical team had (in BP's old culture style) come up with a gold-plated/bomb-proof solution that would cost many millions of pounds. However, when encouraged to challenge this more creatively and from a zero-based mind-set (i.e. how can we fix it for nothing/little?), the team came up with an alternative and solved the problem at a fraction of the previous cost.

In Figure 8.1 we see the logical chain as being: values shift, behavioural change, critical incidents. This leads to initial value added. A further two stages, which became apparent in the BP case, are those of 'sustainable value' and 'emergent value'.

The 'sustainable value' phase is often neglected. The culture change team (or equivalent) pack up and go home, or go off to new organizations; old behaviours then recur, and the incremental economic value diminishes. That is, of course, unless (a) there is further reinforcement of the change, and/or (b) the culture change is something that really feeds on the organization's natural agendas, as it did at Tesco – where staff *wanted* to produce world-class service, because *it made them feel better about themselves.*

Now whilst these things cannot easily be financially modelled with precision, we can get a grip on them by stretching our value-over-time curves (see Chapter 6) under different organizational scenarios/intervention scenarios.

Finally, 'emergent' value (our sixth stage) is perhaps even more interesting. The more effective interventions typically bring out from the organization its natural inclinations and energies (once called 'outerventions' – Grundy, 1993), and can generate considerable unexpected value.

Going back to BP, in the 1990s BP went from being 'Bloody Profitable' (a joke often told at the pre-project 1990 boozy BP lunches in city pubs) to not so profitable at all. The early 1990s recession hit BP very hard indeed, slashing its profits. However, BP management, now softened up by culture change and by structural change at Head Office (there was considerable downsizing, shift change and management process simplification), was then able to come through the recession in better shape than many other oil majors. This, and a number of well-timed and well-managed acquisitions (for example, Amoco), made BP Amoco the world's second biggest oil company

173

by 2002, and a very successful performer in terms of shareholder value creation.

Had BP *not* initiated and relatively effectively implemented Project 1990, it appears doubtful that:

- It would have so successfully weathered the difficult 1990–1993 recession, and it might even have lost its independence
- It would have built a world-class management capability that could then put it towards the top of the league (one of the authors was a manager at BP during 1980–82, some years earlier; it was his first management experience, and with little (then) to compare it with it felt very much like being in the second division whilst ensconced managers thought they were actually at the top of the premiership).

The lesson here is that we should look at emergent change from a number of perspectives:

1. What economic value might be lost over time through long-term decline, in the event that no intervention is made?
2. What new opportunities exist in the future that can only really be successfully exploited through having a new culture/capability?

Besides value creation, we must not forget the negative side to cultural change interventions. For example, they are costly in terms of organizational development/consultancy resources and in terms of management time. They may also require costly venues, overnight stays, etc. When you are dealing with a large population of managers, this can become a very expensive process.

Worse, there may be significant distraction costs – as managers are encouraged to think and behave in new ways, ongoing imperatives may be neglected. Certainly at Mercury Communications in the mid-1990s, its 'Ignite' programme clearly did not help maintain the management focus at a time of mounting organizational challenge and change.

This all leads to the conclusion that there is a need to draw up a kind of 'culture change' profit and loss account, so to speak, for the intervention.

Our BP case thus raised a number of interesting points:

1. To put a value on 'culture change' (or similar wide-ranging interventions), you need to go down the change process to look at the impact behavioural shifts have on specific incidents/events
2. In addition, there is harder-to-quantify value through the change's sustainable effect, and through further value emerging later (using scenarios will help here)
3. The economic value of culture change might only be realized if interdependent initiatives are mounted – at BP, for example, these were:
   - Structure change

- A major downsizing
- Management process re-engineering
- The introduction of value-based-management (see Chapter 2) as an incisive/challenging management tool
- An ongoing focus on 'the learning organization'
- Changes in the pattern and style of career development at BP, which in the past had been very driven by the organization (people were posted hither and thither, rather than having shared ownership of their careers)

4. A 'profit and loss' account of major interventions like change management needs to be drawn up.

CHAMPNEYS HEALTH RESORT

Having rehearsed some of the issues and processes of culture change with the Tesco and BP case studies, we will now look at a smaller-scale example of how HR strategy provided the vehicle for culture and strategic change at Champneys Health Resort. This case also illustrates how HR strategy can be turned into implementation. This case study is based on a documentary on BBC television in 1996 and also on interviews with the (then) Chief Executive of Champneys. This will help you to practise your skills as a strategic HR consultant.

The case study shows how the main ingredients of strategic change (including culture change) need to be interpreted. Figure 8.2 shows how strategic change is impacted by:

- Environment: the external market place
- Strategy: the company's competitive scope and positioning
- Culture: the underlying values, beliefs and attitudes that shape behaviour
- Leadership: the overall direction and inspiration within the company
- Agendas: the things that inspire people to act, or prevent them from acting
- Structure: how people are organized, and power is exercised
- Processes: how decisions are taken, managed, and monitored
- Careers: how managers get on in the company
- Legacy: the company's past successes, failures and resource base.

It also illustrates and introduces a new technique (more sophisticated than AID analysis) for appraising options; the need to project manage HR strategy implementation.

In the case study we will see that there is a two-way flow from competitive strategy to HR strategy, and back from the HR strategy into creating *new* competitive strategy.

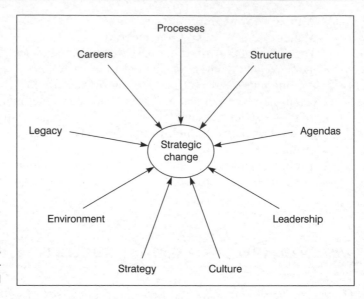

Processes

Careers

Structure

Legacy

Strategic change

Agendas

Environment

Leadership

Figure 8.2
Strategic change –
a model

Strategy

Culture

Background

Champneys Health Resort is located at Tring, in Hertfordshire (UK). Champneys is a select rural retreat for its members, who reside principally in and around the Home Counties. Traditionally it is a most exclusive retreat, charging near-Savoy prices for its luxurious and relatively exotic services in body and skin care generally.

However, by the recession of the 1990s Champneys was suffering considerably. Falling demand meant that its cash flow had deteriorated to the point where it experienced an annual cash deficit of £1 million. Its previous owners decided that enough was enough, and sold out to foreign investors.

In both business and organizational terms, Champneys was in the situation of a strategic turnaround. Its new investors therefore decided that a new breath of life was required to secure Champneys' future. The choice of a new leader was the first key strategic decision, as the particular appointment would shape how future strategy would both evolve and be implemented.

As Champneys had recently been acquired by a new owner, in effect this case study is also about acquisition integration. The integration of acquisitions is a key issue in HR strategy, particularly because it often entails changes in leadership, structure, skills and culture – and often also in operational processes. Many acquisitions are badly handled in the integration phase, primarily due to the lack of a robust HR strategy.

In late 1995, Savoy-trained Lord Thurso was recruited to spearhead Champneys' recovery, and as its integration manager. As its new Chief Executive, Lord Thurso set about formulating a turnaround plan that would secure Champneys a viable future. At this time Champneys also featured on a BBC2 production, *Trouble at the Top*. Some of Lord Thurso's comments quoted here are taken from that television programme, and some from interviews with the authors.

Because Champneys prided itself on its exclusive customer service, this turnaround strategy needed to be managed with great sensitivity to the HR-related issues.

Strategic diagnosis

In the tradition of turnaround specialists, Lord Thurso set himself a tight deadline to formulate and project manage his strategic turnaround plan. This was just 1 month. In the course of that month Lord Thurso was to spend the bulk of his time listening to Champneys' various stakeholders, particularly:

- Its members and its regular customers
- Its staff
- Its current managers.

A number of strategic projects were born out of Lord Thurso's strategic thinking, including HR-related strategic projects (asterisked):

- Sampling Champneys treatments (by Lord Thurso)
- Simplifying management processes
- Improving management reporting processes, and more commercial focus and style*
- Management restructuring*
- Management recruitment*
- The communication plan*
- The strategic vision*
- Developing a business strategy*
- Customer database
- Maintaining organizational morale*
- Culture change*
- Getting rid of the 'Health for Life' timeshare scheme
- Premises strategy
- The business case and its approval.

To start with, Lord Thurso, who weighed 16 stone when he took over Champneys, undertook to reduce this weight – coincidentally in parallel with what became Champneys' own corporate slimming exercise. Most important in those early days for Lord Thurso was sampling Champneys' exotic, health-generating treatments – this being his first project to help turn around the business. This was a very useful process in helping Lord Thurso to understand the organizations' current capabilities and weaknesses, and areas of opportunity to exploit its skills.

Lord Thurso's early diagnosis within the turnaround project indicated that

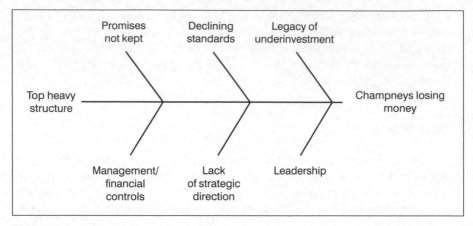

Figure 8.3
Champneys fishbone

Champneys suffered from a number of underlying problems (see Figure 8.3), some of which were more business-focused and some HR-based. These included:

- A legacy of under-investment (and decay)
- A decline in standards generally
- An over-zealous attempt to market Champneys timeshares to customers outside Champneys' core customer base
- Promises made to members that could not be kept
- A top-heavy management structure
- Relatively poor (or inappropriate) management and financial controls
- A lack of sense of strategic direction generally.

Lord Thurso wisely negotiated a remuneration package that would not disadvantage him in recommending possibly unpalatable options – highlighting the linkages between strategic thinking and reward structure that must be an essential part of any effective HR strategy.

Reflecting on this situation in 2000, Lord Thurso elaborated:

There isn't any money and my job is to get the value out – bang, bang, bang. To take difficult decisions with easy. In a way, what I was doing was not far short of that. You arrive, the thing is absolutely bleeding to death and the shareholders are not going to be able to bale it out a great deal more, and you have to have a plan for dealing with an emergency situation. That's when you whip the patient into an ambulance and off to hospital. The thing was absolutely in the shit – that is a technical term.

To which his interviewer replied:

Yes, it is a technical term – it stands for Strategic Health in Trouble.

Lord Thurso continued:

When I first started I had an option, which was to recommend closing the business down, and I would be paid, I would have a kind of parachute, so I was free to say: 'Look, I am sorry, I don't feel that the business is viable, the only way out is to chop it up and sell all the bits off . . .

On his first inspection of the property after taking over in 1995, Lord Thurso commented:

It is clearly very tired. These rooms would have been considered five star when they were built, but clearly the expectations of five star has changed. It is bland, it is grey, it is a very dead, dull room, it has no colour and it has zero on the excitement scale.

Champneys strategic positioning itself also seemed to be unclear, as was apparent from the organizational mind-set:

I have asked the question of everybody, 'what are we selling?', and I get a lot of long-winded answers; the real answer is that no-one has thought about it.

Interviewed on BBC2 in 1997, Lord Thurso reflected:

And I had also decided – it was as plain as day as the previous strategy, there was this wonderful name 'Champneys', which is true, it is the great opportunity. But what had been created in the past was the infrastructure for a £100 million company even though it was only a £10 million company.

It had all these people here who were called brand managers. And none of them understood what a brand was. And that was the extraordinary thing. None of them understood the elementary concept of a brand being a promise made to customers that has values and a character. If you said to them, 'what does Champneys mean?', the answer was, they hadn't thought it through.

It would thus appear that the organizational mind-set that Champneys could expand easily, on the back of its brand and existing skills, had played a major role in taking the company to the edge. Framing the organizational mind-set appropriately is a key part of any HR strategy.

Many of these issues must have been apparent almost as soon as Lord Thurso drove up Champneys' drive. To diagnose HR issues it is often useful just to observe some of the initial cultural artefacts around the organization. For instance, as soon as he arrived he found a mass of memos from his managers. Lord Thurso commented:

There are piles and piles of paper. It is a fairly classic thing. There are too many managers sending memos to each other. And I am suspicious of any company that is capable of generating so much paper when they are told they are expecting a new Chief Executive.

He continued:

When I arrived here, there were huge reports on everything. I said to them, 'look I just don't read them. I don't mind reading a novel by Tolstoy or Dick Francis, but I am not going to read *that*!

The following reveals Lord Thurso's quite different management style:

I tend to communicate by getting up and sitting in someone's office. I loathe memos. In my last company I banned them completely for 2 months. I said 'the next person who writes a memo will be fired' – it was amazing, we didn't have a single memo written for 2 months. It was brilliant, people actually started talking to one another.

The above thinking clearly flagged up two significant strategic projects – simplifying management processes and improving management reporting processes – in calculating a more commercially-focused mind-set.

At the same time, management lacked the fundamental information that it required:

We do not have good financial information – in fact not only is it not good, it is actually awful. The management accounts that I have seen are mathematically correct, but they are not informative.

These accounts gave Thurso some advanced knowledge that he might need to make some changes within the finance function:

The management reports were gibberish. I asked simple questions – 'do you know what your cash flow is?' – and the guy couldn't tell me. . . . They didn't produce balance sheets. They produced huge, thick reports, full of graphs, trend analysis. But the one thing that they didn't do was to produce reports where you could find profit, where you could find cash flow. I said, we will really have to start from scratch.

I remember sitting on the lawn on holiday wearing my Panama hat and a tee-shirt and my kilt, and smoking a cigar, trying to read through 2 years of drivel, the management accounts . . . I can usually work things out, and I just couldn't make it work.

However, instead of rolling out a turnaround plan straight away, Lord Thurso spent precious time soliciting the views of *all* its key stakeholders –

especially its disgruntled customers. This enabled him not only to be absolutely sure that his chosen path was the right one, but also that, in behavioural terms, it was owned.

This period of listening was primarily so that Lord Thurso could establish a rapport with his new staff and thus to provide a platform for influencing them effectively. To develop a set of externally or internally faced strategies requires as much attention to the people-related process as it does to the content. Indeed, the way in which the strategy process is conducted is frequently a key HR breakthrough.

In 1997, Lord Thurso said:

> To be honest, I had already made up my mind before I arrived here what I would do. I had actually decided before the day that I started that I was going to take a million pounds out of the costs.

He continued, reflecting on the obvious sensitivity of the HR process:

> I wanted them to have thought that I had thought it through. They wouldn't have understood that I was capable of thinking it through very quickly, and that it was really clear what had to be done. It was really a very simple problem, and it needed some pretty straightforward solutions.
>
> After I arrived, I said, 'I will have a month and I will take no decisions until the end of the month.' It was a good thing. I did fractionally amend certain decisions, but 90 per cent of it was exactly what I had thought previously.

Lord Thurso realized intuitively that Champneys was in the kind of situation that could easily blow up if a number of stakeholders decided, rightly or wrongly, that he was 'the wrong man for the job'. Quite quickly Lord Thurso concluded from his own personal course of treatments that his operational staff were a real asset, to be retained, nurtured and grown. Indeed, this capability base provided the foundation of its future competitive strategy. According to Lord Thurso:

> The closer I get to the front line the better I find the troops are. And that is very pleasing, because if you have good officers and lousy soldiers you have got a lot of work to do, but if you have good soldiers and lousy officers, then you have to work to train or change the officers.

In contrast, Lord Thurso found that the management he inherited was, although up to the task of managing in a more steady state environment, not really up to a turnaround. The top-heavy management structure was not only an expense that the business could not afford; it also impeded the recovery plan, inviting two further interrelated HR projects – *management restructuring and management recruitment*.

Lord Thurso reflected in late 1997 just how serious the problems at the old Head Office had become – and attributed this to organizational culture and mind-set:

> And there was a business over there that had been completely neglected at Head Office. There was a flipchart in every office, which to me was a symptom of this very introverted style – the moment anybody had a meeting, someone was on a flipchart. The whole thing was driven by the processes rather than by the objectives. If there were objectives, they were tacked onto the process.
>
> People worked hard and interacted and interfaced, and essentially went around in circles. There was no questioning of 'why are we here?' or 'what is the meaning of the universe?'
>
> It was quite clear that I had to be very clear, that I had to make a very definitive statement that there was a complete change coming. It wasn't quite as bloody as it looked, because I re-deployed quite a lot of the people I had here back into the units. That refocused them on where the action was.
>
> I described it once as 'this Head Office was once a great black hole which sucked energy out of the units. Things vanished into it never to be seen again'. Whereas my idea of a Head Office is that it should be a tiny, tiny star in the sky, twinkling light down, completely out of the way.

The above suggests that a key HR strategy issue is often 'how do management themselves add economic value to the business strategy?' This question is much more direct, challenging and testing than simply asking 'what roles are appropriate?' To pull his commentary together let us return to Figure 8.2, which gave us a model for strategic change. Before Lord Thurso's arrival, Champneys' situation could be characterized as follows:

- Environment: recession had reduced volumes
- Strategy: it had also lost its focus, and was not delivering value for money to its target customers
- Leadership: this was in a state of drift
- Agendas: these were more personal than commercial
- Structure: this was very complex, bureaucratic and hierarchical
- Processes: these were very slow and rigid
- Careers: empire building
- Legacy: changing ownership, in the past involving private ownership (it was owned by the same family on two occasions), and ownership by two bigger groups.

Our verdict on this is that Champneys was in an advanced stage of 'strategic drift', where the organization was out of sync with its environment.

Strategic options and vision

As Lord Thurso said in 2000:

I think life is all about circles and not straight lines. You can jump onto the circle anywhere you like. Number one, it is having a vision – call it a vision, call it an objective, call it a goal, it is the idea of where you want to go. The beginning of strategic thinking is where you are working out the vision, then map out the ways in which you could deliver that, like policies you put in place. Overall, a series of moves in chess is a strategy. Each move is a tactic.

The leader has to ensure that there is a vision, that there is a clear idea. Whether the leader dreams that idea up himself, or whether that idea is produced by a process of consultation, it doesn't really matter. He then has to make sure that there is a strategy for prosecuting it.

At this point it is worth doing an exercise to consider the possible strategic options facing Champneys. This can be done at three levels:

1. Options for competitive strategy
2. Options for organizational strategy
3. Options for the change process.

To help you to think about the first level, consider once again the lines of enquiry for the business, which might include:

- Which market sectors should Champneys be in?
- Where (geographic options)?
- Which customers should it target, and what areas of value creation?
- Are there different means of value delivery and resource bases?
- Are there alliance or acquisition possibilities?
- Might Champneys divest or outsource any activities?
- Given its capability base, what would the most 'natural' strategy be for Champneys (the 'natural' strategy test – i.e. what things would it be naturally very good at, and not bad at?). This final question is of most concern where HR strategy can shape competitive strategy proactively, rather than *vice versa*.

Here we see the need to be quite creative and fluid in strategic thinking about the organization and its vision. As Lord Thurso reflected in 2000:

The guy at the top must always be mentally in the future.

Figure 8.4 provides a technique that can be used not only for competitive strategy options but also for the organizational strategy options – the 'strategic option grid'. This displays a number of options against some generic criteria. The scores are normally:

✓✓✓   High attractiveness
✓✓   Medium attractiveness
✓   Low attractiveness

(half scores are possible, too).

Options / Criteria	Option 1	Option 2	Option 3	Option 4
Strategic attractiveness				
Financial attractiveness*				
Implementation difficulty				
Uncertainty and risk				
Stakeholder acceptability				

* Benefits less costs, cash flows relative to investment

Figure 8.4
Strategic option grid

When each box has been scored, each column is added up to give a total, which provides a rough prioritization on the basis of critical, first-cut thinking. A second cut is to look at how you might increase the scores with your 'cunning plan' (see Chapter 1). A third cut is to consider the potential impact of different scenarios on the scores – to perform resilience testing.

A quick further point is that the criteria 'implementation difficulty' and 'uncertainty and risk' are scored in reverse – that is, high difficulty is low attractiveness, and high uncertainty and risk is low attractiveness too.

The various criteria can be defined as follows:

■ 'Strategic attractiveness' means positioning ourselves in growing, less competitive markets when we have real edge and many opportunities.
■ 'Financial attractiveness' means benefits less costs (in cash flow terms ultimately) relative to investment (use value and cost drivers, and the value-over-time curve).
■ 'Implementation difficulty' means the sum of difficulty over time to achieve the desired result (use force field analysis or difficulty over time curve).
■ 'Uncertainty and risk' means the extent to which key assumptions are certain/uncertain (use the uncertainty grid).
■ 'Stakeholder acceptability' means the buy-in of all the stakeholders, weighted for their degree of influence on the issue (use stakeholder analysis/agenda analysis).

Exercise: Champneys – options for competitive strategy

Based on the case study so far:

1. What key strategic options can you think of for Champneys, based on what might be a most 'natural' strategy for the organization? (use the strategic option grid).
2. Can you think of any ways to increase the scores on the strategic option grid (through the 'cunning plan')?
3. How might these scores come down through an adverse scenario (resilience testing)?
4. Were Champneys to acquire some new skills, could this generate some further, interesting options for competitive strategy?

   This kind of reflection needs to be done in some specially created thought or 'helicopter' space (and time). In 2000, Lord Thurso reflected:

> The guy at the top is probably the only person spending his time thinking 6 to 9 months ahead of the business. The most important single thing is thinking ahead. . . . The first thing is, with door shut, with 'phone switched off, gazing at this ceiling, running 'what-ifs' through my mind. . . .

Turning to organizational structure, assuming that you are going to reposition Champneys back to its traditional upmarket focus, what future organization would you 'really, really want' (the 'Spice Girl' strategy)?

Exercise: Champneys – options for organizational structure

1. What key value-creating activities would you need in the future (say, over the next 3 years)?
2. What likely roles would be needed to deliver these value-creating activities?
3. How could you deliver these in the organization, with least resources?
4. What numbers of managers would this imply?
5. For one or more alternative organizational strategies, how do these appear on the strategic option grid?

The implementation process

This posed a major dilemma for Lord Thurso – if he were to move very fast and introduce a new, slimmed-down management structure, the shock might topple the organization, undermining morale at the cutting edge of customer service. In such a situation there is probably no single 'right answer'.

185

Arguably, by leaving the Champneys managers in suspense for 1 month, he prolonged the agony of uncertainty. On the other hand, by at least listening to them over this period he would have a better idea of who was and was not able to make the transition, and also how many, in simple financial terms, he could take with him.

In 1997 he commented:

> First of all I wanted a huge change, and I wanted that to sink in quickly. I wanted the troops, the army in the resort, to go, 'Hey this guy might know what he is talking about!'
>
> I also felt that I only wanted to do it once. I wanted it to be viciously quick for two reasons; one was to make a point, and the other thing was to say to people 'that's it, it is done.' And that undoubtedly worked.

Lord Thurso decided that above all, Champneys needed a new strategic vision.

Strategic vision

Lord Thurso's own vision for Champneys was profoundly simple. He preferred the idea of 'vision' to 'mission', principally because mission statements are harder to grasp, particularly in terms of the *behaviours* that are implied by them:

> If you cannot remember a mission statement (I cannot remember our old one), if you have to refer to something, that's wrong. To me, any mission statement which is 'we will have care for our customers, be nice to our staff, be nice to grey squirrels on Sundays', you know, you have gone to sleep.
>
> It has got to be something that encapsulates the spirit. 'Nowhere else makes you feel this good' – yes, it is a spirit statement. That's why NASA's 'To get a man on the moon' makes sense. At Champneys it is: 'Nowhere else makes you feel this good' – and that should apply to the staff as well.

Frequently 'mission' and 'values' are at the very heart of a company's HR strategies. However, this can easily result in an introverted and potentially static and rigid view of what should drive the organization.

Lord Thurso potentially faced major resistance to his plan, especially from his senior managers, who expressed their loyalty to their previous MD and to past strategy during the television documentary. In business terms there was little alternative but to reduce severely the number of his central management team. In the 1997 documentary, Lord Thurso addressed the team at a management meeting:

> Please view my arrival not as something disastrous but actually as an expression of support by our shareholders.

The problem in a nutshell is that we are losing money. You are all intelligent people, and therefore you will know that there will be a cost-cutting exercise. We have an expression in the fitness centre of 'no pain, no gain', but there will be pain.

We are, with the cost of Head Office, losing as a company approximately £1 million in cash terms per year. It is my intention and target that by the end of the next year we will be cash-breakeven. The direction I have decided to follow is to put Champneys absolutely and without doubt at the top of the tree.

He had decided to tell them collectively of his decision so that he delivered two clear and separate messages. The first message was that there was an impelling need to restructure and reduce the management resource. The second message was to specific individuals – that they were, or were not, to be members of the future team. Within the restructuring project there would be two sub-projects: diagnosing current skills, and defining the future skills needed to deliver the strategy. Indeed, besides developing an internal strategic vision for the organization, a further project was also required – developing a business strategy.

Figure 8.5 represents this strategic vision as a wishbone analysis. This analysis highlights the key factors that needed to line up to deliver the vision of Champneys' financial turnaround – through 'Nowhere else makes you feel this good' – as being:

- Restructuring and cost reduction
- An appropriate business strategy
- Promises now fulfilled – through the exit from the 'Health for Life' timeshare scheme

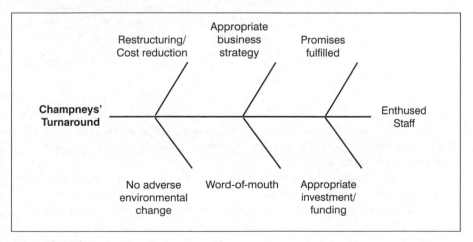

Figure 8.5
Champneys' wishbone

- A new management team
- Enthused staff
- Sufficient financial support for development
- Appropriate investment decisions
- The resumption of 'word-of-mouth' recommendation
- No major adverse environmental change.

Returning to Champneys' change process, Lord Thurso had a number of options in communicating his strategy. One alternative would have been to speak to individuals separately, both to communicate the need for the change and to let them know whether or not they still had a job. This approach would have had the merit of removing the period of uncertainty whilst managers were concerned about their job security. However, it would also have meant that some managers would have heard about the organizational change sooner than the others.

These simple logistics highlight the HR-related implications of making a strategic change in an organization. Whichever way Lord Thurso played it, the effect on individuals' feelings – perhaps of hurt and fear – might have ramifications in their future and also that of the remaining team. Thinking through options in this area is always of major importance when applying strategic thinking.

The impact of these redundancies was obviously severe for the managers. Champneys' Property Manager, Willie Serplis, attempted to put a brave face on it as he came smiling to the television interview following his meeting with Lord Thurso. His smile quickly faded as he told us:

> Do you want to ask the question then . . . 'How are you?' Not very happy. I just lost my job – it is better knowing, but what can I do? You want to be angry with someone or something, but it doesn't make sense. You can dress it up in all the esoteric bullshit you know – downsizing, redundancy – but the reality is, through no fault of my own I have just been fired . . ..

Lord Thurso himself looked emotionally strained when he was asked how he felt about this part of the process:

> I would find it hard to sleep if I felt that anything I was doing was wrong in any way. I dislike doing it, but it is a necessary operation that has to be done on the company. All that one can do is to do it as humanely and professionally as one can.
>
> Most of them have been angry because at the end of the day we all like to think that we have a value in an organization, and effectively when you are made redundant someone is saying that you don't have a value in the organization. When I say that 'it isn't to do with your performance, it is entirely to do with the financial structure of the company' it actually doesn't help them very much.

HR strategy may thus have to deal with some very difficult and sensitive issues that have a major impact on the individuals involved, and on their lives. This underlines the need to bring in stakeholder analysis as much as possible when thinking about how to move HR strategy forward in as restructuring context.

It is easy to imagine the atmosphere within the management block at Champneys as the reality sank in that it was the end of an era. Those staying also realized that they would be expected to achieve a quantum shift in the level of effectiveness, if the business were to come back into profit.

(The above account highlights a further, short-term HR project: maintaining organizational morale.)

It was then Lord Thurso's turn to address his operational staff. He appeared to be in a lighter mood as he informed his staff not merely about the severity of the situation, but also of the fact that he was planning other job cuts. He continued:

> The last part of the strategy and the bit that does concern all of you is that New Court and the concept of a headquarters is going to be quite radically scaled down. There are 22 people sitting here, and we have probably half that as the number of places that I actually have available. You are intelligent and you will have worked this out. And therefore some people are going to have to be made redundant. . . . And I do recognize the pain that this will cause you. I am sorry that some of you will be going, but please understand that it is nothing to do with you and your capability. It is simply about how this business has been run over the past few years, and the requirement to put it on a proper cash footing.
>
> Finally, I would like to give you a little thought. All my life I have been involved in giving first-class service to people, and I believe it is a wonderful thing to do. Be always ready to say 'yes' whenever a client or guest comes to see you and asks for something and you are tempted to say 'no'. Stop, think, and that will help us to create a level of service unheard of in this country.
>
> It is a tremendous culture change.

The above shows how the best HR strategies are essentially very simple – to deliver superior value required a flexible attitude amongst staff, which could be secured essentially through training and appropriate recruitment.

Besides dealing with internal stakeholders, Lord Thurso had to manage the expectations of the Champneys members, whose business was needed to secure a successful future. These members had been disappointed in the past by the previous management, who had perhaps set up expectations about improvements in standards that had not been (or could not be) delivered. Lord Thurso then decided to end the previous management's scheme for timesharing, not only by stopping the sales activities but also by buying-back the timeshares. Getting out of this business area proved to be one of the most difficult projects, because of stakeholder agendas.

Lord Thurso was quick to realize that 'the Health for Life' timeshare scheme needed to be halted:

> From what I have seen, the constant push–push–push on 'Health for Life' has given the wrong impression in the market-place. I think maybe we should cut that right back.

Apparently this was an issue that emerged only during his fact finding. After being assured by his senior managers that there were no more burning issues to be brought to his attention ('other than the cash flow', said his finance director), he said in 2000 that he discovered that:

> Some of the key issues I did not realize until later. The fact that the timeshare was totally critical and I would need to do that was something which I didn't realize. When I first got here one thought 'yes, that's a timeshare business, I will have to rev it up'.

The 'Health for Life' business is an example perhaps of where HR strategy was driven by structural issues:

> Once sales staff were deployed in numbers, they then had to stick with a business strategy that really was not working. Human momentum (and fear of losing one's job) appeared to prevent a review of their strategy – so badly needed – from happening.

To achieve these plans Lord Thurso needed to build the confidence of his investors – who might well have thought that a turnaround was possible *without* major investment. To build this confidence he needed to produce a robust business case, and to support this Lord Thurso realized that he would need to achieve a number of things:

1. The restructuring of management had to be implemented successfully
2. Better financial planning and control needed to be stabilized, with the help of the new Finance Director (who Lord Thurso had brought in)
3. His restructuring would need to have delivered the required cost savings
4. Although a gap still remained (to break even) with these cost savings, this gap would need to be closed by expanding revenues
5. To achieve this, the quality of service and standards generally at Champneys had to improve considerably – to the point where existing members felt a real difference, and new members were brought in.

The above implementation areas highlight how inextricably HR strategy is linked with both the competitive and financial strategies.

Although cost savings of half a million pounds per annum were achieved relatively quickly, it proved much harder to increase sales through improving customer confidence. However, within a year Champneys was managing to break even, and Lord Thurso was therefore able to then put into effect his plan to obtain enough investment to reposition Champneys as an outstanding health resort.

The overseas investors were able to give Lord Thurso the vote of confidence he needed in order to move into stage two of the turnaround – a major upgrading programme, whose implementation became a further strategic project. At last all the planks of Lord Thurso's future strategy were in place.

We have told the story of Champneys' strategic turnaround, but mainly from the point of view of the business. However, if we look at this situation from a more behavioural point of view, we find that this dimension has perhaps even more importance than more tangible areas of change.

Implementing the strategic breakthroughs

The key three strategic breakthroughs for Champneys comprised:

1. A new competitive strategy
2. An effective resource base
3. A responsive organization.

These will be fleshed out in a later section, which summarizes the key strategic projects.

The key forces enabling Champneys' change programme included Lord Thurso's leadership, the clarity of the strategy, and the support of lower-level operational staff. The most important forces were thus more behavioural in nature. These are represented in Figure 8.6, a force field analysis, and highlight that:

▪ Lord Thurso had introduced a number of key enablers into the strategic change through his own leadership, a new strategy, a thorough restructuring

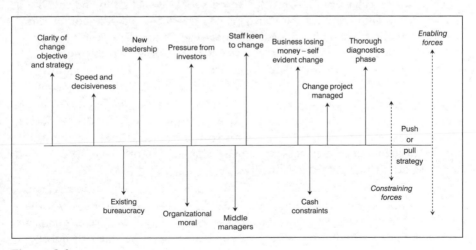

Figure 8.6
Champneys' force field analysis

and, particularly, in making some fresh appointments (this was, in effect, a 'cunning plan').

■ Whilst there were a number of constraining forces, these were overall weaker than the enabling forces. Even these, Lord Thurso managed to eradicate or mitigate with his cunning plan.

However, as stated previously, we always need to ask the question, 'What is the One Big Thing we have forgotten?' Probably the traditional culture of Champneys was the missing constraining force from the 1998 picture seen in Figure 8.6. This highlights the need always to take the HR strategy perspective, as otherwise a critical constraint on strategic change may well be missed.

Lord Thurso's own larger-than-life character was a crucial ingredient in signalling that the changes necessary were very, very real. In 1997 he reflected on the progress of his customer service project, which was also closely linked to the ongoing project of culture change, which appeared to go through a number of future phases:

But the key at the top should have a kind of evangelical fanaticism about what the strategy is. Unless you have this, you are not going to manage to convince people. For example, last year I called our plans 'Going from Good to Great'. And we didn't go from Good to Great, we got better. So I said 'This is Good to Great' part two. We could be back here next year doing part three or even part four. But one day *we will get there*, and I ain't leaving here until we do.

I believe that all human beings are capable of change for the better. This may be an optimistic view. But I therefore start from the premise that it is better to work with people rather than change them. I find that the grass on the other side of the fence is not often greener.

When you are sorting out a business and getting the headcount right, yes, you have to cut to get it right. But some people would go in and say, 'I can't work with that General Manager' and fire them and get another one. And then after 6 months you get another one. Personally I prefer to say 'why is this not working? Let us look at it and actually help this person'. I find that you then get staff who are more loyal.

However, this involves recognizing that the staff's agendas may not be nicely aligned with the vision. HR strategy thus needs to drill down to agendas at the personal level. Lord Thurso went on to talk about the practicalities of achieving the necessary culture change – another key project – to shift old behaviour patterns radically:

If I am honest with you I am only a small part of the way through. All the things, these wonderful things that managers do, that is all part of our game. But the guy at the bottom says 'Sod you, I only have 40 hours to do my job'. What he is saying to you is, 'if you want me to do this, give me a reason'.

> And that guy at the bottom isn't going to say, 'wow, that guy at the top
> – he is a "zing", now I will suddenly smile at customers'. There has got to
> be something in it for him. And part of it is being controlled, led, cajoled,
> pushed into it. And a part of it is being rewarded, feeling nice, all of the
> rest of it. It is a huge culture change that virtually every company in this
> country needs to actually genuinely understand what a customer-orientated
> organization is. I have grave difficulty in thinking of a truly customer-
> orientated organization in the United Kingdom. I mean, there must be one
> somewhere.

The difficulty of achieving this in the UK context is highlighted by the
authors' experience when visiting various Champneys sites over 1997–2002
to help benchmark HR service levels as part of this case study. They
experienced:

- A rebuke for using a mobile telephone just to pull down messages (it was
  simply assumed that visitors would not use one)
- A treatments mix-up on timing (by the health farm), followed by being
  told that 'you have to pay anyway – you were late'
- A massage treatment inappropriately conducted.

Indeed, none of their visits had zero defects!

Again in 1997, Lord Thurso reflected on the need to take HR strategy a
step at a time, recognizing that there would inevitably be a degree of incremental thinking and action at work:

> You do have to have a strategy. You can fight battles without a strategy and
> have success, but it is a pretty haphazard thing. You have got to have a
> clear idea of where you are going, but equally you have to recognize that
> the achievement of the strategy will be a series of tactical steps.

It is also necessary to look at how implementation difficulty changes over
time. Initially Lord Thurso's turnaround project faced severe difficulties, but
once the new structure was put in place and Lord Thurso's new vision for
the organization had been unveiled, this difficulty was mitigated. Figure 8.7
gives us an illustrated view of this difficulty, over the period 1996–2000.

As time progressed this difficulty increased at certain periods as the
organization found a new stability and sought to resist further changes. The
difficulty was in turn reduced once Lord Thurso's programmes to improve
customer service and to shift attitudes began to bite.

Looking now at the key stakeholders who had an influence on this strategic change, we see that:

- Before Lord Thurso unveiled his turnaround project, the balance of influence in the organization was against him (especially among the existing
  middle and senior managers)

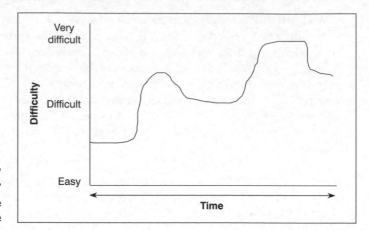

Figure 8.7
Champneys'
difficulty-over-time
curve

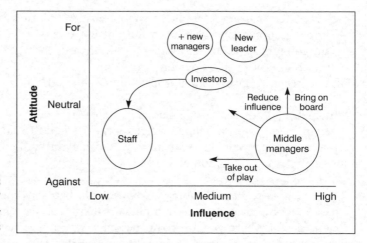

Figure 8.8
Champneys'
stakeholder
analysis

■ By introducing new stakeholders (including two new senior managers), exiting some old ones, and appealing directly to the staff, the balance of influence was reversed and moved in Lord Thurso's favour (see Figure 8.8).

Figure 8.8 shows an impressive turnaround in the balance of power within the organization – and again this was down to Lord Thurso's cunning plan.

To understand the influence patterns of these stakeholders, we must also bear in mind some additional factors:

■ The agendas of stakeholders are not fixed but will change over time *vis-à-vis* the various HR strategy projects as new issues arise and as perceptions change within the organization.

■ At any point in time agendas may be fluid and ambiguous, particularly at the start of the turnaround. Key stakeholders, particularly middle managers, *may not have any clear attitude at all*. Although they may have some case agendas (such as 'I want to hang onto my job'), these might be very limited. And even here, core agendas might be conditional on Champneys being seen as a congenial atmosphere to work in, given its new leadership. Never assume therefore that the attitudes and underlying agendas of stakeholders are always givens.

■ Individuals within one group will influence the agendas of others within the group. Through an informal network, opinion leaders will signal their approval or disapproval of particular actions.

■ You may need to break down the project into a number of sub-projects, as stakeholder positions will vary according to what is being implemented. For instance, a stakeholder may approve of Lord Thurso's plans to renovate the buildings and of his plans to end the 'Health for Life' promotion, but be violently against running a smaller department.

Besides Lord Thurso's management of the key stakeholders, it is also worthwhile pausing to reflect for a moment on the impact of team roles and style – which has an impact on the extent to which a team can think and manage strategically.

Lord Thurso's own role came over very strongly as being that of coordinator (or 'Chairman'). He combined both plant and shaper characteristics in his visionary skills. He exuded personal charisma, and was able to carry a considerable number of stakeholders with him. His new General Manager appeared (in the TV programme) to be a shaper and completer–finisher. His new Finance Director appeared to be a very strong monitor–evaluator, and his existing Marketing Manager an implementer and team worker. So with even a small team base most of the roles appeared to be well covered, helping to provide a good behavioural base for future strategic thinking. (We will return to this in the case postscript, which is based on an interview with Lord Thurso in late 2000.)

Summary of Champneys' strategic change projects

Listing Champneys' strategic change projects according to the categories of 'strategic', 'operational' and 'organizational', they run as follows:

1. *Strategic projects – for a new strategy*
   ■ Business strategy
   ■ Marketing strategy, involving market research and brand strategy
   ■ Business case
   ■ Exit timesharing
2. *Operational and systems projects – for an effective resource base*
   ■ Sampling of services
   ■ Customer service improvement
   ■ Premises upgrade
   ■ Management process simplification
   ■ Management reporting
   ■ Customer database enhancement

3. *Organizational projects – for a responsive organization*
   - Management re-structuring
   - Management recruitment
   - Maintaining staff morale
   - Culture change
   - Communication plan
   - Organizational skills diagnosis.

These are inextricably linked in showing the need to manage HR strategy in effect as an 'organization and people strategy'.

The strategic programmes described above also gain in attractiveness through being part of a set of aligned and mutually supportive projects that together (and not separately) add economic value (the 'strategic project set'). They also gain through reduced implementation difficulty.

Key lessons

In summary, the key lessons on managing strategic change, and especially those that impact on people and behaviour specifically, are as follows:

- Stakeholder analysis is absolutely central to managing the various strategic HR projects effectively. Accordingly, sufficient strategic thinking time should be devoted to analysing the current and potentially future positions of stakeholders and their driving agendas.
- Leadership is crucial in a situation where stakeholders are likely actively to resist implementation efforts. This leadership requires a degree of evangelical enthusiasm, a great practical tenacity in implementing that vision, and a continual openness to the environment of strategic change through strategic thinking.
- Achieving headway depends on building a sufficient 'stakeholder platform' to leverage off. This involved (at Champneys) the key appointments of a new Finance Director and Property Manager, and winning over Champneys' front-line staff.
- The difficulty-over-time of a strategic change or particular strategic project will vary over time. The shifts in difficulty need to be anticipated and managed rather than just coped with, which requires strategic thinking in order to sense the future.
- There are invariably more options that can be addressed through strategic thinking than most managers normally think about.

Champneys' excellence in skills across a variety of treatments and customer services invites us to think about how, based on its competencies, it could develop the most 'natural' strategies. This follows on from the thinking (see Chapter 2) that organizational diagnosis can actually help to create new competitive strategies, rather than *vice versa*. However, we will next take a look at competitive strategy options, and then at organization/HR strategy options.

Natural options for competitive strategy

A considerable range of options has been suggested over the years by managers regarding what Champneys might have done (or might still do). These have included:

1. *Market sectors/segments*
   - The corporate market
   - The younger market
   - Professionals, generally
   - The 'mass' market (but not necessarily downmarket)
2. *Geography*
   - The US tourist market
   - The Middle-Eastern market
   - Continental Europe
   - Via franchise (on cruise liners)
3. *Customers*
   - The 'pamper yourself' customer
   - The stressed-out person
   - The exploratory, alternative treatments type
   - The health fanatic
   - Men (in their own right)
4. *Value creation*
   - More focus on guiding customers through treatments
   - Aftercare between visits, as part of a continual 'better life' process (e.g. through help-lines, home visits)
   - More focus on stress and lifestyle
   - Change of use to, for example, a management centre; an upmarket retreat; therapy for worn out rich people (including pop stars and football stars); the corporate market; younger, single professionals (and couples); US market (and tourism to the UK)
5. *Value delivery*
   - Franchising
   - Smaller Champneys centres (actually now implemented)
6. *Alliances*
   - With a food company, to market the Champneys brand (Champneys food is outstanding)
   - With a restaurant company (who might deliver food to Champneys' recipes)
   - With a cruise line or other upmarket leisure providers
7. *Acquisitions*
   - To acquire and develop a second site with a different catchment area (for example, in the North of England or in Scotland).

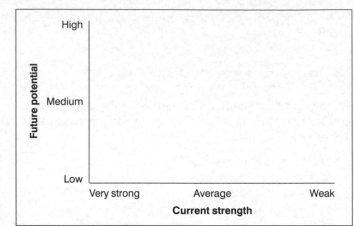

Figure 8.9
Management strength versus potential (original grid by General Electric)

Options / Criteria	Sell now	Sell 3 years	Up market	Extend segments
Strategic attractiveness	✓✓	✓✓	✓ ½	✓✓✓
Financial attractiveness	✓	✓✓✓	✓ ½	✓✓✓
Implementation difficulty	✓✓✓	✓✓✓	✓✓✓	✓✓
Uncertainty and risk	✓✓✓	✓✓✓	✓✓✓	✓ ½
Stakeholder acceptability	✓ ½	✓✓	✓✓✓	✓ ½
Score	10½	13	12	11

Figure 8.10
Champneys strategic option grid – competitive strategy

Figure 8.9 looks at some of these options on a notional capability grid. Here the vertical axis looks at *future* capability (to do a strategy naturally well), based on cunning skills-acquisition and judgement plans. The horizontal axis looks at *current* capability to do a strategy naturally really well. Again, this uses HR strategy to help to generate, screen and improve competitive strategy (rather than the other way around).

Interestingly, the most common 'option' the majority of students come up with is 'to make Champneys more exclusive and to re-market it to its core market', which is actually the option that Lord Thurso adopted (see Figure 8.10 for a completed, strategic option grid).

Most groups underestimate the cost of this strategy (Champneys invested around £6.75 million), and fail to think through the possibility of Champneys coming under greater competitive pressure. Also, Champneys' traditional positioning might (some day) not quite fit with customer demand. Perhaps Champneys might now consider a strategy that involves building new capabilities rather than focusing on existing strategies and national capability.

Some lines of enquiry may open up then peter out. For instance, in 2000 Lord Thurso reflected:

> For example, we looked at opening restaurants. Now I am not saying that we won't open restaurants, but I have put it to one side for a while. We happen to produce stunningly good food.

Here we can perhaps only realistically consider these options on the basis of a more effective and visionary management team being in place, for example with acquisition/other skills. (So here HR strategy can enable competitive strategy).

> I have had conversations with a supermarket chain, but at the end of the day ... if you go to Birds Eye, for example, or Nestlé ... they very quickly say 'actually, we can invent a brand and in the short term your name, Champneys, won't help us'. It is an area which remains of interest to me.

However, unless a strategy fits in naturally with the agendas, mind-set and 'strategic recipes' of the Chief Executive, it will probably not be pursued with tenacity. ('Strategic recipes' are the conscious and unconscious rules of what things 'work' or 'don't work' strategically within the mind of the Chief Executive and his management team. When a CEO appointment is made (as part of HR strategy), you are effectively committing to these recipes, and to a probably course of strategic action.)

The range of options that can be generated for Champneys underlines the need to think much more broadly about 'options', through strategic thinking, than is conventionally done. Each of these options can then be mixed with others through a mix-and-match process – for example, Champneys could hold alternative treatment sessions for professional, stressed-out people (with their partners) on one-day visits, delivered through an alliance with an upmarket hotel group.

Organization/HR strategy options

When doing the exercise on organizational strategy, no one has ever wanted to keep the organization much as it was. Invariably managers go for *at least* halving current numbers, and some take it down as far as six or even less.

Whilst Champneys delivers very high levels of service in comparison with other organizations, its value-creating activities are, if broken down, not unduly complex. Furthermore, apart from IT there is currently a relatively limited technology base to manage and develop.

The main roles that are often identified are:

- Managing Director, to provide leadership, strategic thinking and challenge
- A General Manager, to deliver day-to-day excellent service
- A Financial and Commercial Director
- A Marketing and Sales Manager, perhaps reporting to the Financial and Commercial Director
- An HR Manager.

Breaking this down into sub-options:

- The Finance Director might have been supplied for the first 9 months on a loan basis, to help sort Champneys out. Once Champneys became steady-state, a Financial Manager could suffice.
- The HR Manager's role might be part-time, subsumed into that of the General Manager and supported with some outside HR consultancy.

It would be crucial that the Financial and Commercial Director or the Marketing and Sales Manager had the competencies to develop the sales database.

Here we see conventional structure semi-dissolving into fluid, strategic projects, rather than making the assumption that for every value-creating activity there must be a role, that there must therefore be an incremental person, and that therefore there must be a cost.

Figure 8.11 gives some worked examples using the strategic option grid. Interestingly, minor versus major downsizing have the same scores – so you then have to stand back and say, 'what are the most important/least important criteria in this case?' Arguably these should (here) be 'strategic' and 'financial' attractiveness, making the major downsizing most attractive.

Once again, we would make the point that if future competencies were to be acquired, this would open up new options for competitive strategy –

Exercise: reflections on the Champneys' case

1. What parallels are there (if any) between Champneys' organization and your own in terms of HR strategy issues (for example, in its strategic drift, its internal rigidities, and its focus on the internal environment over and above the outside world)?
2. What parallels are there between Champneys' strategic change process and the way change is managed in your own area?
3. Using the strategic option grid, either on your competitive strategy or for a variety of structure options, what does this tell you?

Options Criteria	Minor downsizing	Major downsizing
Strategic attractiveness	✓✓	✓✓✓
Financial attractiveness	✓✓	✓✓✓
Implementation difficulty	✓✓	✓
Uncertainty and risk	✓✓	✓✓
Stakeholder acceptability	✓✓	✓
Score	10	10

Figure 8.11
Champneys'
strategic option
grid –
organizational
strategy

meaning that HR strategy can actually *create* competitive strategy, rather than *vice versa*.

Case conclusion

The Champneys case study gives us a fascinating real-time account of how HR strategy is integral with culture and strategic change. It also highlights that there may be many options that can be created, even in an apparently tightly constrained situation. These options can then be manipulated by 'mix and match' to evolve even better, and potentially cunning, combination strategies.

The study also highlights the equal importance of thinking through cunning options for implementation.

Finally, the Champneys case underlined the need to create a joint sense of personal and business need to do strategic thinking. Lord Thurso's final reflection was:

> There are very, very few people who just do that [think strategically] with no pressure at all. If you are comfortable, well paid, good job, and good prospects on the horizon, where the company's making money, unless someone says growth is necessary then you won't think about it.

Case postscript

In 2001 Lord Thurso became a full time Member of Parliament, and opted to leave Champneys (with much sadness) to pursue a political career. The then Non-Executive Chairman of Champneys (since 1995) slipped into his role. In August 2002 the consortium that owned Champneys sold the business to the middle-market Purdew Health Farm Group, which owns Henlow Grange and Forest Mere – with a turnover of £45 million.

CONCLUSION

Key points from this chapter include the following:

- Culture change can be valued economically, but by focusing on critical breakthrough incidents, sustainable changes and emergent changes.
- Culture change can also be costly and distracting, destroying shareholder value.
- Strategic change often demands a complex set of external and internal breakthroughs – all of which need to be skilfully prioritised.
- Its value is inevitably part of a set alongside other interrelated initiatives.
- Fishbone analysis helps to diagnose the current situation very quickly and easily. This needs to be accompanied by active contact with customers, managers and staff in order to gain a clearer sense of what has gone wrong, and why.
- It will have more value if it appeals to the positive agendas that exist in the organization.
- Whilst there were a considerable number of strategic options for Champneys, it was probably even more important to apply strategic thinking to the implementation process than it was to identify the 'perfect strategy' (assuming of course that such a thing actually exists).
- The strategic option grid is a particularly useful method for evaluating difficult dilemmas over future structure.
- Organizational structure issues are perhaps best addressed through the idea of determining 'what do we really, really want?' rather than making incremental changes.
- It is imperative to have an overarching vision to guide strategic thinking about the implementation process.
- Strategic thoughts need (at some stage) to find a home in specific strategic projects.
- Strategic thinking needs to focus very much on finding the optimal communication plan (and style) for the strategy.
- Champneys could potentially have gone for a wider set of strategic options. Usually there are many possibilities, which need to be stored up as latent strategies for the future.
- Stakeholder agendas need skilful sensing through strategic thinking.

CHAPTER 9

HR succession planning and development

INTRODUCTION

As a key plank of an HR strategy, creating a superior management resource is worthy of expansion in its own right. Some writers have sought to move around this impasse by putting forward strategic HR planning systems as an 'issue-led' process. However, we currently lack the frameworks, tools and case histories (with lessons) to encourage both line and human resource managers to experiment with strategic HR succession planning and development in practice.

This section represents an important step towards defining a process for both strategic HR succession planning and development. This process also includes developing organizational scenarios, which are equally helpful for developing an overall, HR strategy (see Chapter 2). Development is included as an integral part of the planning process. HR development is felt to be a key ingredient in bridging strategic HR planning with its implementation.

The strategic HR planning and development (HRPD) process is a very useful one for the strategic HR consultant to experiment with, and to tailor and develop.

The Nycomed Amersham case illustrated in this chapter shows how strategic HRPD can be applied in practice, demonstrating the benefits and feasibility of the process.

STRATEGIC HR PLANNING AND DEVELOPMENT

The close relationship between strategic human resources and competitive strategy is in turn closely related to the business environment, and also to organizational position and development. Figure 9.1 shows how competitive strategy (which may be deliberate or emergent) influences (and is influenced by) the current organizational position and its stage of development. Figure 9.1 also highlights how the business environment may exert a direct influence on thinking about the current organizational position. This is more likely to

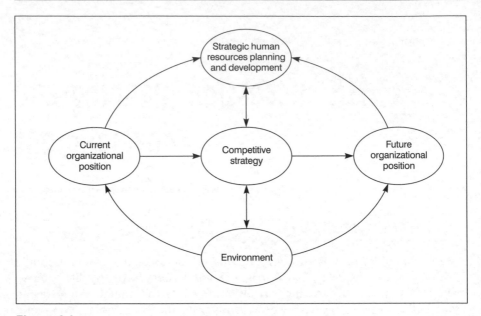

Figure 9.1
Strategic HR planning and development, organization and strategy

trigger a management review where environmental change is major and disruptive.

Figure 9.2 expands this analysis by looking at some of the key linkages between strategic HRPD and competitive strategy. A major link between competitive strategy and strategic HRPD is strategy implementation. The quality of strategic implementation will be influenced by any new, emergent strategies, especially for organic and acquisitive development, as these emergent strategies may easily distract or deflect strategy implementation programmes.

Strategic HRPD also provides an important vehicle for mobilizing competitive strategy through the development and exploitation of underlying competencies. Applying these competencies to live strategic challenges provides the key means through which the economic value of strategic HRPD is harvested.

Figure 9.3 explores how this value may crystallize. Value may crystallize via incremental customer value being created (and harvested). For instance, taking a major hotel chain like Intercontinental, by having a genuinely superior standard of customer service it is able to:

- Build customer loyalty, leading to further sales and to cost avoidance (as new customers cost money to acquire).
- Charge premium prices (over lesser hotels). Alternatively value might be captured by lowering the cost base. In both cases (differentiation and low-cost strategies), complex interdependencies may also need to be orchestrated to avoid undermining the overall strategy.

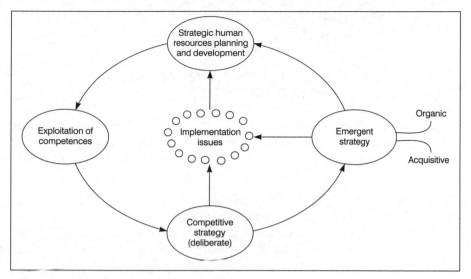

Figure 9.2
Strategic HRPD and competitive strategy

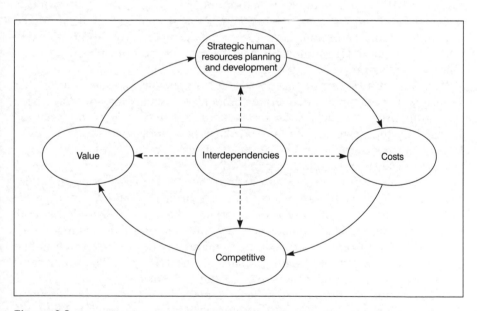

Figure 9.3
Strategic HRPD – value, costs and interdependencies

In summary, strategic HRPD entails the close integration of thinking about *future* HR needs with thinking about competitive strategy, organizational strategy and the business environment. This is indeed a far cry from traditional manpower planning, where business plans are closely integrated to financial thinking but are loosely influenced by (some) business strategic thinking.

A STRATEGIC HR PLANNING AND DEVELOPMENT PROCESS

Figure 9.4 shows a strategic HRPD process, which was developed based on existing theory and frameworks, for a major (UK) international company. It identifies four key stages in strategic HRPD (prior to the actual implementation phase):

1. Review of the strategic business issues
2. Review of the key organizational issues
3. Analysis of the current organizational position
4. Recruitment, development (and deployment) plans.

Review of strategic business issues

Strategic HRPD gathers inputs from a number of sources. First, it obviously needs to distil inputs from the existing strategic plan. This may not be straightforward. The existing strategic plan may imperfectly capture thinking about those softer HR strategic issues that are on the critical path of strategic implementation.

This lack of awareness of softer strategic issues may be due to a number of factors. For example, a deliberate competitive strategy may not have been tested out, even superficially, against the crucial test of 'can we do it and do it well?' Or the strategic plan may not have been translated into a series of breakthrough programmes and projects. Hence some of the key people resource issues may remain to be identified.

These issues can be separated out into those that are obvious and those that are less obvious. It may also be fruitful to distinguish those that are more important from those that are less important. The area of issue that is both most important and least obvious is clearly the area of greatest vulnerability.

Besides input from the strategic plan, there may be future strategies that emerge and then put additional pressure on the HR base. These emergent strategies can be organic, acquisitive, or a mixture of both.

Many companies do not think hard enough about the HR requirements for integrating acquisitions until after a deal is consummated. Until the point of deal consummation, the strategy is still essentially contingent. Nevertheless, a company or group can be easily burdened by even one major acquisition or by an over-ambitious organic development programme – for example, BMW's cross-border acquisition of Rover Group, where BMW had to deploy a considerable proportion of source design resource in order to develop Rover Car's portfolio, before its subsequent disposal of Rover in 2000.

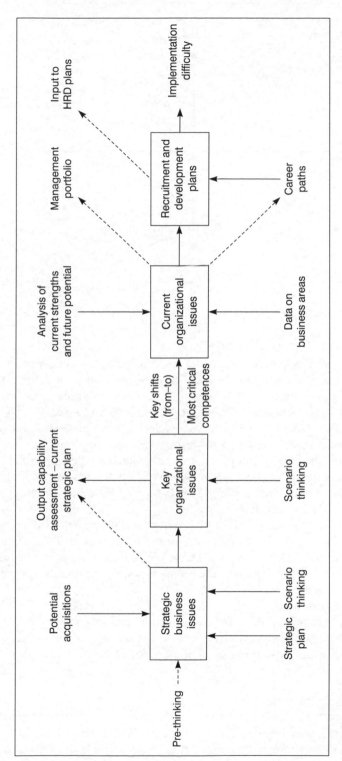

Figure 9.4
HRPD process strategy

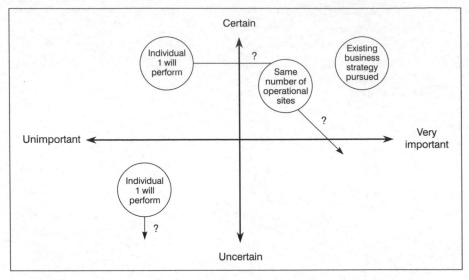

Figure 9.5
Operational assumptions underlying HR development strategy

Strategies that may emerge therefore need to be anticipated just as much as existing, deliberate strategies. The HR requirements of both deliberate and emergent strategies can then be assessed by scenario thinking – for instance, managers can be encouraged to 'story-tell' possible strategic and organizational futures (see Chapter 4) This involves fleshing out plausible and consistent stories of the future, and also requires testing assumptions like 'we have enough of the right kind of people at the right place at the right time'.

Contrary to expectations, scenario development for organizational states can be performed relatively quickly. This can be achieved as an integral part of a strategic HRPD workshop.

In order to test out the areas of greatest vulnerability, the Mitroff uncertainty–importance grid should be used (see Chapters 4 and 7). Figure 9.5 shows an illustrated example of this. Here, the region of most important and most uncertain assumptions (or 'the danger zone') highlights several key constraints that are particularly critical.

Finally, it is essential for the managers (line and HR) involved in the process to perform pre-thinking individually, and prior to any workshop. This thinking can fruitfully focus on any specific 'hot spots' (either occurring now or in the future) that pose a major challenge for HR resources.

Key organizational skills

The key organizational issues facing strategic HRPD may be produced in part from the prior strategic business issues. Also, further thinking about the organization's future is needed. This again invites some storytelling to help draw out pictures (organizational scenarios) of the future.

Key organizational issues that may well materialize at this stage and perhaps adjust existing thinking about organizational capability are, for example:

- A need for major simplification of middle management and front line management structures, to reduce cost and to increase market and customer responsiveness
- New competencies that need to be acquired or developed in order to penetrate new markets
- Marketing skills, to move from being more production-led to market-led (see Chapter 3).

Existing organizational capability needs to be assessed against not merely current but also future needs. There will therefore be two gap analyses, one between *present* capability and *present* need, and another between *present* capability and *future* need (the gap between present and future often being greater in magnitude).

Indeed, these organizational gaps might be so big that either of two things may be realized:

1. It may become evident that the assumption that the business strategy will be effectively implemented is uncertain (due to HR constraints).
2. Although there may be a yawning gap between present capability and future need, this may result in the realization (if not shock) that major development and change is needed. (This may involve changing the structure, shift, skills and culture of the organization.)

Invariably there will be significant output from this review of organizational capability into the strategic plan. This again suggests that ideally any review of key organizational issues *should be a core part of the strategic planning process in any event* (reinforcing our earlier thoughts). Only where this does not occur (and this is a real second test) are we forced to place this as a major phase of a separate strategic HRPD process. All too often these issues are dealt with poorly (if at all) in conventional strategic business planning.

A further key output from this stage is an analysis of the key shifts (froms and tos; see Chapter 6 for FT analysis) implied by our vision of future organizational shape. These 'froms and tos' provide the backdrop for a more in-depth assessment of organizational position.

Current organizational position

The review of the current organizational position relies on inputs from a number of sources, particularly:

- Analysing the current strengths and weaknesses of the organization
- Analysing its potential for future development (taking each key area of the organization in turn).

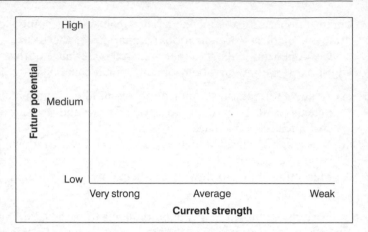

Figure 9.6
Analysis of
strength against
future potential
(original grid by
General Electric –
also seen as Figure
8.9 earlier)

By analysing these strengths and weaknesses across the organization, the major 'hot spots' requiring thought and attention should fairly readily drop out. Managers are likely to find 'what to do' with these hot spots a more contentious issue. This may invite careful thinking through the options for dealing with the threats or weaknesses. Wherever possible, threats or weaknesses should be turned around to become organizational opportunities. This requires an obsessive pursuit of the 'zero-weakness' organization – however elusive this vision may seem to be at times.

Clearly, if we have followed the suggested HRPD strategy process covered in our introduction, a lot of these data would already be available.

A more in-depth review of organizational strengths and weaknesses may well go down as far as dealing with some individual-by-individual issues. This needs to be carried out very selectively, to avoid descending to a trivial level of detail. This in-depth analysis may yield:

■ Initial views of the management portfolio (for instance, its existing strength against its future potential – see Figure 9.6)
■ Possible generic career paths that could help to develop key targets, individuals or groupings in that portfolio
■ Recruitment and development plans.

CREATING ORGANIZATIONAL SUCCESSION SCENARIOS

A tangible way of exploring 'organizational what-ifs' is to create a number of flipcharts to represent different parts of the current organizational structure. On the flipcharts, using large yellow 'Post-its', senior managers place their current higher potential manager and existing incumbents. Senior managers may then negotiate with one another key organizational transfers, to simulate 'what might happen in the future, given the strategy, organizational shifts, and desired career paths'. Specific transfers of key individuals may enable them:

■ To perform in their new role sufficiently well

■ To be targeted to ensure that they develop in the longer-term sense.

This process also needs to take cognisance of the career paths that have already emerged and are more desirable for the future.

Where future organizational shape may look significantly different from the present, two sets of flipcharts can be created – one for the old organization and one for the new. The yellow 'Post-its' are *all* moved to the new flipcharts. In practical terms this involves sticking the flipcharts all around the workshop room as 'strategic wallpaper' – although of course if this is to be done the workshop should be held off-site, for obvious confidentiality reasons. (Note: owing to shortage of time, this process was only applied in a much abbreviated form in the later case study on Amersham Pharmaceuticals.)

Besides providing output into formal HR development plans and programmes, this process may open up managers' minds to different kinds of job moves from those prevailing currently. This can stretch their thinking further into the future, and also help them to see individual moves more as part of a pattern. Assuming all the key senior players are here in the same room at the same time, the potential for 'behind the scenes' power play (or 'tug-of-war' activities to retain or capture hot talent) is considerably diminished.

Senior managers' assumptions about future operations and organizations can also be tested by the key players working as a single group. These assumptions might include, for instance:

■ That the existing strategy will be pursued 'as is', or will swerve off into new emergent directions

■ As to the number and locations of operational sites

■ That particular individuals can deliver adequate performance in particular roles

■ That apparent 'readiness for promotion' assessments of key individuals are valid.

Having analysed a number of key individuals, it may also be fruitful to prioritize HR-related actions or programmes to develop these same individuals, in terms of their importance and urgency. Particular programmes may then need to be appraised with their attractiveness (in terms of net benefits less costs) set against their implementation difficulty, using attractiveness–implementation difficulty (AID) analysis (see Chapter 6). This helps to identify key barriers or constraints, as well as to prioritize organizational benefit.

Having described the strategic HRPD process at length, we will now turn to a case study of Nycomed Amersham, which follows very closely the outline of possible best practice.

 AMERSHAM PHARMACEUTICALS LIFE SCIENCES

Amersham is a pharmaceutical company with technology, marketing, distribution and manufacturing activities, serving markets worldwide. Its worldwide operations are based in the UK, and it has a small number of key divisions.

This particular review focuses on Amersham Pharmaceuticals (formerly Amersham International). In the past Amersham had instituted 'human asset' review processes, and this had met with varying success. Although it identified some important management succession issues, it was perhaps not quite as effective in looking at 'the bigger picture' rather than just certain individuals and their possible career futures.

Amersham's strategic HRPD followed substantially the process as is outlined in Figure 9.7. The core of this process was a two-day workshop attended by a number of senior line managers within Amersham. In addition they were joined by one of the current authors, as co-designer and off-line monitor of the process, and with an emergent role as action researcher (and not as a facilitator as such)

The key outputs for the workshop were envisaged as:

- Key shifts in the organization, as a backdrop to prioritizing HR development
- A listing of the most critical competencies by function in the organization, and of the biggest gaps (present and future)
- Initial views of the future organizational structure
- Thinking on the implications of a number of deliberate changes and moves of key individuals, to test out what might happen or be feasible over 2 years – and the implications of these possibilities
- A review of the succession plan (and planned career moves in the short-term – the next 12 months)
- An overall plan to address organizational gaps and development needs.

Strategic business issues were thus elicited using the following key questions:

1. What are the key external and internal strategic issues facing Nycomed Amersham over the next 5 years?
2. What would be the key implications for the organization from these developments?
3. What areas of the strategy will be hardest to implement, and what gaps in organizational capability do we need to address?

A number of pre-prepared inputs were distilled from the discussions with the HR managers and knowledge of Amersham's strategic plan, and were then fed into the workshop by the HR managers. These were presented as a number of key shifts, expressed as 'froms–tos' as follows:

- Key business shifts – these included, for example, changes in the mix of business, the margin mix, business complexity, the cost base, operational flexibility, the mix of organic versus acquisition development and, finally, marketing and manufacturing strategy.
- Key organizational shifts – these included, for example, the relative degree of hierarchy, the degree of centralization, functional versus cross-

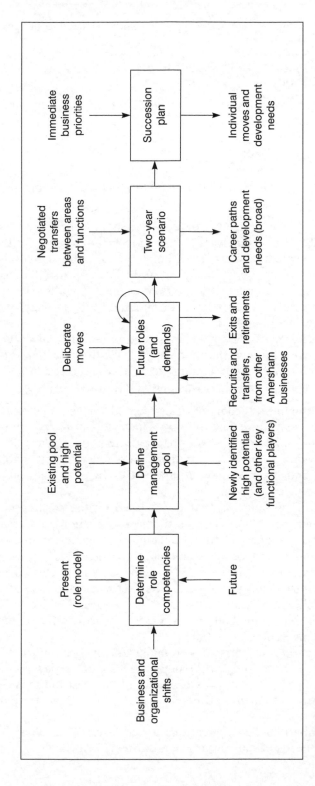

Figure 9.7
Review of management portfolio and succession and development planning – key steps

functional working, typical career paths, and working practices at an operational level.

Debate regarding the current organizational position then addressed the following key questions:

1. What new roles does our review of strategic and organizational issues/shifts imply
   - In terms of numbers
   - In terms of type of role?
2. What existing roles may change or disappear?
3. What kind of overall organizational shape (and structure) does this look like?

This point was reached in the Nycomed Amersham workshop towards the end of the first day. Interestingly, the workshop facilitators felt at the time that the line-management team was spending too long on debate at this stage. That evening, however, the line manager said how useful they had found it, not only in painting a common picture of their organizational world – present and future – but also for their own team-building. HR strategy work can therefore produce some important strategic insights generally.

Based on a backdrop of the key business and organizational shifts, it was then possible to work through the management portfolio or 'pool' (i.e. the current set of senior and middle managers) and also succession and development planning (Figure 9.7). This was addressed in five key stages:

- *Stage 1*: determining the competencies needed for generic roles (based on the present *and* future role models. This role model required identifying a current individual who was particularly good at the role, isolating that individual's top three to five competencies that enabled the performance, and scanning new competencies (if any) relevant to that future role.
- *Stage 2*: defining the management pool, based on the existing pool and others with high potential. (Besides the core operational line managers the team also considered other outstanding managers in specialist functions, including finance, personnel and logistics.)
- *Stage 3*: fleshing out future roles, role demands and likely moves. This involved defining managers' roles, then conjecturing a number of (simulated) deliberate moves. This led on to anticipating likely recruits, transfers, exits and retirements against this scenario (some assumptions needed to be made here).
- *Stage 4*: negotiating transfers of key managers (in line with key organizational skills and desired career paths). This was carried out relative to a 2-year scenario (2 years was probably the longest but most feasible time horizon for meaningful strategic thinking for HR in this particular context).
- *Stage 5*: drawing out the implications for the succession plan, and also reflecting the needs of more immediate business priorities.

Stage 4 was subdivided into five smaller steps, which were structured as follows:

- Step 1: considering your current management pool, what key option for moves (not too many) can you think of? (Note: it is perfectly possible here to vary organizational structure.)
- Step 2: identify any key gaps you might seek to fill from other areas of the division (or from outside).
- Step 3: discussion between different areas of the organization.
- Step 4: agreement between different areas of the organization as to the logic of individual transfers now being conjectured, and then make assumptions that these transfers are actually made (justifying your rationale).
- Step 5: determine your final choices of people to be given roles (making recruitment, attribution, transfers, assumptions).
- Step 6: share the development and other career path needs arising from these intended strategies.

A critical issue in Stage 4 was how the team might cope with situations where there was excess demand for a particular individual because of his or her strong personal competencies. Three guidelines were laid down in advance to cope with this. These were that the team should:

1. Think about how they could make the most impact on the business
2. Think about what provides them with a really big contribution to their personal development (present and future)
3. Disregard the fact that he (she) would be difficult to replace with someone just as good (in the short term).

One of the major points of debate was this area of excess demand for particular individuals. Ian Parkes, the then HR Development Manager of Amersham, said:

> There were a number of instances where we might say, for instance, look, we could really use manager Z for a particular idea. But then who would be available to play Z's role, and what developmental effort and other cost would be needed to achieve this? By looking at these indirect effects we were much more able to draw out the implications of a particular appointment.

Ian Parkes was effectively discussing the key impact of interdependencies on the value of a particular HR investment decision. Besides the direct value generated, he also highlighted the need to think about possible value dilution or destruction elsewhere. This suggests that a particular appointment should be evaluated not as a stand-alone, incremental investment decision, but potentially as part of a set of interdependent strategic HR projects. When an HR project is an integral part of a set of closely interdependent projects, or of a programme, its economic value should be estimated at the level of the programme, rather than taking each project one by one.

There was further debate in Stage 4 about career paths. The line team were asked:

- What will they be, and how will they be different from the past?
- What do we need to do to support them?
- What key constraints could block them, and how must we head these off?

Following the workshop, Ian Parkes was also interviewed to elicit his views of the strengths and weaknesses of the process:

> I think there were a number of parts to it. First, there is the 'big picture' stuff – the overall strategy, the organizational shifts, and the implications of those shifts. Second, there were the things which we used to bring the thinking forward – like the workshop itself and, in parallel with that, management competencies.
>
> But another ingredient was the actual people element, the people reality, the individuals and where they were. Another thing which we perhaps were not so strong on was the platform for talking about those kinds of issues. I mean, we need the backbone of understanding and talking about management competencies, which is where we are working now. As far as the workshop went, although we did not perhaps get quite as far and as deep as we would have liked, we did cover a lot of ground, especially as this was a new way of thinking in the organization. Although at some times it was difficult to lift the discussion from specific individuals, and at some times the discussion was too general, we did arrive at some tangible and specific priorities. In particular, the urgency–importance grid was invaluable in identifying short- and medium-term priorities and, more importantly, their knock-on implications. This helped us to prioritize and to fulfil my own goal of being realistic in what we can do.
>
> There is certainly a lot in the process – it is chunky, and involves a good deal of subprocess. It is going to take a fair bit of time and a lot of facilitation. The workshop began with a lot of divergent thinking, which normally doesn't add value and needs facilitation to keep it on path. Also, as you go further and further down, the issues can actually get more rather than less complex. For instance, you might conjecture that manager X could benefit from an international move, whilst the reality is that his/her spouse and children would not strongly favour this. So we need to find a way of bringing in the views of these managers on their future.

This highlights the need to work through HR strategy at a number of levels, rather than seeing strategy merely as a 'big picture'.

What emerges, therefore, is that strategy HRPD involves four major elements:

1. The overall strategy
2. Its tools and process
3. The people reality
4. Creating platforms for discussion.

This invites a suitable infrastructure for managing HR development in a more strategic way in the organization, created perhaps out of:

- The strategic HRPD process itself
- Management competencies
- Career development workshops
- Management skills development
- Mentoring and boss support.

CONCLUSION

The key lessons from this chapter are as follows:

- Strategic HRPD can (and should) play a key role in the evolution of specific competitive stratcgies.
- Strategic HRPD can also be instrumental in pinpointing areas of weakness or gaps in implementing major changes, developing future competencies, and in more tactical implementation.
- Its potential economic value is considerable, and can be harvested through highlighting major likely future shortages in management resources; through challenging assumptions that source management resources will be deployed in certain ways (for instance several senior managers in the organization may be counting on having a particularly talented person, even though this is plainly not feasible); and through freeing up career paths so that key individuals can move between functions, business units and geographics, helping to develop and retain them and also increasing their general and international management skills.
- Strategic HRPD is feasible provided that line managers are prepared to invest some time in strategic thinking. This time investment can be focused carefully through an issue-driven process.
- This requires balanced input from line and HR managers – the line managers driving the analysis and decisions, and HR managers orchestrating and structuring the process.
- Strategic HRPD ideally is an integral part of business strategic planning, and not a follow-on, an afterthought or a sideshow.
- There needs to be a balance between the wider backdrop and longer term, and work on more specific, detailed and shorter-term HR issues.
- There needs to be strong follow-through and follow-up.

Amplifying the last point, Ian Parkes of Amersham reflected:

You have to have a number of building blocks in place to actually get the most out of Strategic Human Resource Planning and Development. We have scoped out our work for a considerable period of time ahead. But the real

217

work has hardly even begun, as we need to get the input and active involvement in the process of many of our middle managers. This requires them to think about their own career strategies – not just discussing them as 'human assets', which we are moving well away from.

Strategic HRPD therefore provides a refreshing approach to harvesting the human element of strategy. However, once again it highlights the need to provide a clear and sustained implementation focus within a crucial area of HR strategy – one of paramount importance.

CHAPTER 10

Value-added management development and training strategy

■ INTRODUCTION

Even before the recession of the early 1990s, managers were becoming increasingly alert to the need to take more control and to have more influence over their development. Previously there was more emphasis on the individual's organization being the primary guardian of development.

For example, when one of the authors worked for the BP Group in the early 1980s, each new manager had an individual programme of development laid out – in keeping with the organizational hierarchy (of the time). At that time self-development was not on the radar map. For example, the very idea of individuals deciding to put themselves on an MBA was almost unthinkable.

One of the authors used to joke at the time (of that hierarchy):

> By the time I get into a really senior position at BP and get a company car I will probably have to drive a Reliant Robin.

Since then organizations and careers have changed and become far more uncertain, generating a surge of interest in the individuals driving their own development. Since the mid-1990s there has been a surge in growth of public courses (especially short courses – which mean that managers do not have to catch up too much with their work when they go back). These changes have mixed benefits/costs, and successful individual development is often accompanied by organization-wide support for learning and development – and as part of a coherent strategy.

Although a wide variety of development strategies for the individual exist (courses, projects, MBAs, secondments, coaching and monitoring), the default solution is very often still the training course. In many ways this is a pity, because it is not always the case that training generates significant learning – and it is learning that produces a real change in capability and in action, thus developing the individual, the group, and the wider organization.

Table 10.1
Significance of the major courses undertaken by one of the authors

Course	Major benefit
First degree – Behavioural Sciences	Analytical understanding
Chartered Accountant	Financial and business awareness/analysis
MBA	Strategic thinking and confidence
	Entry to strategy consultancy
PhD – Strategic Management	New frameworks/products
	Credibility as a strategy consultant
	Entry to business school lecturing
	Confidence as a writer
	Two books authored
MPhil – Strategic Management	Greater strategy facilitation capability
	One book authored
MSc – Organizational Behaviour	HR strategy product

Indeed the very notion that *everyday work* presents one of the best possible developmental activities seems to have gone by the board. Perhaps better still is where individuals work in learning groups in the organization to resolve key issues, and gain organizational learning, too.

Don't get us wrong; courses do have their own role to play – especially at the start and during the early middle phases of a career it is useful to digest sufficient mental frameworks and maps to be able to deal with complex issues easily and quickly and, above all, with confidence. However, everyday work (and especially group learning projects) often provides the best opportunity for learning and development.

So what economic value does development bring? Let us touch on the career of one of the authors (see Table 10.1).

It is interesting at this point to reflect on the value (and we mean the economic value) of this kind of development, possibly amounting to a doubling of income (relative to a less stretching personal developmental strategy). Each one of these courses generated an incremental income stream.

This brings us to a number of key points:

■ Development investment by the individual (or groups of individuals) can potentially produce a huge economic pay-off.
■ Development activities need to form part of a longer-term strategy. Also they typically add value through being part of a set, rather than having a relatively isolated contribution.
■ This development strategy should be thought through as a series of stages, or as a sequence of pre-orchestrated moves.

We will now turn to strategies for developing the individual, and then go on to consider the value added by individual development. After that we will look at some key concepts in management development strategy (including the learning organization, competencies, and training needs analysis).

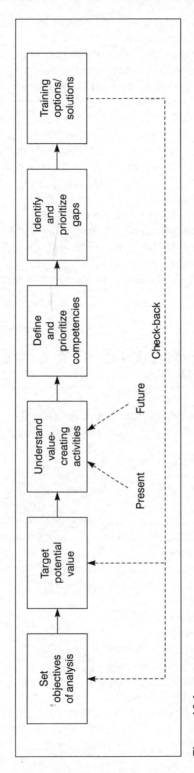

Figure 10.1
The process for competency analysis

Management development strategy is illustrated by an organizational intervention at Mercury Communications.

The chapter will help you a lot in the organizational development role of a strategic HR consultant, especially through the Mercury Communications case.

Figure 10.1 shows that competencies form the core of the process. Besides defining existing competencies, we also need to look at those of the future. These overall competencies need to be prioritized in terms of criticality/importance. In defining these competencies we also need to identify the key value-creating activities of each role. Next, the gap between the vision for future competencies *vis-à-vis* the present position is identified, with inputs from the business strategy. Our competency definition may also provide input to challenge and build the business strategies.

The competing gaps are then prioritized (in terms of both their importance and also our relative strength). This leads on into implementation options and their evaluation (perhaps with AID analysis), and then into implementation and learning.

The above process should be used in creating a management development plan.

STRATEGIC OPTIONS FOR DEVELOPING THE INDIVIDUAL

There are a number of strategic options for developing the individual, or groups of individuals, some of which have already been touched upon. These include:

- On-the-job development
- In-company training
- Public training programmes
- Consortia programmes
- Formal management education – including professional qualifications; an MBA; an MSc in a specialist area such as corporate finance, HR development, or strategic change
- Actually reading (and digesting) quality management books, and articles
- Working on a (real) strategic change project
- A group project (learning)
- An individual project (learning)
- Benchmarking opportunities
- Shadowing someone in another industry
- Mentoring with a senior line manager
- Coaching, perhaps with a specialist, outside the company
- A secondment within the company
- A secondment outside the company
- A particular challenging short-term role (to develop a targeted number of competencies).

Each of the strategies needs to be evaluated for each and every individual. However, at a more generic level we can still characterize these strategies for development as in Table 10.2.

Table 10.2
Strategies for development of individuals

Training	Advantages	Disadvantages
On-the-job development	Has immediate benefits	Real-life experiment is perceived as 'too dangerous'
In-company-training	Should be highly relevant to the work we actually do	It doesn't (easily) bring in an external perspective
Public training programmes	Mixing with people from other companies	This is typically 'low reality learning'
Development consortia	Gets the best of both worlds (in-company and public course training)	These are typically difficult to set up – and to sustain
Professional qualifications	Can give a tangible edge in terms of both role and rewards (depending upon the qualification)	Might well limit career opportunities (subsequently) to a specific type of role)
MBA	A high status qualification	This might be pursued as an end in itself
	Salary premium	Not always as high as you might think
	Learning and increased capability	Lots and lots of time input
MSc	Signals a higher level of competence	Sometimes overly academic
	Quicker than an MBA (and less time input)	Might not have the status of an MBA

Table 10.3
Various forms of learning and development processes

Projects	Advantages	Disadvantages
Group projects (learning)	More learning in teams	More time-consuming, and potentially difficult behaviourally politically
Individual projects (learning)	Personal sense of stretch and achievement	Might be more difficult analytically
Real strategic change projects	Real business value added	Can get so real that learning disappears from the agenda
	Highly stretching developmentally	Might be a high career risk

Table 10.4
Other development processes

Other processes	Advantages	Disadvantages
Shadowing – in another industry	Very powerful and enlightening learning experience	Benefits might not be so obvious (before the event)
Mentoring	Can be a great all-around and personalized development experience	Shortage of decent/appropriate mentors
Coaching	Provides a sounding board from outside the organization	Likely to be reasonably expensive

Ideally, individuals should pick from the most appropriate of the above opportunities, depending upon their situation. For instance, if an individual is seeking exposure to the thinking in another company, then a public training programme, an MBA or a consortia (if available) could be ideal.

Also, a professional qualification might be more appropriate at an earlier career stage. However, an MBA, an MSc or a public general management course might be more useful during the transition from early to mid-career.

Table 10.3 lists some other forms of learning and development projects.

From this we can see that the choice of project will depend upon the degree of stretch being sought, and also the level of pre-existing self-confidence.

Table 10.4 moves on to other development processes:

Shadowing entails spending a day or a couple of days with a manager in another industry. Mentoring is an internal process, and works well if there is a very close trust between the mentor and the manager, and if the mentor is highly motivated to add value. Coaching (usually external) can integrate a whole variety of approaches, including personal/management style analysis (with psychometrics), support in defining role and tasks, problem-solving and prioritization, and strategic thinking.

Table 10.5 looks at developmental roles.

Table 10.5
Developmental roles

Roles	Advantages	Disadvantages
Secondment within the company	Broadens experience without leaving the company	It may not be for long enough
Secondment outside the company	More scope to manage differently and exposure to different ways of thinking	You might not wish to come back!/re-entry problems
A challenging short-term role	Excellent for developing specific target skills	Risks of failure in the role may be high (without support, e.g. mentoring)

Table 10.6
Developmental mix of a chartered accountant between the ages of 24 and 39

Age (years)	Development
24	Qualified as a chartered accountant
25	Management development course – in-company (management and leadership skills)
26	Public programmes in marketing and in IT strategy
27–28	MBA (part-time)
27	Secondment to a line position
28	Led a strategic change project
29	Promoted to business level FD
29	Mentored by a Divisional CEO
30	International assignment
32	Appointed Divisional Finance Director within another Group
32–33	MSc (part-time) in Corporate Finance
34	Secondment as Group Head of Acquisitions and Business Development
35	MD of a significant operating unit
38	Promoted as Group Financial Director
39	Coaching programme – preparation for being Group CEO potentially

Once again there are many trade-offs to be made, but each one of these roles can often accelerate learning much more effectively than formal training (and related approaches).

Let us now take a quick look at the developmental mix. Table 10.6 provides the example of a high-flying accountant between the ages of 24 and 39.

Notice how these training and other developmental activities are carefully sequenced and timed (for example, an MBA after the age of 35 might be spurious for this high flyer).

ECONOMIC VALUE ADDED BY INDIVIDUAL DEVELOPMENT

The value added by individual development occurs in a multitude of ways. First, benefits to the individual include:

1. Better performance on the job
    - Increases job satisfaction
    - Increases the probability of promotion
    - Brings forward the likelihood of promotion
    - Produces a solid track record as a basis for applying for better jobs in other (and perhaps more attractive) organizations
    - Reduces stress
    - Reduces time-on-the job

2. Higher salary and/or bonuses
3. A sounder base for attracting further developmental opportunities (e.g. general management courses or an MBA).

The value added to the company can take other, although related, forms:

1. Better performance in current roles
2. Creating a bigger pool of strong executive talent (really excellent senior managers are still hard to find)
3. Maintaining employee satisfaction
4. A more open, challenging culture in the organization
5. Better key employee retention
6. Attraction of high calibre recruits, through a genuine commitment to investing in individual development.

INDIVIDUAL DEVELOPMENT AND BREAKTHROUGH THINKING

A development breakthrough can be defined as:

An initiative or action that produces a very major shift in performance or in capability – at the organizational, developmental, team or individual level.

As already explained, an interesting feature of breakthroughs is that they typically have to be relatively small in number to prove effective. In fact, breakthrough theory (or *hoshin*, the Japanese word for 'breakthrough') suggests that only between one and three breakthroughs can be pursued both simultaneously and effectively.

As an example, Table 10.7 shows the personal career breakthroughs over the last decade for one of the authors

Table 10.7
Example of career breakthroughs

Date	Breakthrough
1990–1992	Acquiring independent consulting skills
	Acquiring research skills (PhD)
	Writing my first management book
1993–1994	Developing consultancy products/strategy skills
	Becoming a business school lecturer
1994–1995	Acquiring more all-round facilitation skills
	Becoming less of a workaholic
1998–2001	Acquiring skills for helping to manage energy levels (my own and others)
2002–2003	Developing skills in writing practical management guides
	Strategic coaching skills

Exercise I

1. What are the three skills breakthroughs that would advance you more in relation to your next possible career move?
2. What are your options for achieving these breakthroughs?
3. What might the value be (to you and to your organization)?
4. What might the business case look like for one or more of these?

Notice that at times the author focused on just one skill breakthrough, and at other times on two or three – but never on four, five, six or seven.

To summarize so far, flatter, changing organizations have meant that individual development is not just an 'add-on' but is an essential part of career development. Whilst the default development path is often one of formal training, there are typically a wide variety of developmental options that need to be tailored to the individual. Most managers and many HR professionals consider far too narrow a range of options here.

It is important therefore that individuals should create their own developmental mix, rather than getting sucked into the question of 'what training should I ask for?'. This learning and development should be focused primarily on a small number (maximum three) of learning and development breakthroughs.

We will now move on to key concepts in management development.

KEY CONCEPTS IN MANAGEMENT DEVELOPMENT

Key concepts include:

- Development
- Learning
- The learning organization
- Competencies (with a pharmaceuticals case study)
- Gap analysis
- Training needs analysis.

Development

Development can now be defined as:

The process of transforming an individual (or group) from one level of capability to another.

Development is a slightly different concept from training, as it is:

227

- More broad-based, covering not just one skill or a number of specific skills, but a more generic capability (like leadership)
- Long term in its focus (frequently over a year and perhaps longer)
- Generally more concerned with acquiring new skills or applying existing skills in new ways.

Development is perhaps best seen as being a process that might be made up of a number of phases. For example, to develop an effective general manager might require:

- Phase 1 – induction into the company/industry
- Phase 2 – first supervisory role
- Phase 3 – specialist functional management skills
- Phase 4 – general management training (formal education)
- Phase 5 – transition to first general management role (with mentoring)
- Phase 6 – move to overseas company to acquire international experience.

Within each of the above phases there may well typically be more specific training on perhaps five or more key competencies.

Learning

Learning can now be defined as:

> A conscious or subconscious process of developing or adapting perspectives to make better sense of the world, and ultimately to become more effective.

Learning may thus occur at a conscious or at a subconscious level. Indeed, highly successful managers are typically excellent at subconscious learning – indeed, learning is built into their everyday routines for doing virtually everything.

Learning is not merely about adding to a stock of knowledge, but is frequently about changing it. The more successful learners are able to re-examine beliefs and thought processes, and discard them where they are no longer appropriate or applicable.

For instance, in Phase 2 (first supervisory role) of the individual's development illustrated above, a successful belief would be:

> I need actually to do things myself to make sure that things get done – when these have not been done by other people.

First-line supervisors cannot delegate everything – they need to provide a focus for action. However, in Phase 5, where the individual now takes a general management role, this hands-on style would not only be unproductive but it could even be a disaster. A successful general manager usually needs to step back from the detail and provide overall direction, intervening only selectively in what their staff are doing. Such interventions should be more concerned with steering staff processes and motivating them, rather than in the detailed content of their actions.

The above point was once put in a very direct way as, 'Why have a dog and bark yourself?'

The learning organization

Much has been made of the learning organization, but few organizations appear to have been able to take on this model successfully. A learning organization can be defined as:

An organization that uses organizational, group and individual learning to continually transform itself and to meet its ongoing challenges – both consciously and unconsciously.

In an ideal learning organization:

- Learning and experimentation are prized highly
- Learning is seen explicitly as producing better performance, and is conspicuously invested in
- Action and learning are equally valued
- Mistakes are recognized as inevitabilities and as potential positives, rather than as evils
- Individuals and groups are actually encouraged to develop and to adapt
- Rigid mind-sets and structures are regarded as no-nos.

Unfortunately, it is easier to paint an idealistic picture of an learning organization than it is actually to create and sustain one. In reality there are three schools of management thinking on the learning organization:

1. The *prescriptive* school believes that organizations must learn in order to survive and to thrive and become 'learning organizations'.
2. The *impossibility* school believes that attempts to spread learning throughout any complex organization will founder upon a number of obstacles – for instance, denial of error, avoidance of uncertainty and ambiguity, or pure business politics.
3. The *pragmatic* school believes that although there are many barriers to learning, islands or pools of learning can be created within an organization. These islands need a lot of effort if learning is to be developed and sustained. However, with continual effort, learning routines become built in to 'how we do things around here', and may ultimately reach a critical mass to form joined-up, learning continents.

The problem with the prescriptive school ideal is that managers may be unable or unwilling to lead by example in changing their style. Without appropriate support and without mobilization as teams of 'open thinkers', individual action is very likely to be frustrated.

The impossibility school, by contrast, suggests that complex forms of (strategic) learning are highly unstable and are very difficult to share and sustain within an organization. Argyris (1991) argued that most managers are comfortable with simpler forms of learning, where the task on which the learning centres is repeated essentially in the same form or the same loop ('single-loop' learning). However, managers are much less comfortable with more open and unpredictable learning.

Later in this chapter we will put the argument for the pragmatic school (to which both authors subscribe).

Just because organizations are not the most natural homes for learners, this does not mean that they cannot become learning organizations. Companies that have sought to introduce learning processes into the heart of organizational life include Coca Cola, the Prudential, and Tesco.

Competencies

There is a very extensive literature on management competencies – indeed, competencies can give rise to almost a new industry of effort, as they can demand considerable effort to define, diagnose and to evaluate.

A competence can be defined as:

An area of skill that adds value (either now or potentially) to the organization.

Competencies are thus not just things that you can do well or not so well, but they also have a very direct relevance to the organization and to the way it generates economic value. Whilst the idea is more specific than that of 'skills', ambiguity sometimes gives rise to nostalgia for the rather easier to grasp notion of 'skills', which once upon a time seemed to do the job.

Tesco has avoided the term 'competencies' and adapted instead 'success factors', thus making sure that they make sense to their primary users – the line managers.

Unfortunately the word 'competence' does seem to be rather technical, and may suggest more complexity than is actually needed. This in turn might lead HR staff (or the line managers) to produce excessively elaborate competency frameworks – sometimes with as many as 50 or so key competencies.

Whilst it is absolutely true that many management roles are highly complex skill-sets, it is nevertheless likely that perhaps 20 per cent of these competencies are in the areas where the biggest gaps exist. Of these areas, maybe 20 per cent are greater importance. This complexity can thus be dealt with by focusing on the $20\% \times 20\% = 4\%$ of competencies that both have big gaps, and some of the most important gaps.

The key thing with competency analysis is to ask the question, 'so what?'. This 'So what?' entails:

- Looking for patterns in underlying weaknesses across a number of competencies
- Seeking out one or a very small number of areas of major breakthrough that can add the most value
- Anticipating which kind of training and development options might be most suitable in locating the major (and important) competency gaps in the organization (e.g. in-company courses, mentoring, culture change initiatives, changes in performance management and other developmental processes etc.).

Example of a general management competency framework

The following provides a brief example of how a broad-ranging competency framework can be defined:

1. *Strategic thinking*
   - Strategic analysis
   - Creativity
   - Strategic facilitation
2. *Leadership and change management*
   - Visionary skills
   - Personal charisma
   - Leadership style
   - Change management
   - Project management
3. *Commercial skills*
   - Marketing skills and customer focus
   - Financial planning
   - Negotiating skills
   - International vision
4. *Problem-solving skills*
   - Problem diagnosis
   - Data collection and analysis skills
   - Prioritization
5. *Personal and interpersonal skills*
   - Drive
   - Time management
   - Influencing
   - Communication
   - Empathy.

Here we have limited ourselves to just twenty key competencies. Whilst only a limited number of competencies are more emotional in nature than cognitive, these conditional competencies can prove more decisive in sustaining senior performance. (This is sometimes known as 'emotional intelligence' – see Goleman, 1995). Examples in this domain include personal charisma, drive, and empathy.

Let us now illustrate the competency framework with a short case study on competencies from the pharmaceutical industry.

Case study: Pharmatech competencies

A complex pharmaceuticals company needed to define its competency gaps across a divergent range of departments and roles, and in a number of international locations.

The hoped-for benefits of this initiative were:

- Improved performance through increased knowledge, and greater efficiency, effectiveness and responsiveness
- Improved compliance with regulatory requirements and technical requirements
- Improved individual and team performance
- Recognition of individual and team performance
- Improved working cross-culturally
- Training certification
- Integration of training with other organizational initiatives and HR processes.

It was envisaged that besides competencies this would be used as a training needs analysis.

As can be imagined, the competencies were highly complicated and amounted to no less than 53 areas. These were then mapped out in a matrix of competence against role, ticking off each box that was important (see Figure 10.2). A sub-set of these ticks was then scrutinized to see where competency gaps existed. By doing this in a two-dimensional matrix (and visually) it was much easier to helicopter over the analysis and identify the key areas (across roles) where there were common gaps.

Competency \ Roles	1	2	3
A	✓	✓	
B		✓	✓
C	✓	✓	
D			✓

Figure 10.2 A competency matrix

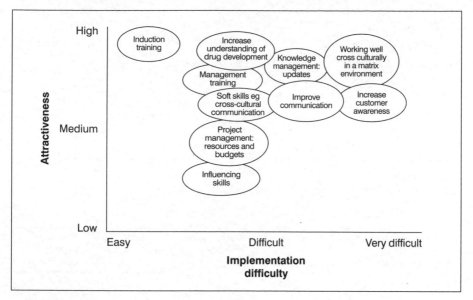

Figure 10.3
Attractiveness–implementation difficulty analysis for key training priorities

In identifying possible training solutions, the company then used AID analysis (see Figure 10.3) for a few examples. This really helped to focus training initiatives subsequently. This analysis task took quite a long time – several weeks, including many interviews, to gain a representative view – even though it was very well targeted and at each stage there was clear link back to objectives and priorities.

This highlights that competency analysis can so easily become a complex exercise. It is crucial, therefore, to ensure that its economic value is carefully pre-targeted and monitored, particularly during the transition to implementing training solutions. Arguably, if you are only going to implement 20 per cent of these (vis-à-vis needs) then it might be a thought to focus the analysis on fewer things and lower competencies, rather than try to map the whole picture.

In making the link with possible solutions, the following two-stage process was performed, identifying the general competency theme, some specifics, and then some possible solutions (each of which could be appraised using AID analysis):

General area	Specifics	Possible solutions
Interpersonal skills (generic)	Communication, Influencing, Managing upwards. Conflict resolution. Teamwork	Either a generic course or a series of sub-modules covering most relevant topics, with common 'culture change' one day. Supported by other company initiatives (company values etc.?) Plus performance management and mentoring.

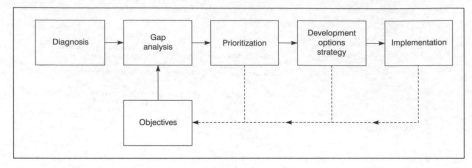

Figure 10.4
Competency prioritization

Key programmes Key objectives	Interpersonal and team-working	Knowledge management and induction	Drug development	Resource/ general management
1a	Common culture	✓	✓		✓
1b	Common skills		✓	✓	✓
2	Flexibility and mobility	✓	✓		✓
3	Processes consistent		✓	✓	
4	External compliance		✓	✓	
5	Efficiency and effectiveness – clinical development	✓	✓	✓	✓

Figure 10.5
An objectives/training needs matrix

Because of the complexity of the task, a final piece of analysis was done to check back to the company's original objectives (see Figures 10.4 and 10.5).

Gap analysis

Gap analysis goes back in time to the beginning of corporate planning in the 1960s. It can be defined as:

> The difference between where you are now and where you need to be or want to be in terms of capability at some future time.

Gap analysis is inseparable from 'understanding what business you are in' (see the final section of this chapter).

The need for a particular competency will change over time, for example with the growing demand for strategic thinking. Ten years ago strategic thinking was hardly on the agenda of most organizations, let alone on that of individual managers, except for a very small minority of potential high flyers. However, nowadays strategic thinking is increasingly recognized by individuals, by HR developers and by senior line management as being a critical skill.

Training needs analysis

Training needs analysis (TNA) is a rather posh way of saying 'skills diagnosis'. A TNA can be defined as:

> A systematic process for diagnosing current and potential future competency groups, prioritizing them, and suggesting some possible training options and solutions.

Because the three words 'training', 'needs' and 'analysis' sound more technical when bundled together in this sequence, it might appear that a TNA is of necessity complex, time-consuming and difficult. This is not necessarily the case. Again, if operating according to the Pareto principle (that 20 per cent of things by number in any given population usually represent 80 per cent of what is really important), then much of the work entailed in TNA can be focused relatively sharply. Also, as suggested earlier, the most important thing is to look for the big 'so whats?'. This entails identifying lines of enquiry (in the style of being a detective) as to which area of competency might generate the biggest wins.

Training needs analyses are usually carried out via a mixture of interviews and questionnaires. Generally speaking, interviews coupled with a semi-structured questionnaire appear to be a more successful approach than just questionnaires, as frequently the terms used in questionnaires will require explanation.

THE EVOLUTION OF MANAGEMENT DEVELOPMENT

In this section we will examine:

- From on-the-job training to training programmes
- From training programmes to training interventions
- From company-led development to individual-led development
- From tactical to strategic development.

From on-the-job training to training programmes

Much training is traditionally initiated on an on-the-job basis. This can take a variety of forms, including:

- Setting objectives for future performance improvement
- Regular reviews of performance, both against these objectives and in relation to specific job tasks
- Annual performance reviews
- On-the-job projects
- Operating procedures guides.

Setting objectives for future performance improvement

Setting objectives for future performance improvement is one of the most immediate and practical ways of developing the individual. This can be used to:

- Set stretching performance goals, notionally aimed at shorter-term performance, but also for learning and development generally
- Prioritize these objectives (a good rule of thumb is to choose *no more than three* stretching objectives to focus on within a particular 6- to 9-month period
- Help in identifying *how* the individual will teach these goals effectively
- Identify the kind of support needed from their boss and from other key people.

Regular reviews of performance

Regular reviews of the performance of an individual (which may be done monthly) can then help to:

- Identify unexpected difficulties in performing tasks really well
- Resolve these problems
- Reprioritize these where necessary
- Provide positive reinforcement of ongoing achievements.

For example, when one of the authors had his senior management role, as Head of Finance and Planning, ICI International Seeds, he had weekly meetings with the Deputy Divisional Finance Director of ICI Agrochemicals. These sessions continued over a 6-month period of secondment from KPMG Management Consultants. In the course of these sessions they were able to sort out:

- Acquisition integration issues with a recent £50m acquisition in Belgium and a £30m acquisition in the US

- Reporting issues (he was reporting effectively to two bosses, making the work focus difficult)
- Major transfer pricing issues in UK operations, where there were disputes with other parts of ICI
- Smooth delivery of the 3-year plan for ICI Seeds
- Quarterly reporting of results – especially how to position certain areas of not-so-good performance.

Looking back, and given his limited competency base for this job, he found it hard to imagine how he did such a difficult job. This role had entailed him being involved in:

- His first very senior line financial position
- A major change in focus from his consultancy role
- An industry he had previously known nothing about
- Acquisition management, about which he had previously known next to nothing
- Cross-border (and multicultural) management.

Regular performance meetings like this with a helpful coach can not only produce superior performance, but also greatly accelerated development.

Annual performance reviews

Annual performance reviews should be higher-level versions of the ongoing performance meetings we covered earlier. Differences might include:

- More emphasis on looking at patterns in performance blockages rather than in isolated problems (which should be covered in more regular reviews)
- More time spent on the individual's development options and strategy
- More focus on specific off-the-job training opportunities.

Obviously because these reviews are often linked to salary rises and provide input to potential promotion they are more sensitive in nature, and if handled badly can cause sudden switches in career direction.

On-the-job projects

On-the-job projects are a much under-utilized area of development for the individual. These can take the form of:

- Market research
- A quality management review
- A restructuring
- Product development
- An acquisition

- Business process re-engineering
- An IT project
- A business plan.

With projects of this kind it is important to set both business and learning objectives, otherwise the business imperative will be considered to crowd out the learning focus.

However, the beauty of projects is that to a very great extent they can be self-driven. This improves the individual's ability to *learn how to learn* – which is a higher order management competence normally associated with high flyers. Learning to learn entails:

- Being able to monitor your learning
- Being able to make your learning much more efficient (i.e. getting the learning with less effort)
- Being able to make your learning considerably more effective (i.e. getting more value out of the learning, subsequently).

Operating procedure guides

Mention the words 'operating procedure guides', and people may well start to yawn. However, where these are appropriately written they can provide an excellent way of helping the individual to pick up the culture and routines of a new organization. Also, in the right hands they can provide a living guide to 'how to do things effectively around here'.

For example, some operating processes that are now used extensively in organizations in an ongoing way include:

- Guides to strategic thinking – especially at Diageo, Standard Life and Tesco

Table 10.8
Advantages and disadvantages of on-the-job training and of training programmes

	Advantages	Disadvantages
On-the-job training	Has immediate application	Too much of a focus on performance can drive out learning
	Tangible pay-off short/pay-back	Usually has short-term focus
	Performance improvements on everyone's agendas	Perceived as time-consuming for the developer's manager
Training programmes	More far-reaching scope	Can be too diffuse, unrelated to specific action
	Longer-term development	Longer-term, potentially dubious pay-back
	Benefits from safe, socially-based learning	Can be treated as a 'management holiday'

- Guides to project management – for example, as used at Tesco on major projects since 1997, and at Amgen (a leading biotech company
- An HR consulting guide – at the Royal Bank of Scotland Group.

These guides are no longer paper artefacts but are in electronic format, effectively representing a simple form of computer-based training. These are useful aids to on-the-job training.

Whilst on-the-job training has a very valuable and often overlooked role in development, it does need to be complemented by training programmes. Some of the advantages and disadvantages of both forms of development are shown in Table 10.8.

From training programmes to training interventions

A training programme usually takes the form of a short course, of maybe 1, 2 or even 3 days, with:

- Pre-work
- Goals and objectives
- Conceptual and practical input
- Practical group exercises
- Feedback sessions
- Distillation of learning lessons (at group and individual levels)
- Action plan
- Handouts and checklists
- Feedback (or 'happy') forms.

Training programmes are typically relatively self-contained. Attendees are rarely met individually or interviewed by training deliverers, unless a full training needs analysis is undertaken.

Whilst their overall skills gap may be known broadly, it is often not known in detail by individuals. Also, training deliverers (especially where external) may not have detailed knowledge of participants' agendas and mind-sets (are they up for it, or not?). This makes it harder to ensure that the training is well directed and steered towards its real targets.

It is probably a 'no-brainer' from this example that training programmes should:

- Rather than having just superficial pre-work and follow-on work, have a much greater emphasis on this – *even if this requires more effort from HR*. (A suggestion here is for HR to run fewer and higher quality training courses rather than 'putting bums on seats').
- Be positioned not as a welcome break from normal work, but as an integral part of future management process and of 'how we do things around here'
- Do a more thorough appraisal of the training need.

Table 10.9
Differences between a training programme and a training intervention

Training programme	Training intervention
Relatively stand-alone	A series of workshops/other interventions
Quick-and-dirty training needs assessment	A fuller, training needs analysis is conducted
Narrow objectives – to deal with a specific symptom/problem	Integrated with organizational goals/other interventions
Little reinforcement of learning and behavioural change	Considerable reinforcement of these shifts
Positioned by HR	Positioned by senior line management
Lower reality exercises	High reality work – on major operational/organizational issues
Outputs presented to senior management as 'interesting things to think about – and maybe forget'	Management actions and decisions actually change as a result

When the above points are in place, we can begin to see the training programme as more of a 'training intervention'. The key differences between the two are shown in Table 10.9.

A training intervention is thus very much a different beast to a training programme. An excellent example of a far-reaching training intervention is that of Mercury Communications, which we will see later in this chapter. This intervention had:

■ Very clear business goals
■ A number of phases (there were a series of interventions over a period of about 4 months)
■ Positioning by the general manager, and active involvement throughout
■ Real and tangible improvements to performance as a result
■ Major shifts in capability of middle managers.

From company-led development to individual-led development

Whilst a high percentage of development is still organized for groups within an organization (as training programmes/interventions), there is an increasing focus on individual-led development. This is partly as a result of a greater focus on empowerment (or enabling individuals to take more responsibility and control over their roles and their careers in general). Also, individuals are increasingly eager for this following the massive restructurings and redundancies of the 1990s and early 2000s.

Table 10.10 contrasts the philosophies of company-led versus individual-led development.

Table 10.10
Company-led versus individual-led development

	Company-led development	Individual-led development
Developmental plans	Done mainly by the company	Done mainly by individuals (with their boss)
Training resources	Controlled by the company	Controlled at least in part by individuals
Training programmes	In-company programmes mainly Delivered mainly through training courses	More public course, or MBAs A wider variety of inter- ventions (e.g. mentoring etc.)
Career pattern	Assumed to be within the company	Portable capabilities/portable career

From tactical to strategic development

Tactical development aims to achieve performance shifts within 3 to 6 months. Strategic development aims to achieve performance skills over a 3- to 18-month period, and capability skills within a time horizon of 1 to 6 years. Tactical development is also more typically focused on narrower, relatively stand-alone objectives, whilst strategic development typically has a broader range of goals, and also is likely to be interdependent with other initiative, support processes and interventions.

More narrow ranges of objectives are often associated with, for example:

- Technical training
- Presentation skills
- Influencing skills
- Supervisory skills
- Functional skills.

Wider-ranging objectives might be:

- Facilitating organizational change
- Making people more innovative
- Introducing project management processes
- Team-building
- Improving communication
- Strategic thinking
- Commercial awareness and skills.

The latter objectives will typically require more time to deliver their full economic value. They are also likely to require a training intervention rather than a discrete training programme, and they are more likely to have tangible business goals, as well as learning and development goals. Finally, they are more likely to require a high level of consultancy diagnostic skills within

HR, rather than being a case of doing a training needs analysis of *the need as defined by management*.

Consultancy skills require more contact with line managers, deeper knowledge of their business and organizational issues, and a lot more time investment. (The latter is a big problem for HR staff, who are still expected to do operational personnel roles, meaning that they are continually dragged into HR fire-fighting.)

Case study: the Royal Bank of Scotland Group

Around 2000, the Royal Bank of Scotland Group, which had recently bought the NatWest Group, decided to enhance the consulting skills of all of its key HR managers.

The 'Consulting diagnostics' module within this programme consisted of:

- What is strategy/HR strategy?
- Understanding business performance – performance drivers
- HR strategy in acquisitions – BMW/Rover case
- Creating and evaluating strategic options
- HR strategy in corporate turnaround/post-acquisition – Champneys case study
- Diagnostic work on an HR issue
- Option generation – own HR issues
- Implementation analysis – own HR issues
- Stakeholder analysis – own HR issues
- Uncertainty analysis – own HR issues.

This module is now supported by the RBS group's (or the Group's) HR consulting diagnostics tool kit.

Companies vary considerably in their degree of sophistication in this development area. There is a lot to learn by networking/benchmarking approaches, both with other companies and with industries.

To summarize so far, developing the individual has resulted in a number of major shifts in the development mix. Stand-alone, in-company programmes are now managed more frequently as training interventions – and of a strategic rather than a more tactical type.

Also, at a micro-level there is more of a role for individual-led development, manifested in the growth of short, public courses, so that individuals can mix with staff from other companies and other industries.

With the spread of mentoring and coaching, the distinction the between on-the-job and off-the-job training has become more blurred.

DEVELOPING A PERSONAL MANAGEMENT DEVELOPMENT STRATEGY

Having exhaustively covered more individually focused development strategies, we will now look at developmental interventions – particularly the case of Mercury Communications.

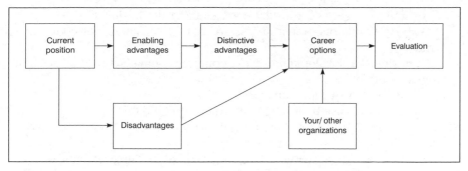

Figure 10.6
Self-development process

Effective self-development involves using strategic learning to evolve your capability to a higher level. This is illustrated in Figure 10.6.

Figure 10.6 begins with understanding your current position and how you add economic value. This involves identifying both your 'enabling advantages' (for instance, core functional skills) and your distinctive advantage (for example, political skills or vision). It also requires analysis of your personal competitive disadvantages. It then explores what your career strategy might be. Depending upon the point you have already reached in your career and aspirations, this might have a three- to five-year timescale – or possibly even longer.

What business are you in?

When defining your organizational role, it is rarely self-evident as to 'what business you are in'. Although many roles are relatively fluid, it is still necessary to have a clear understanding of what is (or should be) at the core of this role.

The traditional way of defining roles – for instance, in terms of defining your key, fixed responsibilities – is less relevant in an environment of continual change – which most managers now find themselves facing. Nevertheless, even in a fluid environment it is essential to understand how you currently *add value* to the organization, and how you could *add more*. This 'added value' test is extremely useful, as it reinforces activities that you should be doing and questions activities of a less valuable or more dubious nature.

For instance, in an ideal world a financial director might add value by:

■ Providing input into the strategic decision-making process
■ Suggesting new areas for business development
■ Keeping track of financial performance
■ Interpreting this performance so that operational managers can take rapid corrective action

- Providing internal and external confidence in the business
- Satisfying regulatory requirements so that the business can continue to trade
- Optimizing the development of the company's financial resources – long and short term
- Promoting a cost-aware culture
- Helping to avoid both strategic and tactical blunders
- Developing staff so that they understand the business and its finances.

Some of the above elements will not appear to be particularly 'new'. However, some finance directors may place much emphasis on certain areas, but less on others. For instance, many financial directors may not see it as their role to be suggesting new areas for business development, or they may see this as incidental. This may be related partly to the role expectations set by the discipline, and partly to those set by the organization. Yet financial directors may be particularly well placed to identify possible profit-making opportunities.

In addition, financial directors may not see their position as a consultancy role. More typically, the their function may be seen as a 'controlling role', hardly conducive to having a consultancy style. Furthermore, the burden of regulatory requirements may drive out other value-adding activities. This may be even though this function adds value purely by via keeping the organization in business. Figure 10.7 represents a financial director's 'business value system'.

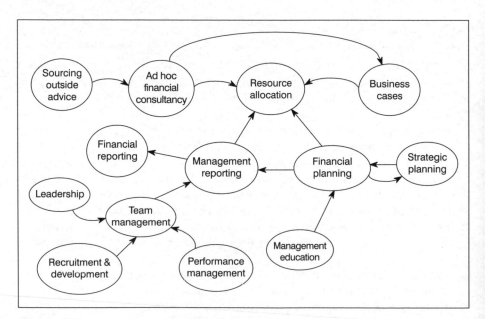

Figure 10.7
Business value system of a finance director

A typical pattern is thus one where individuals – like many businesses – lack a clear focus on 'what business they are in', and also 'where they can add most value'. This lack of focus means that, while they are able to satisfy more routine demands, there is an acute lack of time and energy to deviate to activities of a more strategic nature where they may add more value. As a result, they may begin to lack personal competitive advantage and thus be 'me-too' players in the organization.

Exercise 2 (10 minutes)

1. What value do you generate in your own role? (Do a business value system, as in Figure 10.7.)
2. How can you reshape your role to add more value, and possibly *distinctive value*?
3. How could you now develop your personal competitive advantage?

Following Exercise 2, you may have identified some key shifts in what you do, and also how it is prioritized. In order to achieve these shifts in 'how I do things around here', you may need to programme how you can *stop* doing things that do not add value and *start* doing new things that add very high value.

One of the most difficult parts of all, however, is to stop doing things that actually *destroy value*. If we return to our notional case of the financial director, there are a number of ways in which he or she may destroy value – for example by:

- Adopting an excessively tight approach to financial controls, which results in gross inflexibility
- Imposing over-complex financial controls in, for instance, authorizing investment or costs
- Slowing down the decision-making process to a snail's pace
- Intimidating champions of new and value ideas
- Adopting a policing rather than a consulting role

and so on . . .

Exercise 3 gives you the opportunity to reflect on those areas in which you may be destroying value.

Exercise 3 (5 minutes)

1. How are you inadvertently destroying value in your organization?
2. What causes you to do this? Is it your personal or professional style, or is this the way people customarily behave in the organization?
3. Is this because your role overlaps with that of other managers, or because tensions and conflicts are allowed to get out of hand?

An honest response to Exercise 3 should highlight at least one (and possibly several) areas where you are destroying value. The incidence of value destruction may be rife in the organization. This helps to explain why, when a well-focused 10–20 per cent reduction in managers within an organization is coupled with a shift in style and refocusing of activities, little seems to suffer.

The analysis of how you create and destroy value in the organization leads us to the next topic: looking at your personal competitive advantage.

What is your personal competitive advantage?

Although the idea of competitive advantage is by now widely spread in management thinking, it has yet to crystallize in how individual managers think about their personal capability. Over the past few years much energy has been expended in identifying and seeking to develop management competencies. However, many of these initiatives have absorbed a great deal of analysis, while the outputs have been slow to arrive, often cumbersome, and usually cluttered.

Effective management behaviour is complex, but there may be a relatively small number of key ingredients that offer personal competitive advantage. These key ingredients may account for 80 per cent of what might be a distinctive (as opposed to a mediocre) performance, yet account for only 20 per cent of possible competencies. For instance, many managers contemplate, at some stage in their careers, 'going independent as a management consultant'. They may (erroneously) believe that the most critical competencies will be found in the area of functional skills and excellence. However, from a *customer's point of view*, these competencies are often regarded as merely getting the player into the game – they are purely *enabling*. More *distinctive* skills of an independent consultant include:

1. *Holistic vision* – being able to see problems holistically, across functions, in their historical and political context.
2. *Implementation focus* – understanding the issues associated with implementing change to resolve these problems, and also to facilitate this change in addition to having 'expert skills'.
3. *Distinctive, interrelated skills* – having a core of well-honed skills that form a *distinctive cluster* – i.e. part of a distinctive set.
4. *Presentation of self* – as an independent consultant you would need to have (or develop) some sense of personal distinctiveness that fits your personal style and target clients. This might, for instance, embrace becoming an acknowledged expert in the field in the public domain, finely honing your interpersonal skills, and being flexible enough to tackle 'how you come over' to match individual client styles.
5. *Networking* – the ability to gather information and build relationships is crucial in order to help get people to come to you with their problems, as opposed to you chasing around to find them with their problems.

6. *Flexibility* – in order to provide a preferred alternative to the larger consulting firms, you would need to develop flexibility to be able to respond in a more relevant and rapid mode.

You may wish to reflect now about how your own enabling competencies differ from your (possibly) distinctive competencies. Try Exercise 4.

Exercise 4 (20 minutes)

1. What are the sources of personal competitive advantage that *enable* you to execute your role competently, for instance, in your:
   - Functional skills
   - Knowledge of how the business works
   - Interpersonal skills
   - Project/management skills
   - Skills in planning and controlling resources
   - Communication skills?
2. What are your sources of personal competitive advantage that give you a distinctive capability, for instance, in your:
   - Ability to look at problems cross-functionally and to analyse these strategically
   - Leading-edge knowledge base (and one which is particularly relevant to resolving key business problems)
   - Leadership ability and strategic vision
   - Competence in facilitating change
   - Knowledge of the industry, your customers, competitors, suppliers, etc.
   - International experience and fluency in particular languages and culture
   - Unusually strong network of relationships, giving you the capacity to influence decisions and thinking at senior management level?
3. What are your key sources of personal *competitive disadvantage*? For instance, do you have:
   - Specific skills where you are weak in areas that are regarded as fundamental by the customers who in effect buy your services
   - Mainly a single-function vision
   - Major knowledge gaps – for instance, in marketing, IT or finance
   - Lack of exposure to how things are done elsewhere in the organization
   - Low awareness of how other companies work, especially in your field of expertise
   - Lack of experience of front-line management (for advisory staff who may not appreciate the pressures that line managers often face)
   - Acute aversion to risk and to making errors
   - A tendency to deny or oversimplify problems
   - An apparent inability to plan ahead further than a few months?

LEARNING, DEVELOPMENT AND OPERATIONS AT MERCURY COMMUNICATIONS

Introduction and background

Mercury Communications was, at the time of this case study, the subsidiary of the multinational company. Mercury's operations were principally in the UK, and Mercury had made major inroads to the UK telecommunications market. Mercury Communications had expanded extremely rapidly, reaching a turnover of well over £1 billion by the mid-1990s.

This success story takes us right into the heart of Mercury Communications, and into a key business unit – Mercury Messaging. This intervention added major economic value through simplifying and improving key decision-making processes, through cutting out value-destroying or diluting projects, and through improved cost management.

Mercury Messaging's senior team was already well advanced in devising a strategy for future development of the business. Here the need was one of helping to improve the quality of operations, particularly by improving organizational capability, and to translate this into economic value added.

The case highlights how Mercury Messaging became a more 'learning' and 'earning' organization – at the same time.

Origins and scope of the learning and development initiative

The general manager of Mercury Messaging, John Mittens, was becoming concerned about his staff's ability to implement the strategy, which was likely to stretch their capabilities much more than in the past. Many staff in the organization appeared to be focused mainly on striving to be more efficient rather than more effective.

Very few staff had had much formal management development – their training had been primarily of a sales or technical nature. Most worked long hours, and some of this time was spent in resolving tactical problems rather than trying to understand and rectify the underlying causes of these problems. This produced (unquantifiable) economic value dilution and destruction in the organization.

All these symptoms seemed to point to a major management skills gap in the organization, and there was a danger that this gap might widen when the organization tried to implement its strategy for further development. John Mittens and Mercury Messaging's human resources manager, Russell Connor, met to discuss how they might tackle this issue.

Connor's views of the problem were as follows:

> We have a number of staff, particularly those whose backgrounds are mainly sales/technical, who we try to coach and direct, but due to their limited experience they are often unable to come to grips with the basics of good management. For instance, when we pursue market opportunity they hardly

seem to pause for breath before they are in the middle of the project. The result is that we have too many projects, many of which don't really fit with what we are trying to achieve overall. And the good ones we do have become disrupted when someone gets pulled off to do something more urgent.

Many of our staff are still relatively young, and are in danger of continuing like this unless they can somehow switch over to a different way of managing.

A learning and development programme was then put together to work on some live business issues. This consisted of three parts. First, it would not just involve individual learning, but also team and organizational learning. Second, it would involve action-working on live issues with a view, subsequently, to implementing appropriate changes. Third, it would be business-focused, so that it would not be just action learning for the individuals involved *but would also help John Mittens to solve some of Mercury Messaging's most important business issues, and simultaneously* – thus adding real economic value to the business.

This was to be a modular programme; it would not simply be a course, but a series of workshops and projects. This would help to reinforce the change.

The learning and development process

The overall learning and development process that helped Mercury Messaging to become a learning organization is shown in Figure 10.8. Prior

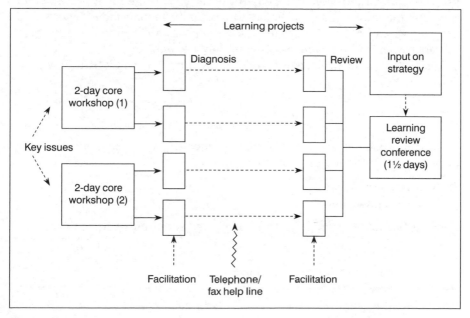

Figure 10.8
Mercury messaging process

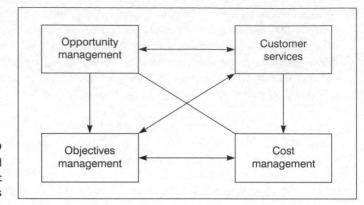

Figure 10.9
Learning and
development
projects

to the core workshop a series of four questions was defined, one for each of the four learning projects.

The four issues that were chosen were as follows:

1. Opportunity management
2. Objectives management
3. Customer services
4. Cost management.

Figure 10.9 shows the four interdependent learning and development projects networked together. Of these four learning and development projects, the core issue was that of opportunity management. This was an area with greatest economic value added impact on the business. It was also the area where *most change* was eventually accomplished.

Each of the four projects was defined by a key question, as follows.

Learning project 1: opportunity management

How can we improve our process for identifying, screening, evaluating, deciding on and finally programming:

- Strategic opportunity
- Tactical opportunity?

What barriers to change would need to be surmounted to achieve this?

Learning project 2: objectives management

What should be the role of 'objectives' (strategic, operational and financial) be in steering a path through future change, and how can these objectives be used to greater effect in the business?

Learning project 3: cost management

How can this we reduce our expenses without damaging the business:

- Short term?
- Long term?

In what specific areas are there possibilities for improving leverage between the use of resource and value added?

Learning project 4: people management

In what areas can we improve the people management process in order to generate further competitive and financial benefits, at minimum cost, and what barriers to change might need to be overcome?

The core workshops

About a dozen managers attended each of the two core workshops, which were run on alternate weeks, and covered competitive change, financial awareness and opportunity development.

Following the core workshops, each learning project team spent approximately half a week in sessions as a group to work on the project issue. In addition, they spent some individual time in further analysis. The workshops extended over a two-and-a-half-month period, and were facilitated with an independent consultant via a telephone/fax helpline, which was very actively used.

It was felt best to give the groups in each team between 2 and 3 months to work on their learning projects, as a shorter period would have not done justice to the issues, and a longer period would probably have resulted in a loss of momentum.

Each project had a learning project plan and an appointed project co-ordinator. The managers were also given on-line access to John Mittens, as key stakeholder and as mentor. In order to enhance learning on working in teams, all participants took a Belbin team role test. This proved very useful, not so much in stereotyping individuals as 'only a plant', 'only a shaper' or 'only a chairman', but because individuals were encouraged to develop those team roles that did not come quite as naturally to them.

The project activities culminated in a project review workshop. Here the outside facilitator provided input to test and reshape presentations, taking care not to over-facilitate and over-intrude on each team's ownership of outputs.

Finally, all four learning projects were presented at a review conference attended by all managers in a hotel at the top of Richmond Hill. This conference lasted an intensive one-and-a-half days, beginning at 5 pm. The format for the presentations was:

- Present the project outputs: 'What we found out'
- Present 'What we learned about the process, tools, etc., and about wider organizational issues'
- Debate and constructive critique(
- The facilitator's summary on the outputs *and* on the process.

In addition, John Mittens was able to spend time formulating a strategic overview that put the projects into a wider context.

Mercury Messaging then decided to extend the learning process into a second phase. The four learning projects were re-labelled as 'change projects', signalling their transformation into high reality and into action.

Making it happen

John Mittens played a key role as sponsor in ensuring that the learning/change projects did not terminate prematurely just after the Richmond conference. It would have been very easy for him to have expected 'things simply to happen', but he maintained an active involvement in the initial stages of implementation.

A number of *process* lessons emerged from the four projects:

1. During the diagnosis stage, the definition of the problem changed quite considerably. In some cases, the scope of the problem (and thus the project) seemed to grow. Learning project teams need to understand that to a degree this is inevitable, as they learn more about the issues and their underlying causes.
2. Teams devoted at least half a day per week to the projects together (in addition to further investigations carried out individually). This put an additional burden on their workload. Again, it is essential to set their expectations realistically for the level of input required for the projects. It may be useful to couple this with a renewed effort in task effectiveness and time management in their day-to-day responsibilities. Also, at times it was difficult to get the teams together as a quorum because of other business pressures. This highlights the need to give (and sustain) a sufficiently high level of priority for the projects *vis-à-vis* other activities.
3. Cynicism that management are serious in desiring this change is highly likely to surface at some stage. Management needs to be aware of these perceived discrepancies and prepared to address them positively rather than compartmentalizing them. Staff, in turn, need to manage any tendencies towards cynicism and put themselves in the position of more senior management, who may seek to change behaviour and management style but quickly suffer relapse.

Extracting the economic value

The key benefits from the four learning and change projects are detailed below.

Opportunity management

Mercury Messaging created a more formal and thorough process for screening and evaluating new product/market/technology opportunities. This involved looking not merely at the financial and sales projections, but also at the inherent strategic attractiveness of the opportunity externally, and at Mercury Messaging's competitive position and to what extent this could be sustained.

A series of bullet-point questions was drawn up and tested against past opportunities (good and not so good) in order to pilot the appraisal device. A common framework was adopted for both better screening and detailed evaluation, structured according to four key questions:

1. Is the market that the opportunity addresses inherently attractive, and thereby offering above-average profitability?
2. Do we have competitive advantage, and can this be sustained?
3. Will the financial returns be sufficient?
4. Given our resources and capability, can we implement it effectively?

This cut out a considerable number of potentially value-destroying projects.

This process was facilitated by the declaration of a 'learning amnesty': that Mercury Messaging managers could be totally open about lessons from past projects without fear of retribution.

Objectives management

It was slightly more difficult to achieve progress on this particular issue. The project team and senior management agreed that staff ought to have a clearer framework of individual and team objectives, linked to business objectives. They also agreed on the *content* of these objectives. What was more difficult, however, was resolving the issue of *flexibility*. On the one hand, Mercury Messaging wanted to preserve as much flexibility of goals and objectives as possible. On the other, everyone realized that, taken to an extreme, this fluidity made it more difficult to achieve goals, owing to ever-changing priorities. This feature is by no means unique to Mercury Messaging; to a lesser or greater extent all organizations face the same dilemma. When a company is grappling with major external (and internal) change, this dilemma can become acute.

Cost management

Although the members of this team had a particularly difficult time at the early, diagnosis stage, they went on to produce some very useful insights, and identified a number of areas for more effective cost management. The following were some of the key outputs from the project:

1. A number of areas were identified where *cost monitoring systems* could be significantly improved
2. A much more *cost-aware* culture was created, where staff began to challenge, continuously, whether objectives could be achieved with less cost
3. In one specific area, the potential for some *very major* cost savings (of several million pounds per annum) was highlighted.

Customer services

This project was a mixture of customer-focus issues, and organization and cost issues. The project team had to ensure that a clear focus was retained throughout, as a result of this diversity of issues. Nevertheless, it proved possible to crystallize a number of options for refocusing and concentrating the resources of Mercury Messaging's customer services activities.

CONCLUSION

Management development strategy is an essential part of value-based HR strategy. This can be defined the levels of:

- The entire organization
- A department
- A functional discipline
- A cross-functional team
- The individual.

We began by explaining the strategy process for creating a management development strategy, and then examined development options, principally at the individual level, and found that there were invariably many more developmental options than were normally considered. We then looked at some key management development concepts before turning to the value-creating intervention at Mercury Communications – which resulted in it becoming simultaneously a learning and an earning organization.

The few exercises on developing a strategy for yourself as an individual, which were just before the Mercury Communications case, are likely to add real economic value to your personal situation. Having looked at individual and group development, we will move on to strategic team building in Chapter 11.

Value-added strategic team-building

INTRODUCTION

A key theme in HR strategy is often that of team-building, when this can have a major impact on economic value creation in formulating and implementing a specific strategy.

Strategic team-building is defined here as meaning:

Developing a teams' behavioural alignment in order to achieve acquisition improvement in its capability as a unit, its positioning in the organization, and the economic value of its outputs.

Whilst there has been ample research on team building, there has been relatively little associated with building a strategic team. What specific behaviours are at work when senior managers work together to formulate and/or implement a strategy? Again, this is an area that has been explored little – at least in a systematic fashion. In this chapter we focus on the new notion of 'strategic behaviour', which is extremely helpful in strategic team-building.

One of the authors therefore performed extensive research into the role of strategic behaviour in team-building within a division of BT. This research (and its outputs) complements our discussions in Chapter 12 on the value of strategic thinking. For unless a team can behave strategically, it is unlikely that it will be able to think strategically very efficiently as a unit, either.

Our focus now is much more on this as a behavioural, emotional, and political topic, as opposed to being mainly a cognitive one.

Although managers know they are expected to act strategically, they frequently don't know what this entails – in short, they don't know how to do it, and especially how to behave strategically. This is not merely a case of lacking the necessary strategic thinking skills but is more fundamental, as it requires ability to manage strategic behaviour and the wider strategic process.

This chapter should make you far more alert to the dynamics of any meeting or workshop that you may be facilitating as a strategic HR consultant.

Strategic behaviour can be defined as being:

The cognitive, emotional and territorial interplay of managers engaging in strategic thinking.

Mere 'behaviour' has been expanded here to encompass 'the cognitive, emotional and territorial interplay' of managers. This stresses that there are several factors at work, and that these are extremely closely interwoven. These interrelationships between cognition, feelings and territorial interplay are appropriately called 'the behavioural cocktail'.

 ## WHY IS STRATEGIC BEHAVIOUR IMPORTANT?

If we take it as read that strategic behaviour is the behavioural context for strategic thinking, why is it important?

Strategic behaviour is important in shaping strategic thinking (and thus building a truly strategic team) and thereby adding economic value to the organization for the following key reasons:

1. *Informal decision-making within the team.* Too frequently, one (or more) manager is more vocal and dominant in a team than the others, resulting in the arguments and concerns of other members being marginalized, or in them not even being expressed at all. This creates an unbalanced political climate within the team. Where strategic behaviour is managed well there should be a more favourable climate for well-focused strategic thinking, which results in more informed and appropriate decision-making – thus generating more economic value.

2. *Speed of decision making by the team.* Relatively turbulent strategic behaviour is very likely to slow, or even halt, the progress of decision-making in a team. This produces a backlog of undigested strategic ideas, and also reduces the strategic responsiveness of the team – which has a knock-on negative effect on the responsiveness of the rest of the organization. It also gives an opportunity for the wrong kind of organizational politics to thrive. Slow strategic decision-making will dilute or destroy economic value.

3. *Decisions are actually made, not deferred by the team.* One of the biggest problems in senior management teams is that of actually coming to a decision, even once the strategic issues have been thoroughly explored. This was described graphically by the Head of Strategy of a well-known financial services group:

> When our management team gets together, it is just like Heathrow. More and more aircraft [strategic issues] are coming in, and the air traffic controllers seem to have given up. They just get stacked up and nothing ever seems to be landing.

This means that economic value is continually being diluted by unfocused strategic behaviour within the management team.

4. *Creativity is encouraged within the team.* Where a team's strategic behaviour is more consciously orchestrated, there is perhaps a greater chance of its full creativity being harnessed. This applies both when a team is full of very creative individuals and when it is relatively deficient in that vital creative spark. This helps to avoid strategic thinking being purely analytical in style, and thus barren in generating superior economic value.

5. *Discussing the undiscussible within the team.* Many management teams find certain issues particularly difficult to deal with. These may be associated with strategic projects or programmes that are drifting or appear likely to fail. As soon as this occurs, the ripples of organizational politics begin to spread, building one on the other until they become waves. Where a team finds it hard to harness its strategic behaviour, these kinds of issues are likely to remain in the realm of the undiscussible. Unless this zone of debate is opened up, strategic thinking will remain at best only partly effective. Therefore strategic behaviour here influences the quality of strategic thinking, and thus the generation of economic value.

6. *Mental maps are enriched and shared within the team.* Managers in established teams sometimes tend to assume that everyone in the team sees the world in more or less the same way. The reality, however, is that even in a mature team they often do not. Managers may need to work hard in their interactive behaviour to share and compare their mental maps explicitly. Otherwise, they are likely to run into unduly (and often unnecessarily turbulent) strategic behaviour. Much of what we know as organizational politics is probably caused by mental maps being only partially exposed, thus generating either artificial or exaggerated areas of disagreement – and thus diluting economic value. Interestingly, more open strategic thinking leads to more harmonious strategic behaviour.

7. *Frustration is avoided and energy accumulated in the team.* In a management team facing many intractable strategic issues, and where team behaviour is not really under control, frustration can mount and mount. This frustration can be cognitive, emotional, political, and even personal. Energy then dissipates as problems are not solved, everything appears to take two or three times the time it should, and, very quickly in these circumstances, the team's behaviour becomes fractious. However, where the team can helicopter out of its behavioural difficulties, this can resolve the more business-related complexities and dilemmas. Where frustration builds unduly, top managers may be inclined (in their desperation) to 'drive through' strategies, which may short-circuit true strategic thinking, and thus

destroying shareholder value. This sets up waves of (political) resistance, some of which could be avoided.

8. *Commitment to a strategic course of action can be increased.* Even a relatively strong and open team may struggle when it has to deal with painful options – such as putting a major project on hold, refocusing activities or embarking on a significant downsizing. By being able to steer around the more awkward behavioural blockages, these decisions can be made not only with less difficulty, but also with a better balance of evidence and judgement – again increasing value added.

9. *Creating a platform for influencing for the team.* Many business teams find that they need to influence thinking and feeling about strategic issues elsewhere in the organization. Unless the team's own strategic behaviour is well aligned internally, it may prove difficult for the team to exert its influence in the rest of the organization. In such instances, being able to harmonize its own internal strategic behaviour may reduce the political disadvantages of a department or business unit relative to its organizational peers, thus enabling it to add more value.

10. *Internal politics are channelled more effectively by the team.* Although every team has to deal with its fair share of internal politics, if unchecked, political activity can debilitate it severely. Many of the more dysfunctional aspects of internal politics can then be channelled into a more constructive debate, avoiding value destruction.

Figure 11.1 shows how strategic behaviour and strategic thinking combine to create a strategic team. This is also influenced greatly by the team defining 'what business we are in?', and also its targeted economic value added.

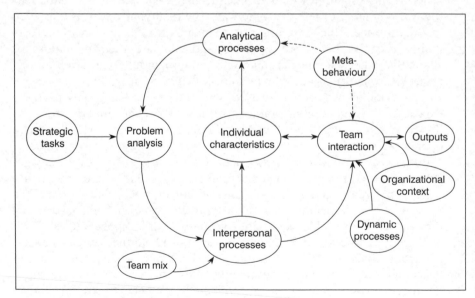

Figure 11.1
Strategic behaviour and team working

WHAT FORMS DOES STRATEGIC BEHAVIOUR TAKE?

From our research, 'strategic behaviour' manifests itself in a variety of forms in practice (see Figure 11.1), including:

- Strategic tasks and problem analysis
- Analytical and interpersonal processes
- Team mix and individual characteristics
- Team interaction and dynamic processes
- Meta-behaviour
- Organizational context
- Outputs.

'Meta-behaviour' represents the higher order behaviours associated with strategic thinking, including summarizing, process management, reflection, etc.

These behavioural groupings are analysed below. The analysis includes questions that will help you to diagnose strategic behaviour (and its influence) in your organization.

Figure 11.1 is an excellent diagnostic technique for understanding not only weaknesses within the team's behavioural system, but also the knock-on effects of any weaknesses within the system.

Strategic tasks and problem analysis

Strategic tasks are essentially the major value-creating activities that a team undertakes. These can include:

- Acquisitions
- Business development programmes
- Business performance reviews
- Cost reviews
- Divestment/rationalization decisions

- Key management appointments
- Reacting to external change
- Resource allocation
- Restructuring decisions.

During these value-creating activities many problems can arise, including, for example, deciding whether to make a senior appointment internally or recruit externally, or, where there are many business development projects, determining which should be given priority.

Questions

1. What are the key strategic activities your team faces over the next 6 to 12 months?
2. Which of these activities are most crucial to the business in the:
   - Medium term
   - Long term?
3. How time-intensive are these activities likely to be, and how should they be programmed?
4. What does the team need to do less of (or stop doing altogether) to devote sufficient time to its truly strategic activities?
5. Which of these activities is liable to generate the most behavioural turbulence, and thus value destruction?
6. What roles should key individuals within the team play (for a specific activity)?
7. What specific problems and dilemmas are likely to come up, and how can these be addressed?
8. What personal agenda factors are likely to come into play, and how should these be managed?
9. What major constraints are likely to be faced, and what options for getting around these are likely to exist?
10. Where are these constraints likely to become virtually impossible to deal with, and how can this be headed off?
11. What is the economic added value from these team activities?

Analytical and interpersonal processes

Addressing these strategic tasks and problems requires both analytical and interpersonal processes. These processes add value through decision-making and speed.

Questions

1. How can problems and dilemmas be anticipated well in advance by the management team?

2. How can your team ensure that it clarifies issues before debating situations, let alone creating options?
3. How can your team avoid tunnel vision and achieve some genuine creative thinking when generating options?
4. How will solutions be challenged and probed, without destructive picking apart?
5. Who will summarize and synthesize a conclusion?
6. How will your team ensure that where people do agree, they say that they agree?
7. When members of the team disagree, will they be expected to also say, in the same breath, why they disagree?
8. How will interruptions be managed so as not to disturb the flow of debate yet still allow valuable, but lateral, thoughts to be heard?
9. How will your key team members allow themselves to be influenced and won over (where appropriate), rather than taking up fixed positions?
10. What economic value are these analytical processes currently creating?

Team mix and individual characteristics

Team mix and individual characteristics, where aligned, can minimize politics and wasteful disagreement.

Questions

1. Is your team mix genuinely in balance, or is there a preponderance of one or two styles (for example, in Belbin terms – see below – too many plants or chairmen)?
2. Is it worthwhile to get your team to check out its team styles (using some psychometrics)?
3. Do individuals with pronounced team styles require one-to-one support (off-line, as it were) to adapt their behaviour, or could they fruitfully simply try out another role?
4. Where your team recruits someone new, what are the preferred team roles, and, assuming this person replaces someone who is leaving the team, will this inadvertently unbalance the team mix and undermine its value creation?
5. What other characteristics of particular individuals might distort the strategic behaviour of the team (for example, their idiosyncratic cognitive style or other personal traits)?
6. Does the professional background of your team members bias them towards certain types of behaviours (for example, towards excessive picking apart of issues, rather than synthesis)?
7. Are there particularly acute 'power contours' surrounding a particular individual (or individuals), where these individuals like to be excessively

powerful and pushy, and how might we moderate these? (Power contours can be thought of as being like isobars on a weather map surrounding a depression or a storm, but in this case they surround an individual. They occur where an individual is particularly strong and is also prepared to make a strong stance to the point of inhibiting or intimidating others from engaging in debate. When you encounter these in reality, they are tangible) What value does this destroy?

8. What are the personal career ambitions of individuals within your team, and how might they influence or distort their behaviours?
9. Are there particularly anxious, vulnerable or sensitive individuals, and how does this need to be managed?
10. Are your team members (either as a group or individually) just that little bit too serious, and is it necessary to oil the flow?
11. Who is likely to succumb to strategic frustration, and on which issues? How can this be headed off?
12. What distinctive economic value does the current team mix add?

Belbin team roles include, for example: *chairman* (a team coordinator); *plant* (an ideas person); *shaper* (an ideas developer and prioritizator); *teamworker* (a generator of team spirit); *resource investigator* (a fact finder); *completer–finisher* (a results person). The main idea behind Belbin team roles is that if there is a predominance of a particular style within a team, then team behaviour will become unbalanced and destroy value through time and energy wasted, through indecision or through strategic errors of judgement.

Team interaction and dynamic processes

Dynamic processes add value through speed, and also through the quality of the decision-making output.

Questions

1. What is likely to generate a particularly high level of behavioural turbulence, and how can these issues or interactions be navigated?
2. If there are specific threats of team breakdown, how can these be facilitated? (What could give rise to these breakdowns? Consider using fishbone analysis to anticipate a breakdown of team behaviour, working backwards to what might have caused this.)
3. Where known or likely areas of conflict or personality clash exist, how can these be averted or controlled? In which behavioural scenarios are these likely to arise?
4. How can levels of excitement be managed so that your team neither flags nor burns up too much energy?

5. Where there is real threat of one or more individuals dominating the conversation (and others probably withdrawing), how can this be minimized?
6. Is there a tendency to dive into issues or to rush their discussion so that problem analysis is incomplete? If so, how can this be averted (for example, by more helicopter-like reflection)?
7. Can your team time be managed more effectively both to avoid slippage and to allow sufficient time to debate the really big issues?
8. What economic value is sometimes destroyed by poor team interaction and lack of decision-making momentum?

Meta-behaviour

Meta-behaviour creates economic value by overall realignment of the team, and through helicopter thinking.

Questions

1. What facilitation is your team likely to need, and when and how should this be provided?
2. Would it be wise to ask your team, before discussing a particularly sensitive topic, what 'P' behaviours it wants to avoid (for example, being political, picky, pessimistic, and so on)?
3. Should your team use any strategic analysis tools or methodologies, and how can it learn to use these consistently? (For example, consider using fishbone analysis for any strategic problem.)
4. Could your team benefit by consciously trying to avoid 'rabbit hole management', and strive instead towards 'helicopter vision'?
5. Would stakeholder analysis or stakeholder agenda analysis be useful in surfacing agendas in your team?
6. How can your team target (in advance) the value of its outputs and monitor these subsequently (for example, by using the 'value over time' curve)?
7. How can your team take up the idea of value destruction and use this idea on an everyday basis to steer debate towards value added?
8. How should your team prioritize its decisions? (For example, by using AID analysis.)
9. How can your team build in time to reflect on the process (even if this is just 5 minutes at the end of a 2-hour meeting)?
10. Can your team usefully introduce more humour to lighten its heavier strategic debates (without being frivolous)?
11. Does your team manifest significant meta-behaviour, and if not, how much economic value is being destroyed?

Organizational context

The organizational content often causes value destruction through distraction, hesitation (to act), and through the costs of changing direction.

Questions

1. Who are the key stakeholders (outside your team) with an influence on the team's strategic activities? What is on their agenda, and how should these agendas be taken into account or proactively influenced?
2. How does the wider organizational and political structure influence what goes on in your team?
3. What factors outside your team are likely to result in inaction, inertia or distraction, and how can these be managed?
4. How does your team interact with strategic processes elsewhere in the organization, and how can these processes be managed more proactively?
5. To what extent does the organizational context facilitate or constrain the economic value added by the latter?

Outputs

Outputs add economic value by focusing effect on real results, rather than on interesting management conversations.

Questions

1. What specific outputs will be needed from key team meetings (for example, decisions to do things, new projects, decisions not to do things, and so on)?
2. How will these outputs be communicated to the rest of the organization?
3. How will the likely reaction of other stakeholders outside the organization be gauged? Will this cause your team to think through its positioning of the messages most carefully?
4. At the end of the day, what are those outputs worth – what economic value have they really added?

STRATEGIC BEHAVIOUR AT BT

The following is an extract from research data on the interaction of the senior team that was responsible for BT's Global Technical strategy. The specific category of behaviour of each team manager is noted in brackets and italics, and this gives us a feel for the preponderance of types of behaviour over this particular workshop (Grundy, 1998). This turned out to be more concerned with microscopic picking apart than it was with genuine synthesis – which inhibited its strategic vision considerably.

One of the authors played the role of facilitator during this tape-recorded session. The workshop was BT's most 'strategic' and value added – earlier ones were characterized by lower-level debate and by more random and divergent strategic team behaviour.

The BT team was led by Andy, and other members were David, Bonnie, Paul, and two Keiths. As we will see, they do have quite different styles of strategic behaviour – which makes for a much more difficult process.

A coding system – of high (H), medium (M) or low (L) level – is used as one means of tracking the dynamics of the debate – which here tends to go from 'high to low' before losing the bigger picture. The code is given at the end of each statement, as well as being summarized at the end of a section. This is because the debate was somewhat jumpy, and a degree of concentration is required in order to make sense of what is going on. In the material later on in this chapter, we will then analyse it. (You would probably find something quite similar if you tape-recorded a session of your senior management team.)

The inspiration for the high, medium and low coding comes from the researcher's acquaintance with the idea (from strategy) of helicopter thinking, or seeing the bigger picture. However, equally important is the need to avoid getting so lost in the detail that you lose your original field of attention. This is humorously called 'rabbit hole discussion'.

Simply introducing a team to these two notions can improve the team's efficiency and effectiveness by around 20–30 per cent. (As team facilitators we use pictures of an Apache helicopter and one from an IBM advert with a man literally sticking his head into a hole in the ground to help the team visualize these ideas. This is normally effective for up to a whole day's work – if shown once.)

Natural management conversation is typically disjoined and haphazard whenever strategic issues are debated, and is actually quite unproductive. Whilst the first workshop (parts one and two) is a little harder to read (as it has been preserved in its natural and unadulterated form), it is suggested that if you are patient with this, the reward comes from the second workshop. In the second workshop we see a good deal of clarity and behavioural flow emerging, largely because of meta-behaviour by Andy, by continued facilitation and, importantly, by the use of some analytical techniques such as AID analysis (see Chapter 6). Surprisingly, these had an amazing calming effect on strategic behaviour within the team, *enabling it to add far more economic value*. Good tools for monitoring the strategic behaviour of a team are:

- The value-over-time curve (see Chapter 6)
- The difficulty-over-time curve (see Chapter 6).

Other tools (which are not shown here but are simply in the same format) include:

- Belief-over-time curves
- Energy-over-time curves
- Frustration-over-time curves.

First workshop – part one

The topics covered in the first workshop (part one) were:

- Strategic roles
- What business we are in?
- What value do we add (and to whom)?
- The role of the department
- Its key priorities – importance and influence
- Process review.

At the end of this chapter (as reward for the reader's patience!) we will draw together the practical implications from this piece of original research.

The value-added roles of the department

Many teams do not explicitly target the value-added role of their unit, causing significant behavioural confusion.

First of all, the team discussed the overall strategic role of the department and its value added. Keith (A) began by questioning the team's assumption that the department was there to create 'all of the strategy' itself:

Keith (A): I think that the message, for me, seems to be that we, in the past, we have tried to do it all ourselves. And, because there is insufficient resource, what we ought to be considering ourselves is as sort of 'strategy facilitators'. *(expanding, strategic roles)* (H)

Andy amplified this point before the facilitator then supported this line of thinking:

Andy: I think that that is the new point that is coming out. We don't have to do it all ourselves, or own it ourselves necessarily. *(expanding, strategic roles, monitoring value)* (H)

Facilitator: Isn't that about leveraging the strategic thinking elsewhere within BT? *(expanding, questioning)* (H)

Andy, Keith, Bonnie and David then reflected:

Andy: Yes, we have been rather jealous of anyone else doing the thinking. *(agreeing, strategic roles)*

Keith (A): Yes, much too jealous. Sitting in a little castle. *(agreeing, strategic roles)* (M)

Bonnie: You have got your own little castle. (M)

David: One of the things that is also an issue here is the level of mature working – I think that if you really want to have an influence on corporate strategy, you really want to talk to people on the main Board. If you are going to have an influence on the main operating business strategy, you have got to have workshops, sessions with their Board. *(influencing)* (M)

David then related this discussion of 'strategic roles' to the discussion in the second workshop about the extent to which the department could really shape BT's overall strategy and, indeed, what forms that strategy would actually take (including deliberate strategy, emergent strategy and so on):

David: They are the people who have to do it. [Naming one senior manager] – it is not us. You know. And that deliberate/emergent strategy distinction, I think, has got a lot to do with that – who has really got the ability to really create strategy for the business. And a department like ourselves does not really have the capability to produce the strategy, except for a few, small, technical areas. (*influencing, judging, strategic roles*) (M)

The need to narrow the focus of work performed by the team was a relatively new line of thinking at this juncture. Initially, the department had seen itself as being the core 'manufacturer' of technical strategy. This is a very common characteristic of strategic planning departments generally – they feel nervous unless it is they (and not line management) that are delivering the strategy. However, now the department was beginning to see itself creating strategy in certain technical areas while also playing the role of facilitating strategic thinking elsewhere in BT.

The pattern of interaction in the initial debate had been at a consistently high level, as shown below:

H K(A) A   T
M   A   K(A) B   D   D
L

Following this early consensus, the course of the debate now turned to what emerged as much more difficult terrain – the question of 'What business are we in?'

What business are we in?

Many teams also do not actually define what business they are in – giving rise to unnecessary politics.

In this discussion, one of the authors was facilitator. First, the facilitator introduced and explained a model for understanding 'what business we are in?' from marketing theory. This model contained three main topics:

1. Who are the customers?
2. What are their specific needs?
3. How are these needs met?

Clarifying mental maps

It is well known (from academic research) that the mental maps of individuals within a team are often very, very different – which gives rise to a lot of fruitless and frustrating disagreement.

Invariably, the questions given in this model are testing and expose uncertainties about why a particular department exists. Ask yourself the questions, 'why does my department exist?', 'What value does it add and to whom?', 'Do others share the same perceptions as us as to what value we add and should add?'

Only when you have reflected on these questions yourself will it be fair for you to evaluate the BT department's clarity of thinking about how it generates value.

Bonnie now began the discussion that follows. The discussion is highly punctuated, with little opportunity created to develop ideas at length.

Bonnie: What does 'what business we are in?' mean? *(clarifying) (H)*

Facilitator: It means what business is the department in. And where could you add most value? *(expanding) (H)*

David: The biggest impact would be on the customer group, which we mentioned the other day. *(diving in) (M)*

Bonnie: Like manager X, manager Y ... *(expanding) (L)*

David: That's interesting, I would actually agree with that. *(agreeing) (L)*

Paul: Who are the customers, first of all? *(questioning) (M)*

David: I don't think everyone would ... *(picking apart) (L)*

Bonnie: I think that it is everyone who ... *(picking apart) (L)*

Andy: Sorry, for us? *(clarifying) (L)*

Facilitator: Yes, for us. *(L)*

Keith (B): For us, the customer is the main operating business Board. *(picking apart) (M)*

David: I don't think that's ... *(disagreeing((M)*

At this point, the discussion seemed to be zigzagging without much feeling that anything clear was being established. The facilitator then tried to intervene:

Facilitator: Let's prioritize them. *(facilitating) (M)*

There was now a spontaneous attempt from a new source to steer the debate. Keith (A) now asks a broader question to try to clarify the discussion.

Keith (A): Can I just ask a question, rather than sort of comment specifically? And that is, one of the things, you know, we haven't actually decided was whether, as one group, we are really supporting main operating business or are we supporting BT as a whole? And I think that is a lack of focus across that dimension. And I think that the focus is on main operating business, but it is not solely main operating business, and that's the issue. *(questioning, judging, challenging) (M)*

This longer input might have provided a cognitive and behavioural anchor. However, Bonnie's fresh input effectively pre-empted the opportunity to set a clear direction for the debate, thus frustrating its productivity:

Bonnie: There is no point in supporting main operating business except to support BT. And from where we are, we ought to function and to see BT's needs, and how main operating business has to function to support that. *(judging) (M)*

The trajectory of the above discussion looks like this:

```
H          B T
M          D P                    K(B)  D T  B  A K(A)  B
L                  B  D  D  B  A  T
```

The facilitator then tried to help the team get more of a focus to their discussions:

Facilitator: This is supposed to be a single task – asking who the customers are. You see you are doing another task, which is to prioritize them. *facilitation) (M)*

Keith (A) reflects on why it is not that straightforward to define, in simple terms, what business they are in:

Keith (A): We are not trying to do that specifically. The trouble is that if you don't bound it when you comment, then you immediately jump in and say, 'Well it's so and . . .' *(facilitation) (M)*

The discussion resumes with Keith (A) linking back to what has already been discussed:

Facilitator: Let's start again. *(H)*

Keith (A): I think that they [the main operating business Board] must come in. *(judging) (M)*

David B: I have a problem with the main operating business Board. *(challenging) (M)*

Bonnie: Put main operating business Board, and then put managers X, Y and Z separately, as well. *(expanding) (L)*

Andy: I don't think we should put P and Q down. *(disagreeing (L)*

The discussion thus becomes focused primarily on specific names of customers, rather than on generic types or generic needs. (Obviously the team could work from the specific back to the general, but the danger of a bottom-up approach is that it could fragment and also fail to identify all clusters of customers.)

David B: Well, these individuals should not be put down because I don't think they would pay for us. *(L)*

Andy: Oh, well, that's a different definition. *(challenging) (M)*

Facilitator: Well there are some customers . . . *(facilitating) (M)*

Bonnie: [Interrupting] We are also saying the BT Board. BT, you know BT? *(expanding) (M)*

David: BT corporate. *(expanding) (M)*

Keith (A): Yes, BT Group. *(agreeing) (M)*

The team's debate produced the following profile for this sequence of interactions:

```
H
M          T  K(A)  T  K(A)              D  A T  B  D  K(A)
L                          D  B  A
```

This shows that the debate is being pulled down to a more detailed level.

One of the major problems here is that the team dived into the analysis without first examining what 'customer' means. Potentially this might have been headed off by more active facilitation, but the problem a facilitator often faces is that it is impossible to see ahead of time all the areas that may be ambiguous. What is perhaps more revealing is that, although the team was obviously struggling to get a hold on the debate, the discussion continued anyway. The debate has here its own 'strategic momentum'. It might have been more helpful to the team to have broken off at that point and reflected on the question, 'If we are having such a difficult time debating this, why is this?'

Key lessons from the debate of the first workshop – part one

This first debate has, frustratingly, not been very productive, for a number of reasons. The following points may help you to avoid these frustrations:

- If you do not define 'the business that your department is in', and its key value-added activities, then your team will invariably engage in behaviours that generate undue heat and tension when discussing strategy issues.
- You will need to examine, quite explicitly, who your customers actually are, and to prioritize their relative importance. Also, you will need to look at all this against your value-creating activities.
- Before you enter this kind of debate, you need to look at 'point of entry' options. If, for instance, you enter the debate at one point (by asking 'Who are our customers?'), where will this lead to versus another point of entry (asking another question, such as 'What are our value-creating activities?'), given the personal and strategic agendas of the key players?

Does this bear any resemblance to teams you work in? If so, try out the diagnostic system (Figure 11.1) and slot in its value- and difficulty-over-time curves in real time.

First workshop – part two

What value do we add (and to whom)?

In this second part of the first workshop, the team continued in more or less the same vein as the first.

The team members turned to the equally difficult (and related) topic of what value the team's activities add. Their facilitator started them off by suggesting that they should put their mind-set in 'customer mode'. Rapidly it became apparent that even the notion of 'value' was unclear and needed to be defined.

Facilitator: What are the biggest areas of value you add? Try to have an 'out-of-body experience' – imagine you are actually the customer. *(H)*

Andy: Well, I don't know. I am not sure which issue we are addressing. At this kind of level, that is the right level – to be against those customers [pointing to the flip chart]. *(clarifying, helicoptering up) (H)*

Bonnie: Well, I think they need to be alerted, to what they haven't seen – to what they don't know yet. *(picking apart) (M)*

Andy: Well, that is a subject in its own right. *(H)*

With hindsight, it was apparent that the department added value in a diversity of ways (and these ways needed to be unravelled). This diversity did not surface in any systematic way, perhaps because the team did not have more complete (and shared) mental maps of its own activities. The facilitator then continued:

Facilitator: So that is something about blind spots? *(clarifying) (H)*

Bonnie: Or simply something that is there, that they haven't taken account of, but you want them to, and you think that they should have been able to see. *(picking apart) (M)*

Facilitator: Whose mind are you now in? *(probing) (H)*

Bonnie: I am in manager X's mind. He can't see everything going on everywhere . . . and something may be happening. *(picking apart) (L)*

Facilitator: Is this an intelligence map? *(probing) (M)*

Bonnie: Yes, yes. *(agreeing) (M)*

David: I don't think that's an issue here. . . *(judging) (M)*

Although the discussion had some focus (on what is on specific customer's minds, using the out-of-body experience technique), it had again become very specific and has thus lost its links to the bigger context. Their facilitator tried to move things on:

Facilitator: Let's carry the flow on. *(H)*

Keith (A): Yes, yeah. *(H)*

David: I think he has got a number of jobs that he has been given to do, which he needs to sort out. *(picking apart) (L)*

Facilitator: We seemed to be up there and now we are back here. I know that there is no right process, but we have got one, so let us stay with it. *(reflecting, facilitation) (H)*

The facilitator again brought it to their attention that the discussion was wandering around, hoping that the team could agree to talk about more specific things. This was echoed by Andy and seized upon by Bonnie.

Andy: I am a bit confused. We are assuming that we are manager X, and what is it that we need from us? *(clarifying, helicoptering up) (M)*

Bonnie: Yes, what does he need from us – a helicopter view? *(questioning, helicoptering up) (M)*

Andy now guided the facilitator:

Andy: I should just put them down, Tony, don't qualify them – the technology X problem [discussed earlier] stands. Bonnie's point is equally valid, so it doesn't negate it. Second operator in Europe. *(facilitating, anchoring) (H)*

Paul now exercised a useful check so that quality control is maintained on the team's debate:

Paul: My worry is that we have gone straight to the main operating business Board. And we have direct reporting to the BT Board. *(picking apart) (M)*

However, then, Bonnie dived down into some specifics, rapidly followed by David, who also defaulted to 'picking apart'. The facilitator was curious here

271

about why the debate was so consistently disjointed, until the thought occurred to him that Bonnie might be working up her next thought rather than actively listening to Paul's contribution, hence leading to dislocation of ideas.

Bonnie: What's going on? Dangers and opportunities are things which ... It is not just the general world around us looking, it is not just the world around us. The Internet is getting bigger ... *(picking apart) (L)*

David: Infrastructure sharing. Working with other companies. *(picking apart) (L)*

The debate at this point contained an effervescence of ideas, reminiscent of a sprinkler system spurting water droplots over a lawn in summer. (Whilst the lawn does get gradually wetter, the effect is diffuse, it takes a long time, and it leaves other parts of the strategic terrain arid.)

The team members are then caught by Keith (A)'s timely intervention:

Keith (A): Gosh, aren't we getting rather specific? *(reflection) (H)*

David: It is. *(agreeing) (H)*

Facilitator: If I am in their heads ... *(facilitating) (H)*

To help give more sense of focus, the facilitator suggested the following line of enquiry:

Facilitator: Are these sort of, it is like the distinction between features and benefits? Are they too specific? Are these rather like activities? What activities are you doing that will really help to add value, and to what specific issues? The issues will change. *(facilitating) (H)*

This debate appeared to have jumped from level to level (with Andy, Keith (A), Tim and the facilitator operating primarily at the 'highest' level) as follows:

```
H   T  K(A)  A  T  T     T  K(A)  T  A  A        K(A)  D  T  T
M      B     B  T  B  D                   B  P
L      B              D                   B  D
```

Here, it was conspicuous that Bonnie tended to worry about more detailed issues (possibly sometimes rightly) and did not seem to be drawn back upwards. Although this was not 'wrong' – as it is crucial in a strategic team that there is someone there to jump on very important details – too much attention to specifics can be counterproductive as the 'big picture' then gets cloudier and cloudier.

David started again, but once more picked up on a very specific activity rather than starting with the 'value to the business' statement. Maybe he saw this as an opportunity to input to the idea of 'the business model', which might have been a particularly important part of his mental map and also played an important role in his personal strategic agenda:

David: I would say more than that because it is actually called the business model. We need to understand the business model of global operations because this business doesn't understand that. *(justifying, mental maps) (M)*

Andy: If we were only in the main operating business we would be purely acting out the role of supplier. We are no longer in that role of supplier. *(strategic role) (M)*

Keith (A): I am surprised. I don't share your view. *(challenging) (M)*
Facilitator: Are we getting confused here? *(questioning, feedback) (H)*

Here the facilitator wanted to check whether or not Andy and Keith were genuinely openly disagreeing with one another.

Andy again tried to grapple with the central issue of the role of the department, pulling back the group discussion into some kind of clearer focus.

Andy: Well, this is the area we need to hammer around because . . . I think we understand this. We could spend all morning arguing over the words, and we will do that, but we understand, more or less, what we were doing before. Right. The issue at stake for us at the moment, it seems to me, is coming back to what Paul was saying. Is, we know we need to make a significant change. It is either in addition to, or a replacement to, the things that we are doing. The organization . . . the new remit . . . to have 'global' in our title and in our job description. Now the issue is, what does that mean? Now we have already got a tension on the table as to whether it is just looking at the global or the technical perspective, all right, or whether we are part of the general thinking on where we are going. *(summarizing) (H)*

Andy was continually having to work really quite hard to give the debate some centre of gravity. It was now taking much input by both Andy and the facilitator to give the team direction.

The facilitator then redoubled his efforts to focus the debate:

Facilitator: What is the product which is adding value to the main operating business? *(H)*

David: It is a model of how the global business operates. *(clarifying, mental maps) (M)*

Keith (A): We are setting direction – to use your analogy . . . *(M)*

Andy: You have moved up a layer, Tony. *(helicoptering up) (H)*

Facilitator: I am trying to get up to the level of, well, if someone says to you, 'Why do you exist?' *(helicoptering up) (H)*

Andy: Ah, well, that is a different matter. *(helicoptering up) (H)*

Although Andy appeared to question the facilitator's line of enquiry, he rapidly latched on to the high-level focus that the facilitator was trying to attain.

The dynamic thus followed this pattern:

H					T	A	T		A	T	A
M		D	A	K(A)				D	K(A)	
L										

Once again, Andy and the facilitator were trying to move the debate up to a higher level. This was with the intent of trying to map the 'bigger picture' issues first, before diving down to the detail.

Then Bonnie dropped down a level of thinking, putting a strain on the sense of continuity but not losing this entirely:

Bonnie: So that manager X can be successful, he can only be successful by understanding what the business needs to be to be global. Understanding his role in that – what is his role in that – and being able to do it. Now, if we come out with 'being able to do it', we come out with, might come out with, helping him to understand what he needs to do to enable BT to participate in global, both from a business point of view and a technical point of view. *(scoping, picking apart) (L)*

However, Andy, determined as ever, challenged the team to go up higher in their thinking on the scheme of things.

Andy: I would move up even a higher notch than that. *(H)*

Paul, however, is left with unresolved issues preoccupying him – highlighting the problems of coping with unfinished business.

Paul: I am confused a bit. I am not too sure whether we are doing technical strategy from the point of view of a supplier or technical strategy from the point of view of a customer or internal customers or are we doing technical strategy for combining both? *(clarification) (M)*

Once again, Andy remained undiverted – he was insistent on getting to the bigger picture:

Andy: I am going to go higher than that. I think that the question that Tony asked is right. We cost about £X million on pay – £X million. What value do we give for £X million per year? If you cut all our throats, what difference would they perceive? Because, Tony was asking, quite rightly, not about what we actually do but why are we actually here. *(helicoptering up) (H)*

Facilitator: Even if we didn't have you, what would be the need, the latent need that isn't being addressed?' *(H)*

Andy: Yes. *(H)*

Now he had them all together, the team was ready to begin a proper debate:

Keith (A): Let's try and . . . *(facilitation) (H)*

Andy: Let's try and answer that question. Then the next layer down. *(helicoptering down) (H)*

Facilitator: One we have got the highest level, then you can try and . . . [is cut off] *(facilitation) (H)*

Bonnie, however, was still circling at another (and lower) level of analysis within the problem architecture. Her thought stream appeared to have its own flight path, and was only gently pulled in a new or different direction. (This suggests that a particular thought stream typically has its own 'cognitive momentum'.)

Bonnie: And it is kind of, what do you want to be successful globally? And we have asked questions like that in the past. We just said that. David said, I said [mentioning enterprise working], he said it probably, had in a way, OK, so its pointing out things with evidence that enabled BT to be successful in attempting to do what it is trying to do. *(Synthesis) (M & L)*

Keith (A) feels impelled to follow Bonnie's course of thinking:

Keith (A): That's right, that's important. Championing change. *(agreeing) (L)*

Facilitator: What kind? *(L)*

Bonnie: It is technical. *(L)*

David: I am not even sure that it is technical. It is change that is to the overall benefit of the shareholders. I mean the enterprise stuff. *(challenging)* *(L)*

Now the facilitator tried again to refocus on the bigger, higher-level question:

Facilitator: You can still think about the £Xm or £Xm that you get paid to do this. *(H)*

Andy, forever patient, now reiterated where he would like to see the discussion going:

Andy: The discussion is wandering around the place. I am saying for starters that the main operating business Board is our customer, for starters. We can't actually get out a simple statement of why the business pays us £X million. *(facilitating)* *(H)*

This debate was thus profoundly sensitive to the pushes and pulls of key individuals – and in this case was often being pulled in habitually opposing and self-cancelling directions. It was evident that, faced with this input, the team found it necessary to fall back on its habitual behaviours. What followed was their habitual recipe – brainstorming.

Keith (B): We need to save the company. *(picking part)* *(M)*

Keith (A): Gosh, no, I don't think that it is as simple as that. *(disagreeing)* *(M)*

Bonnie: Our role is to save the company by championing business and technical change and by improving efficiency and there is also all those other things. *(picking apart)* *(L)*

The facilitator once again intervened, and Andy jumped back in to defend what the team had been doing.

Facilitator: Can I think aloud on this? What we are doing is keeping on throwing things in. No one has said 'What do you mean by ...?' We are fragmenting. *(facilitating)* *(H)*

Andy: Well, you told us Tony, you told us to brainstorm. *(H)*

Facilitator: We are coming off the brainstorming, and, secondly, we are going back to behaviour as normal. *(H)*

Keith (A): Yes, yes. *(agreeing)* *(H)*

Facilitator: But you are right, we are both right. *(H)*

This was interesting from the point of view of how a facilitator operates. At the time the facilitator was thinking, 'How can I help these people to gain a clearer focus and at a higher level of debate?' (The facilitator's role at this point, as researcher, was to see if – with facilitation – the team could shift its behaviours, assuming it wanted to do so.) However, unwittingly, he may have suggested, by implying that they were getting into too much detail, that what he was looking for was a stream of brainstorming. Unless a facilitator can give simultaneously clear signals about what they expect to happen as well as not to happen, then they can generate unintended confusion.

The dynamic of this debate thus jumped down levels suddenly, before recovering at the end somewhat. This is captured below:

```
H   A A T A K(A) A T              T A            T A T K(A) T
M     P                B                    K(B)  K(A)
L     B                    B K(A) T B D              B
```

(Note: as a facilitator it is always useful to model the level of debate, along similar times to the above, to ensure that the 'bigger picture' is not lost sight of, and value destroyed.)

This pattern of dislocation of levels was perhaps even more noticeable than the previous ones. Bonnie's cognitive style appeared to attract her to a more detailed discussion than Andy, Keith (A) and the facilitator were trying to attain. She did not seem to pick up the signals to 'move up' a level. At times, the others were forced to fly down two levels of analysis to maintain the thread of debate.

Andy next took up the theme of 'saving the company', but assumed (apparently erroneously) that 'we all know what we mean here'. This under-scored the importance – not just here but elsewhere – of always defining the meaning of terms, and doing so almost obsessively.

Andy: But let me say, Tony, that we know what Keith means by 'save the company'. *(questioning, probing) (M)*

Bonnie: But I want to ask what he meant. *(questioning) (L)*

Andy: But I honestly think . . . *(judging) (M)*

Bonnie: I am not sure that we all do. I don't know, we do, but Paul . . . *(disagreeing)*

(M)Keith (B): To ensure long-term financial viability of the network business. *(expanding) (M)*

Bonnie: Or BT as a group. *(expanding) (L)*

Keith (B): I am not sure I can do the latter bit. *(picking apart) (L)*

Facilitator: Currently we are focusing on the main operating Board. *(facilitation) (M)*

Bonnie: What the need is. *(expanding) (L)*

Facilitator: But suddenly by talking about BT, we have widened the whole arena of debate. You have got to have discipline in strategic thinking. *(facilitating) (H)*

Andy: Absolutely. *(agreeing) (H)*

The profile of this latter discussion looked like this:

```
H                                       T A
M          A  A  B  K(B)                T
L             B           B  K(B)       B
```

Once more a similar pattern emerged, with discussion torn between Andy and the facilitator attempting to debate at a higher level, and Bonnie at a lower level.

The facilitator was obviously taking some risks in potentially upsetting Bonnie. This risk-taking is intuitive, and is based on the perceived need at the time to get a grip on the debate. Paul now circled back to his earlier questioning:

Paul: That's why I came back to my question of whether we are acting from a supplier perspective or what. *(strategic role) (M)*

The facilitator tried once again to give the debate a direction, suggesting that the brainstorming should be focused more specifically:

Facilitator: Can we go into a more deliberate process of brainstorming, please? *(facilitation) (H)*

Bonnie: Saving the alliance. *(interrupting) (L)*

Facilitator: You see how hard it is to do this, it is almost impossible. Imagine an invisible gag around your mouth and it is only in certain situations that you are allowed to take it off. *(facilitating) (H)*

This highlights how hard team members find it to adapt their behaviour. Again the facilitator took some risks in his feedback, but he felt he had to escalate his directness gradually.

Now David puts the process onto a new trajectory by reading out a policy document – Andy's – effectively cutting across Andy.

David read out of the official document . . .

Andy: Hang on, those are my words you're reading out, David. *(challenging) (H)*

(Presumably David's focus at the time was on making an effective input, but he overlooked – from a process point of view – inputting the words of the team leader without attributing their source.)

Keith (A) now highlighted some unfinished business by once again making a well-targeted, probing comment:

Keith (A): I find it difficult to progress without asking a question, but I think when Keith said 'saving the company', I think he meant from a financial point of view. I think that there are some very specific issues about saving the company from the regulator, the environment, whatever. *(proving, picking apart) (H)*

The final phase in this interaction looked as follows (again reaching a higher level):

$$
\begin{array}{llllll}
H & & T & T & A & K(A) \\
M & P & & & & \\
L & & B & & &
\end{array}
$$

This important debate was obviously a sensitive issue for the team, and one it was hard to be objective about. Owing to its emotiveness and because it clearly impinged on territorial perceptions of the team, discussions were relatively unstable and difficult to steer.

Key lessons from the debate of the first workshop – part two

- When looking at the question 'what value do we add?', always have the 'out-of-body' experience of imagining that you literally are that customer or stakeholder. Get inside their thoughts, agendas, feelings – especially their hopes and fears – and their histories.

- When doing strategic brainstorming, at least set some focus for the brain-storming. Otherwise, it may come up with a real mish-mash of ideas.
- Where the team has, at some stage in the past, hammered out some firm ideas on a particular topic, this must be your starting point. You do not always have to reinvent your thinking.
- Facilitators sometimes need to take risks – they are there to stick their necks out, and managers ought to be tolerant of the occasional mini-blunders. A reasonably humble facilitator can bounce back from making a misjudgement.

At this point, it is worth just pausing for a moment to retrace the order in which strategic issues were discussed. Although the discussions might again have seemed somewhat erratic, there is quite a strong sense of order in the flow. This particular workshop began with the team understanding its scope and then trying to find out who it added value to. This was followed by a discussion (albeit inconclusive) of customer need, before returning to the theme of how value was added. Somewhat tangled up in these discussions were debates about both external (customer) issues and internal issues, and about who the team reported to.

Further discussion

There now follows a useful discussion about the split between 'deliberate' strategy-type work and 'emergent' strategy-type work:

Keith (A): Could we get – in your terms, Andy – a split? *(probing) (M)*

Andy: Well, it will vary depending on the area you are in. *(expanding) (M)*

Keith (A): Across the piece. *(clarifying) (M)*

Andy: An 80 : 20 wouldn't be a bad split. *(strategic role, clarifying) (M)*

Keith (A): OK, fine. *(agreeing) (M)*

Bonnie: But there is a load of other people there to cope with it. *(strategic role) (L)*

Paul: To deliver the strategy component of that. *(strategic role) (L)*

Facilitator: Is Bonnie saying that we see ourselves as partly adding value through other people as well? *(strategic role) (M)*

This conversation led to Bonnie drawing out some practical implications:

Bonnie: In other words, you could spend the 20 per cent and not do anything particularly useful and not deliver anything amazing which in the event is added to shareholder value. On the other hand, that 20 per cent could deliver far more than the 80 per cent. *(strategic role) (M)*

The facilitator then intervened more actively:

Facilitator: But if your mind-set is the set piece battle, with the troops and the tanks there, you might forget the SAS mission where you wiped half their communications behind the lines and . . . because you weren't in the business of that, you were in the business of fighting big wars – and being killed . . . you are just shooting everyone. [Laughter]. *(strategic role) (M)*

David immediately agreed with this perspective:

David: There is a lot of truth in that. Some of these things are big wars. *(agreeing) (M)*

The dynamics of this process were as follows:

```
H
M          K(A)  A  K(A)  A  K(A)        T  B  T  D
L                               B  P
```

The continuity of this debate (at mainly the middle level) suggests that it had been a much more coherent debate than those typical of the earlier workshop session.

Second workshop – part one

The role of the department

Andy now took up the theme of the role of the department, following on from reflections on recent policy statements regarding what this was.

Andy: I mean, I think we are just talking at different levels here, Tony, if I might say so. Let's go back, let's summarize. This one sentence still stands as far as I can see. A lot of what we are talking about, is the following. The prime role of the TSD is to develop, champion and communicate BT's global technical strategy, covering all BT and alliance networks and systems in the UK and overseas. *(summarizing) (H)*

David now amplified Andy's view:

David: Well, you see, that role would actually cover those about saving the company, and it would also cover some of the other things on there. I couldn't even choose between the two. For example, and one of the issues facing us, is we have got to make a choice either between selecting areas to work in, specific areas, we are trying to cover the whole patch. Yes, it seems that both are covered by the role, but for 'save the company' I would argue, goes to the specific areas. *(strategic role, expanding) (H)*

And Andy now continued:

Andy: I fully agree with you David, because I think what we do is. . . . The first sentence that I read out still stands. And the prosaic answer to 'Why?' is, well, we have been asked to do it, we are being paid to do it. Now, the point that you have just described is that, what you then have to apply is deciding that, I have only got so much resource. What is it that we really must do, and that's where the 'Why?' comes in there. *(agreeing, expanding, strategic role) (H)*

We now get the distinct feeling that the debate had moved to more solid ground – it had become anchored (but not rigidly fixed), it had a centre of gravity, and it was building on what had gone before, creating a more solid, strategic architecture.

279

Bonnie and Keith (A) amplified on these themes:

Bonnie: To make BT the best. *(M)*

Keith (A): Exactly, you know, saving the company brings us up to an average, and, if you like, I want to see us move up above the average. So . . . *(expanding, picking apart) (L)*

The team now maintained its strategic formation, with Bonnie complementing Andy's points:

Andy: 'Save the company' actually speaks a mouthful, because it suggests that if we didn't do it, then we fall over a precipice, and that's the point. Doing nothing is not an option. *(L)*

Bonnie: When you said 'we have only got so much resource, you do so much to save the company', you do *sufficient* to save the company, you do sufficient to make us believe that it will work. And those two 'sufficients' might be different things. *(picking apart) (L)*

And the flying formation continued:

Bonnie: Could it be a useful thing for this company, this department, to be doing, to identify those areas of putting effort in which would do both. You know . . .. *(questioning, probing) (M)*

Andy: A double whammy. *(clarifying) (L)*

Bonnie: Where we could be saving the company and making it the best. *(expanding) (L)*

David: I do think that there is a tension between these. *(judging) (L)*

Facilitator: Can we list them out? *(M)*

(They then proceeded to list the issues.)

The whole sequence of the debate was interesting from the point of view of its harmony and sense of purpose. It is not suggested by this that contention is necessarily destructive – far from it. However, a team that spends 80 per cent of its time locked in intense and divergent contention may not prove to be a particularly productive one.

The behavioural sequence here was as follows:

```
H               A  D  A
M                       B              B          K(A)  T
L                     K(A)  A  B      A  B  D
```

So many of the difficulties and frustrations of the group seem to have arisen because of undershared mental maps, the individualistic styles of the team members and because of some personal idiosyncrasies.

Andy now reflected on the level of clarity that has come out of the fog of the discussion, by bringing in the department's formal objectives:

Andy: It seems to me, Tony, that we have got a very nice fit between, these are the objectives of the BT Board, and we have gone through and got a pretty good mapping of this, notwithstanding this . . . there they are, a pretty good mapping of those objectives and the ones that we can see for the main operating business Board, and our role within that. So that has been very helpful in that respect. *(summarizing) (H)*

Bonnie amplified Andy's point:

Bonnie: There is an interesting dynamism issue that . . .. Most of those things are there partly because at an earlier point we said – in some document or another – that they were a good idea. Partly . . . *(expanding) (H)*

Andy now latches on to Bonnie's input, incorporating it immediately into his own mental map of the department's emerging priorities:

Andy: I think that Bonnie has actually put her finger on it, which I tried to say not so well a while ago, which is, most of our work is servicing this lot. But, *en passant,* and in addition, we also need to pull out the new strategic targets which will emerge over the year. *(expanding) (H)*

Keith (A): Yes, fine, fine. *(agreeing) (H)*

Andy now hungered for concrete value to come out of the totality of these discussions:

Andy: But it is very important for us to agree that that is the kind of stance we take, because it then says we focus most of our energy on delivering a strategy there. And I feel we do. Because I feel that I want to get something out of the loop. [Attempted interruptions.] But we also have some of the energy spent on . . . [Keith (A) again tries to interrupt] *(helicoptering up) (H)*

Andy next drew out some potential implications for how the department organizes itself:

Andy: And if you look at the job descriptions, they were very carefully worded with that in mind. So, I think there is a difference between being involved and having the possibility for driving it. *(expanding, strategic role, structure) (M)*

This final sequence of behaviour in this part of the workshop ran at a consistently high level, as follows:

H		A	B	A	K(A)	A
M						A
L						

In summary, the team members initially wrestled to get to grips with the issue of their own role, and what value they added, and to whom. However, Andy then managed to give them sufficient behavioural anchors to conduct a more proactive debate.

Key lessons

- Sort your key strategic tasks into those that are intended and predictable ('deliberate') versus those that are more unpredictable ('emergent'). Think about the kind of team style that best fits your future stream of deliverable versus emergent strategic tasks. Does this shift in mix imply a different mind-set and behaviours?
- Use Pareto thinking to prioritize not only strategic tasks, but also issues for debate (20 per cent of the issues typically constituting 80 per cent of the total importance).

■ Consider what you are currently not doing at all but should be doing – if you take a look at the overall business or group's strategic context.

Second workshop – part two

During this part of the workshop the facilitator indicated that he would not actually be facilitating, other than to provide guidance on the use of a specific management tool – the importance–influence grid (see Figure 11.2) – which was used to understand the priorities of the group. However, during the first phase of this second cycle of discussion he was drawn back in to facilitate in order to establish at least some sense of order. In the second phase, though, the team was able to manage without further intervention.

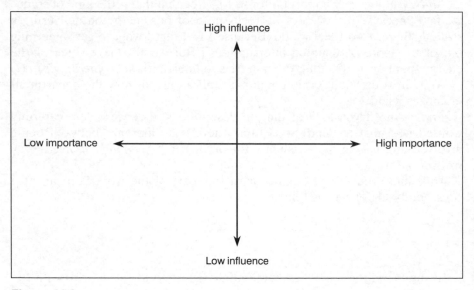

Figure 11.2
Importance–influence grid

Initially, discussions fragmented considerably as the team appeared to succumb to 'diving in' and 'picking apart' their priorities, but they then got to work to break down the issues into manageable units for analysis – in terms of importance and urgency. Their methodical working set the tone for around half-an-hour's discussion.

David: What we actually do have is a list of the priorities in the business that you can use. *(picking apart) (M)*

Keith (A): Could we ... *(L)*

Bonnie: [interrupting] We could have used that in the first place. That is rather circular. *(L)*

Facilitator: Can we get down to this small number of things. *(facilitating) (M)*

Keith (A): Yes. It is no. 2, let us put that as the opposite. *(picking apart)* *(L)*

David: Issue 2 is very big, I would have grouped it with 'broad band.' *(picking apart) (L)*

Keith (A): No, I . . . *(disagreeing) (L)*

Keith (B): Can we tie it into breaking into new revenues? *(proving) (M)*

Facilitator: If we can identify a grouping, then we can split it down later on. *(facilitating) (M)*

Andy: I am not sure. *(disagreeing) (M)*

Although the team members were methodical, they seemed to lose sight of what they were trying to achieve:

Facilitator: Again, you see, we are doing it, aren't we, we are picking. Sometimes you have got to not pick to move on, you can always come back to that. *(H)*

Keith (A): This is not the final list. *(H)*

Facilitator: We have this mind-set that we have got to bottom out everything. But if we can activate strategic patience, and get that into the process. *(H)*

Andy: We will never get . . . *(disagreeing) (H)*

Keith (A): We need to cultivate strategic patience [chuckling]. *(H)*

The team then made better progress for a while, until Bonnie jumped in to disagree – without being very clear why she was disagreeing:

Bonnie: But we just said, sorry David, we just said that the reason that Keith's thingy isn't in there is because . . . *(disagreeing) (L)*

Andy: It is in there. *(arguing) (L)*

Paul: It is in there. *(arguing) (L)*

David: The benefits . . . *(arguing) (L)*

Facilitator: Just in terms of the style here, we seem to focus on areas for possible disagreement rather than hunting for areas where we do agree. *(H)*

This was followed by a discussion where Bonnie tried to defend her intervention by saying that she wanted to understand.

Bonnie: Yes, but I don't understand. *(H)*

Facilitator: Well, it is a style issue, it is to do with going for things rather than saying, 'Let's give someone the benefit of the doubt', maybe they are clear but they haven't expressed it or it is because of the language. Probably if you had had an hour outside then you wouldn't have had any disagreement at all. *(H)*

Bonnie: But you said, if we didn't get clarity, share mind maps. *(clarification) (H)*

Facilitator: True, but it is the way in which you set about that, it is kind of, too almost – er – adversarial. It can get to be counterproductive. *(H)*

Here there seemed to be a relatively slow process of understanding not only what to do in behavioural terms (sharing mental maps), but also how to share this.

The discussion so far had moved through the following levels:

```
H                            T K(A) T A K(A)              T B T B T
M    D        T                  K(B) TA
L       K(A) B    K(A) D K(A)                      B A P D
```

This was a relatively smooth debate, with the 'low' level of debate being dictated by the team task – the prioritization of detailed issues. In the past, the team had not been as able to prioritize its issues effectively. Using a visual prioritization technique appeared to stabilize not merely the team's behaviour, but also its thinking.

Once the task of prioritizing the issues was virtually complete, the discussion then widened to reflect on how these issues sit within the wider context:

David: If you are talking about the means and how to do it, then it is not that at all because I think that a lot of this analysis has already been done. We have a shopping list at corporate, which is generally agreed, which says 'These are the sorts of things that we ought to be doing, chaps' – most of which are on our list, right. There are fourteen items, of which four or five are actually important. *(clarification) (H)*

After this point, Bonnie was still present but was less active in the discussions.

Andy reinforced David's argument, suggesting that the team should sort out what they are not doing as well as what they are doing:

Andy: I think that David has a point. There's a danger in fact. If we stand back a bit, and whilst it is right that we should question things, it is right that we should raise things totally out of court, and that's actually right, I think we should also try not to do the rest of BT's job for them. *(agreeing) (H)*

Andy moved on to more practical terrain by suggesting that their focus of attention should be narrowed down still further:

Andy: And what you could do, for example, is to take the ten points from corporate strategy, which were part of the thinking. And say, 'Of the ten, we are going to address the following four'. Right, that's our agenda. Now that would be a logical way of doing things, it is not presumptuous on our part to be running the whole business. *(prioritization) (H)*

Andy now brought the discussion together as a grand summary, which finally anchored the debate with what had been achieved:

Andy: I want that conversation to finish first, but there is a second question. It seems to be that we have got a loose enough fit. We agreed, a few moments ago, that we didn't need to have a 100 per cent lock-in of all the things that we do. What we have got is a pretty good fit between the company's top objectives and what we think we should be trying to do. Right. There are some bits – the Venn diagram goes beyond what they have got there, which is what you would expect. You would expect us to be looking beyond what has been said explicitly. Now that, I would have thought that an 80:20 fit, is what we have got, is pretty good. *(summarizing, judging) (H)*

Keith (A): It is pretty good. *(agreeing, judging) (H)*

Andy: It is better than we would normally want. *(judging) (H)*

Keith (B): Absolutely. *(agreeing) (H)*

Andy: I have never seen such a good fit before. *(judging) (H)*

The discussion had thus been maintained at a consistently high level:

> *H* D A A A K(A) A K(B) A
>
> *M*
>
> *L*

Andy had steered the team in a real and direct way. They now had better shared mental maps of what the department was about, and were perhaps less prone to unnecessary disagreement on this topic.

The team next prioritized the issues in more detail, using the importance–influence grid. At this point, the team settled down into a much quieter, methodical routine. The downside to this was that they did not actually cross-challenge each other's assumptions on the positioning grid.

The facilitator then attempted to raise the level of debate, trying not to facilitate intrusively as he did so (as this was the team's opportunity for a 'freestyle' discussion):

Facilitator: Can I just make a quick suggestion. What you could do is to say – to get people to position it in their minds, or on a bit of paper – what those were. And you take one of those Post-its, and you say, from someone, 'How do you position it?', and you say 'Why do you position it there?', and 'Why?'. But you first need to identify why the first person said that, so you start off and you say, 'Why did you position it there?', and then you say, 'Why did you position it somewhere else?' And then someone – like Dave – another arbitrator – could say 'Let's move it around', and get a fair balance. *(facilitation) (H)*

So, although the team had taken positive steps to improve its process, there were further areas where they could sharpen it up so that it might result in a richer and more questioning debate. Again, the BT team seemed to view process as relatively simple and mechanical. Instead, a 'process' can be fluid, organic, and consist of a number of ingredients that become more and more effective with learning.

Key lessons from the debate

- A team leader and/or facilitator can add considerable value by providing the occasional summary of what has been said, key points and insights that are emerging, lines of enquiry that have opened up, and things that have crystallized for them – such as decisions, judgements and so on. Earlier, we called this 'meta-behaviour'.
- This summary should be done without distortion: you cannot claim that a group consensus has been achieved when it is just your particular view.
- Where you do want to stake out a decision that runs counter to the agendas of at least part of the group, then this has to be brought out explicitly with a signal, such as 'I am now taking the lead'.

In conclusion, the more structured approach used in the final workshop appeared to have given the team at least the beginnings of a set of priorities. These priorities had eluded them previously. Indeed, this had been the subject of a workshop held during the previous year, when these issues were left substantially unresolved.

Certainly the result was not achieved easily, as it took considerable time – even with Andy present and steering the discussion to a substantial degree – to channel the debate in a meaningful way. These difficulties appear to have had a number of causes, not least of these being the problems of defining the terms that the team members were using and the lack of clarity about which levels of analysis were needed. At times, it felt like a blindfolded person groping around a room to get a feel of its dimensions and of the relationships of objects in the room to each other. There was an apparent absence of problem architecture, and incomplete and differing mental maps within the minds of the individuals there.

Individual members of the team had a tendency to dart off in different directions – especially towards specific ideas that had either just occurred to them or were related to their personal strategic agendas. Andy's persistence (together with David's input on the technical strategy objectives – as set corporately) helped to anchor the debate, along with the use of the importance–influence grid – which calmed individuals down and channelled the thought process.

In the final cycle of debate, the team reflected on its workshop process:

Keith (A): It was nowhere near as contentious as I have seen in the past. *(reflecting) (H)*

However, David pointed out that:

David: The problem that we usually have is we go through this exercise, this prioritization before, the real battles come through when you are actually going through 'why?' . . .. It is only then that you are really challenging people. *(anticipating) (H)*

Andy confirmed David's impression:

Andy: I think there is potential for a lot of conflict, but I think that the real conflict comes when you take the output out of this and use it to influence the allocation of resources in time or budgets. But when it applies to a budget or a departmental resource allocation, the pain comes on. *(control, anticipating, conflict) (H)*

Again, this highlighted that beneath the surface of the behavioural bond there were some very important, if hidden, processes at work. There appeared to be a mixture of personal strategic agendas, anxieties and political manoeuvring.

Conclusion of the BT workshop

The third team workshop offered a further insight into how the team operated in strategy making (and also why it had the difficulties it had). The core topics for debate that surrounded the department's role, the value it added to BT and its priorities were evidently complicated, sometimes not fully mapped out, and frequently emotive.

It would be slightly surprising to see that this territory had been relatively ill mapped out if it were not for the fact that the department had an ambiguous, fluid and changing role. This degree of ambiguity is by no means unknown elsewhere – indeed, because of continual reorganization in some companies, it is almost the norm. In BT, this situation presented the team members with many fuzzy issues, which they seemed to have great difficulty grappling with.

Taking a bird's eye view of the whole debate, it looks as if the team was still working according to the mind-set 'If we just discuss this enough then we will get the answers'. Yet, paradoxically, relatively little of the debate (save for Andy's summaries and the prioritization exercise in the second part) seemed to deliver much concrete output. (The most helpful output seemed to be confirmation that BT's expectations of the department were 'appropriate', but this was based primarily on David's input, and not on any other novel discussion.)

Interestingly, a focused and productive piece of work was achieved as the team members prioritized their issues using the importance–influence grid. However, the distinctive absence of more vigorous debate or contention gave the feel that the team might have been avoiding the really important discussions on its future priorities. (The individuals' subsequent reflections on this team process bore out this impression.)

An additional problem for the team was that its members may have faced a high proportion of emergent strategy dictating their work in the foreseeable future. This not only made the team's role and priorities somewhat harder to tie down, but might also have provided a shelter for Bonnie, Keith (B) and others to 'do the things we are most interested in or committed to'. Andy therefore had a very tough job to reconcile those demands.

On several occasions, the facilitator attempted to flag up this issue of 'avoidance' of the more fundamental issues. David did not respond to this, perhaps because he was keen to get at least some output, or because he wanted to avoid further bouts of erratic discussion or contention. Alternatively, he might simply have been concerned with time pressures. In any event, to have done a first-cut prioritization without significant exploration of why things were positioned how they were meant that further rework was called for, and might actually have made further analysis harder. Having said that, using this kind of management tool was a new experience for the team members and so they might simply have been content to enjoy a welcome 20 minutes of working in what, to them at the time, seemed an effective manner (which it no doubt was compared, to what had happened in the past). Certainly, this tool did seem to act as a profoundly calming influence on the hitherto more usual style of debate.

A final issue was the team's tendency to diverge, not only in terms of actual content of discussion but also in level. Perhaps with practice they might fly more in formation in the future.

Key lessons from this debate

- Where your department or company is being reorganized, invest considerable time defining what business it is in.
- Where boundaries of roles are unclear, iron these out.
- Avoid throwing discussion time at problems. Instead, employ some problem-solving techniques to bottom-out issues quickly and effectively (e.g. AID analysis, the strategic option grid, fishbone analysis, etc.).
- Recognize emergence in your workload in terms of how many issues you have got to work through, and avoid using coping strategies to deal with it.
- Create mini-scenarios to anticipate your workload as best you can (tell stories about how it might develop).
- Do not use excuses to avoid dealing with apparently intractable, 'hot' issues.
- Use prioritization techniques to sort out what you should focus on, and in which order.

Summary

The most valuable questions to ask of a department are 'what business are we in?', 'who are your customers?', and 'what value do you add, and how?'. By applying a clearer process to the use of these questions (and some strategic analysis techniques), BT''s technical strategy department was able to inject more order (and productivity) into its behaviour. This was achieved without any evident loss of creativity.

 THE KEY DIMENSIONS OF STRATEGIC BEHAVIOUR

Figure 11.3 explores some of the more important dimensions of strategic behaviour that emerged from the BT research. Strategic behaviour is an amalgam of cognitive, affective and territorial elements, but, on top of these elements, behavioural momentum is a key variable.

Factors that add energy include, for example, creative thinking, leadership, or simply a sense of urgency. Factors that dissipate energy include having too little process in debate or interactions, generating considerable strategic frustration (for example, where the quality of listening is poor).

Coming back to the BT experience, the field of attention of the BT team was a key dimension. In the BT team this was generally broad, leading to a loss of momentum and diffuse outcomes. Another dimension was clearly the duration of strategic attention – was it sufficient to enable managers to move on thinking, feeling, and territorial agendas on issues in the way they had hoped, or not?

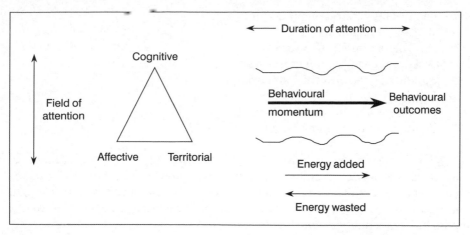

Figure 11.3
Key dimensions of strategic behaviour

Finally, as we have seen, the behavioural outcomes that can accrue as a result of the strategic debate can be very diverse. These may take the form of greater alignment of mind-sets, or feelings about team cohesiveness or about each other.

From Figure 11.3. we can hypothesize that:

1. With attention diffused under a wider range of issues, strategic thinking will be slow and ineffective
2. Where attention is narrow, not only are thought-related outputs likely to be of higher quality, but team behaviour will also be higher – and energy preserved
3. Where territorial and emotional elements in agendas are dominant (either consciously or unconsciously), progress will be slower and energy wasted
4. Where mental maps (and priorities within them) within the team differ, this will cause major frustration and a lack of progress
5. Where cognitive, territorial and emotional elements become interfused, it will become very difficult (if not impossible) to move forward
6. Cognitive confusion will tend to provoke emotional and territorial instability. Equally, emotional attachment and territorial ambiguity will aggravate cognitive confusion, resulting in a soup of strategic agendas.

Why and how is strategic behaviour important for teams? – A summary

It is now possible to explore the more specific reasons for strategic behaviour's importance from the managers' own perspectives – especially in terms of how it might add to or detract from value. These reasons include:

- The quality of strategic thinking
- Sharing of mind-sets
- Creating an imperative to act
- (Possibly) changing territorial barriers
- Building a platform for influencing
- Time expended
- Timeliness and utility of outcomes
- Cognitive and emotional energy expended.

Where strategic behaviour is not particularly well orchestrated, management debate can as a result be too narrowly confined in scope, or too superficial (lacking depth) or fragmented (missing key interconnections). It might also fail to identify strategic blind spots, or it may identify them as vague, possible opportunities and threats, but not have diagnosed them sufficiently in order to add economic value.

Sharing of mind-sets

Linked to both 'quality of strategic thinking' and 'refocusing of attention', the commonality of mind-sets also plays a major role in determining strategic outputs – and their economic value.

Strategic behaviour that is not underpinned by a continual sharing of mind-sets may therefore inhibit a healthy degree of challenge and testing during strategic debate. Poorly shared mind-sets can lead to a hardening of personal strategic agendas, which can then frustrate decision-making action and change, thus destroying economic value.

Mind-sets are therefore the frames of reference that provide a basis for creating shared strategic thinking, and for getting economic value out of it.

Creating an imperative to act

Both managers and strategic management theorists alike are well aware of the frequent gaps that occur between strategic thinking and action, especially when dealing with apparently intractable problems. However, the consequence of this is that, unless the strategic behaviour within a team can create some need to act (even if this action is simply 'to investigate further'), implementation may well not be mobilized – even where it is an organizational imperative. Unless action is instigated, then the economic value will remain latent, and ultimately unrealized.

The feeling of there being a need to act is thus the precursor to action, as a tangible behavioural outcome, and ultimately of value creation.

Changing territorial barriers

An open and cohesive style of strategic behaviour may well be more conducive to reducing territorial barriers. Some of these barriers may be mainly organizational and some mainly cognitive or even emotional, especially when issues exist that individuals have attachments to, given past experiences and investment of effort. Where major territorial barriers exist, it will prove difficult for value to be created effectively within the organization.

Building a platform for influencing

Once again, creating a platform for influencing is a precursor to achieving action, and to economic value creation for the team, especially *vis-à-vis* stakeholders elsewhere in the organization.

Time expended

Time expended by a team will generally obviously govern:

- The number of issues the team covers
- The depth and thoroughness of their investigations
- How many issues exist where thinking is turned into action.

This will not only inhibit the economic value of outputs, but will also drive up underlying costs.

Timeliness and utility of outcomes

Where strategic behaviour becomes increasingly chaotic, this may obviously reduce the effectiveness of the strategy process – which might be frustrating from a team's own perspective. It may result in costly organizational delays as decisions are put off and opportunities slip. While a task-based perspective is by no means the only one, nevertheless it still exists and should not be ignored simply because of the influence of other perspectives – such as the political. The result, once again, will be value destruction.

The timeliness and utility of outcomes thus concerns the final outputs of strategic behaviour and how they are used by the rest of the organization, and what economic value they add.

Cognitive and emotional energy expended

Finally, a management team's mental and emotional resources may be depleted by the frustration of weak control over its strategic behaviour.

Unrelieved frustration levels in other teams might potentially rise to the point at which there is an effective burn-out, especially when a particular issue becomes a 'strategic black hole'. This suggests that controlling strategic behaviour effectively requires an 'energy management' activity. This concerns the less tangible and indirect effects of strategic behaviour rather than the more tangible outcomes. Lower energy will ultimately dilute economic value added.

In summary, strategic behaviour does appear to play a profoundly important and influential role in shaping strategic thinking, and also in adding economic value. Not only does shaping strategic behaviour seem to yield potential benefits, but default behaviours also seem to have costs – for the organization, the team, and the individuals involved.

CONCLUSION

Strategic team-building is another important dimension of HR strategy, and is generated through strategic thinking and strategic behaviour, and by deciding what business we are in (as a team) and what value it will add. Many of the frustrations in getting the value out of strategic thinking are down to behavioural constraints.

Key points are:

- The team mix needs to be managed so that there is a reasonably good balance of skills and style
- The interactive process needs to be monitored for its level of debate
- A richer range of behaviours needs to be created (for example, more 'questioning' and 'probing' types of behaviour)
- The quality and effectiveness of meta-behaviours may need improving
- Behavioural outcomes and breakthroughs may require targeting, and monitoring of the delivery of these against the quality of the behavioural process
- The less transparent aspects of behaviour need to be surfaced and examined
- The team process needs to be orchestrated, including the field and duration of attention, behavioural momentum and energy levels
- Analytical tools (e.g. fishbone analysis) may be required for analysing issues and to help surface assumptions and mental maps (and feelings)
- The team may need to work hard to make sufficient emotional investment to achieve a strategic and/or behavioural breakthrough.

However, perhaps more important than these specific areas is the need to manage strategic behaviour as a total system (see Figure 11.1) in order to add real economic value.

The above list provides a broad range of options for any senior management team to work on, should it feel the need to shape its own strategic behaviour in an active way. However, you might now find it valuable to explore the possibilities of broadening the range of analytical tools managers might use. This obviously raises further issues (and, in effect, political ones) concerning who might do the shaping, to what ends, and how.

'Strategic behaviour' is thus a most fruitful and relevant concept – both in management theory terms and in team-working practice. Strategic behaviour also exhibits some distinctive patterns, in so far as its cognitive, affective, dynamic and political elements are particularly complex, dynamic and hard to manage. These strategic behaviours need to be aligned as a system in order to add full economic value.

Strategic behaviour appears to be important in the strategy-making process on a number of counts, yet seems to be neglected – an area that is seen not so much as one of 'management' or 'control', but rather as something to do with 'shaping'.

At a minimum, it appears that both senior line managers and HR managers should become more aware of their system of strategic behaviour as well as paying attention to strategy contents, context, and the more tangible aspects of strategic decision-making.

Before ending this chapter, it is worth noting that team alignment is a key precondition of getting the value out of strategic thinking (see Chapter 12). Also, we need to have highly developed facilitation from the HR strategy consultant (see Chapter 13).

Value-added strategic thinking

▍INTRODUCTION

Throughout this book we have stressed that organizational mind-set plays a major role in competitive success, and that it should be a central focus for HR strategy. One of the potential breakthroughs that might bring about a shift in organizational mind-set is to facilitate more strategic thinking in the organization. However, how can this be brought about, and with what economic value? This chapter tries to answer this very important question.

Strategic thinking often fails to meet its expectations in delivering economic value in many organizations. This is generally felt to be because strategies are frequently not implemented, or are implemented poorly. Another reason is because managers are unsure about how strategic thinking actually creates economic value. Because 'strategy' is often perceived as relatively intangible and qualitative, the idea of actually putting some financial numbers on strategic thinking (or on strategic thought) may never have occurred to most managers.

To enquire more deeply into this topic the authors conducted in-depth, qualitative research into how five line/HR managers and five strategy academics saw the links between strategic thinking and value creation. The five senior managers were drawn from a variety of industries, each of which was facing rapid external or internal change (or both).

This chapter focuses on the five line/HR managers (findings from them being very closely parallel with those from the five strategy academics, who were also interviewed as a benchmark). Our conclusions (and the implications of these) can be found at the end of this chapter.

Strategic thinking is being seen more and more as a central issue on the organizational agenda. However, it would seem less clear that it is a 'must-do' rather than a 'nice-to-have-and-nice-to-do ancillary process'. Whilst strategic thinking may help to alleviate organizational boredom, how do we put it at the very heart of management's attention? Our answer is that if we were to truly understand the economic value of strategic thinking, it would be obvious why we should all be doing it – and lots of it.

So how can we understand its true value?

Our first step in exploring the value of strategic thinking is to understand what 'value' actually is. For this, we need to recap on value-based management (see Chapter 2).

VALUE-BASED MANAGEMENT

Value-based management emphasizes the need to put a value on strategy. Whilst the focus of value-based management is clearly on managing economic value (or the net present value of the future cash flows from a strategy), these cash flows are frequently difficult to target or measure. However, as strategic thinking is (at least initially) an intangible, let us look at how we can begin to put a value on it.

Instead of there being a single way of coping with intangibles, there are often too many different ways of estimating their value (Grundy, 1992). These can be evaluated through a stage-by-stage process (see Chapter 2) by:

- Identifying what generic kind of intangible it belongs to (for example, is the intangible concerned with the value of a future opportunity, does it protect the existing business, or is it 'intangible' because it adds external customer value – and there is resulting uncertainty about how much of that value will be captured?).
- Next, working out how value might be captured or crystallized in the future.
- Then identifying specific measures or indicators that show value has materialized.

Another approach is to identify specific value and cost drivers, along with the preconditions of getting them aligned (Grundy, 1998; see also Chapter 6). To achieve this we need to isolate the key value-creating activities that might generate value (for example, strategic thinking might avoid strategic errors and help to prioritize resource allocation, etc.). Having looked at this, we should then ask how much value might be created if this value-creating activity were effective and were not frustrated by organizational conditions or other extraneous failings.

Having done this, we can then estimate the value of complete alignment – i.e. where strategic thinking is not only effective and incisive, but also translates into equally effective implementation. We should then compare this wonderful ideal world with the 'base case' (Grundy, 1998) – this is where strategic thinking is not effective, or simply does not get acted upon. An assessment of the difference between both worlds could then potentially be made, if only in broad, financial terms.

To find some clues as to how to put a value on strategic thinking, seven key questions were asked to elicit our data:

1. How do you believe strategic thinking might add value generally?
2. What value (i.e. economic value) might it generate (in each case)?

3. What specific factors are likely to enable or constrain the specific ways in which strategic thinking actually adds that value (using a force field analysis)?
4. In practice, what additional value (if any) tends to emerge (as opposed to being deliberate) from strategic thinking?
5. What value tends to be unrealized, and why?
6. To what extent do the following inhibit its realization?
   - Management distraction
   - Dilution of outputs
   - Defensive routines
7. What could be done to get more value from strategic thinking, and how?

The study enabled identification of ten key factors influencing value creation and capture from strategic thinking:

1. The meaning (of strategic thinking)
2. Its business value
3. The context
4. Thought value
5. Prioritization
6. Core process
7. Process drivers
8. Supporting structure and skills
9. Supporting processes
10. Soft value.

These are shown in Figure 12.1, which effectively represents a system of strategic thinking. We argue that it is only by achieving good alignment within this system that strategic thinking is likely to generate its full potential economic value.

Figure 12.1 also shows the main interdependencies between high-level influences.

'Meaning' was found important, as the meaning of strategic thinking was somewhat unclear. 'Business value' was then segmented by type, and also was broken down into specific categories (e.g. emergent and detergent value).

'Thought value' was also significant in its own right, with strategic thinking helping managers to construct a better ordered and more appropriately focused view of their business. 'Prioritization' was, in itself, of notable value as an activity.

'Core process', as high-level category, contained a variety of sub-categories. These ranged from permission and ownership through to the use of strategic jargon and the physical context of the strategic thinking activity.

There were also a number of process drivers acting on the process, including leadership, management agendas, defensive routines and time constraints.

'Supporting processes' included project management, setting measures (for the value of strategic thinking), and the formal recognition of successful strategic thinking.

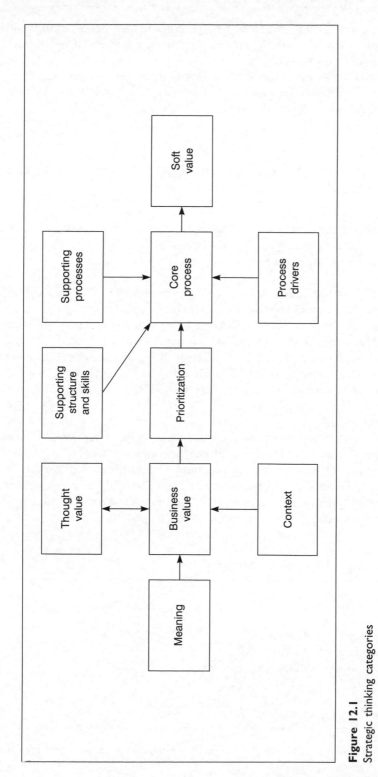

Figure 12.1
Strategic thinking categories

Finally, 'soft value' covered clarity, confidence, belief, and reducing anxiety and stress. Potentially, strategic thinking could be of personal value to the individuals involved, too.

Our framework was then broken down into sub-categories, which are represented in Figures 12.2 and 12.3. The complete framework is contained in Figure 12.4, later in the chapter.

THE VALUE OF STRATEGIC THINKING: CASE STUDY

In this case study we will look at what the senior managers said, and also the work implications for setting a value strategic thinking. The managers involved in the study included:

- Barclays – Steve Landsdown (SL), Senior Manager, Corporate Banking (formerly corporate strategy manager, Group HQ)
- Hewlett Packard – Karen Slatford (KS), then Director and General Manager, Large Systems (Global), Hewlett Packard
- Lex – Lin Kendrick (LK), Group Head of Management Development
- Tesco – Paul Mancey (PM), then Director of Tesco Direct
- Zurich Independent Financial Advisers (ZIFA) – Joe Ranger (JR), Assistant Sales Director.

Over the past 5 years each of these senior managers had been exposed to some formal strategic training, either through a Cranfield School of Management course or through in-company programmes (Lin Kendrick, Joe Ranger), or via one-to-one mentoring (Karen Slatford) or consulting facilitation (Paul Mancey). All the managers had already been exposed to some processes for strategy implementation, and not just formulation.

The meaning of strategic thinking

This section covers:

- Understanding (of strategy)
- The levels of strategic thinking
- Strategy versus tactics.

Understanding (of strategy)

'Strategy' is felt to be inherently bound up with timeframes – and the future:

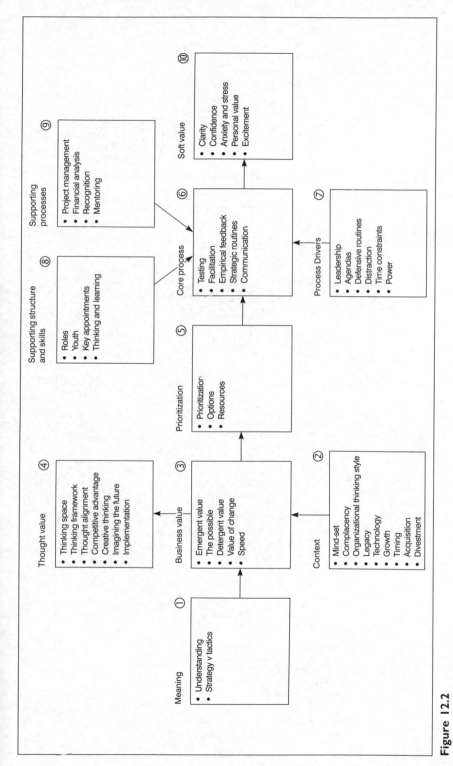

Figure 12.2
The value of strategic thinking: managers' perspectives

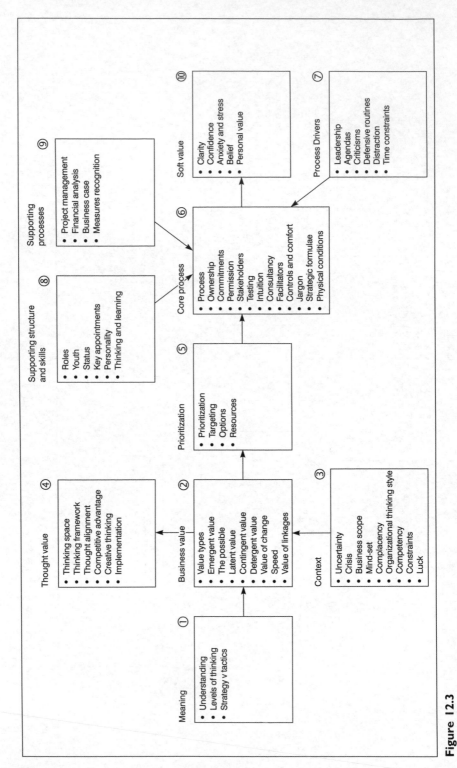

Figure 12.3
The value of strategic thinking: academics' perspectives

> I have never stopped to think what it [strategic thinking] is, although we always talk about it. For me, I think it is about timeframes. One of the significant differences that I see between someone who is being a manager and someone who is being a director is their ability to think in timeframes in which they should think. (LK)

The levels of strategic thinking

There are a number of levels of strategic thinking, as seen in this illustration from Tesco):

> We have used strategic thinking at a higher level as a basis to determine whether to enter the home shopping market. We have then used strategic thinking to determine which non-food markets to enter. At a lower level, we have also used strategic thinking to help us to identify which price and quality positions to adopt at each market. (PM)

This suggests that strategic thinking can add economic value at many levels, and not just at corporate/business strategy levels.

Strategy versus tactics

The levels of strategy are sometimes seen as being distinguished by the concepts of 'strategic' versus 'tactical':

> The word 'strategy' can mean different things to different people, and it is sometimes difficult to differentiate between a strategy and a tactic. Tesco is very, very clear about its top-line strategy and the measures of success. However, delivering the top-line strategy requires strategic thought to choose between the tactical options. (PM)

Nevertheless, confusion around this debate over the meaning of strategy might make the term of self somewhat undervalued. The term 'strategy' itself can dilute the value of true, strategic thinking, because of its ambiguity:

> I think 'strategy' is an unfortunate word. You need a different way of defining it. Because a strategy is a tactic depending upon where you are in the organization, you almost need a different way of defining it. (PM)

> People get confused. They think that tactical thinking is strategic thinking. People say they want to improve their strategic thinking, but they don't allocate the time they need to do something about it. And there aren't the opportunities afforded them to really do [it] because we recognize and value action around here. We far less recognize thinking. And in an organization

when it is all about action and doing, the strategic thinkers get lost, they don't want to be around . . .. (*LK*)

The 'so-whats?' from this analysis are that:

- Strategic thinking needs to be defined much more clearly (especially as managers are often unclear about its true meaning) so that it will be used as an everyday process
- The more tangible its end-goals are, the more managers are likely to be focused on it, and the more economic value they will gain from it.

Business value

This section covers:

- Emergent value
- The art of the possible
- Detergent value
- The value of change.

Emergent value

Emergent value is seen as being created through an openness to learning, but this is inhibited both by frequent organizational career moves, and because learning is not captured from other parts of the organization:

> Part of emergent value is how things work in practice. The value is being able to make mistakes and learn from them and to recognize successes and run with them. (*SL*)

So 'value' may not always be predictable in form, but with emergent value we should be always trying to create the preconditions of some value creation.

The art of the possible

Thinking about the art of the possible can help to generate business value, but again the focus on the Today (internally and externally) inhibits the capture of this value:

> We don't have any of our businesses considering what the art of the possible is. We don't manage our customer data in the way that we could, there isn't a synergy across the group in the way that there should be; we could manage things . . . so we are dealing very much with today, we are

managing the short term. It is a major constraint because our competitors will move well ahead of us. (*Anon*)

Again, this reinforces the need to use strategic thinking to get value by changing organizational mind-set.

Detergent value

At Barclays Bank, 'detergent value' is seen as being a very tangible area where strategic thinking has generated tangible business value:

The economic value analysis suggested that the emerging scenario for this business was dominated by big investment banks. So we reached a fork in the road. We can either invest really heavily to try to rival the big investment banks, and we might just be able to realize value from doing that. The second option was to invest in reaching the scale of the Americans because there are other stronger opportunities for us in the UK. We would get more bang for our buck if we invest in the retail side of the business. (*SL*)

This 'detergent' value was obviously a very key management concern for Barclays in the recent past.

Whilst value is often seen as being drawn out of the new and the incremental, this need not be the case for both strategic thinking and HR strategy generally.

The value of change

Strategic thinking can add more value if managers screen out any change initiatives that are not self-evidently 'positive' or beneficial:

The value of strategic thinking in Tesco is its role in creating positive change for customers . . .. If strategic thinking and positive change is interlinked, then it is very important for everybody to be very innovative in what they do. It is equally important to make sure that it is positive change and not negative, so it is in line with business objectives and what people want. (*PM*)

The above reflects the value of combining strategic thinking and HR strategy – by using the very simple strategic thought of targeting 'positive change', we then focus on more appropriate HR strategic breakthroughs.

Speed

At Tesco, speed is seen as being a very major area where strategic thinking has added value. This is manifest in Tesco's expansion globally into non-food products, and into innovation in supermarket formats:

> For me, it is remarkable that in 5 years Tesco has moved from being a UK-based supermarket chain to become an international mixed retail and services business. This rapid transformation is based on clarity at the top and a tremendous creativity and energy in making it happen quickly . . ..
> Within a couple of years Tesco will have 45 per cent of its space overseas, it is a dramatic transformation in what Tesco is. And that can only be done by firstly clarity at the top in the general direction, and also a great deal of strategic thought in applying it and making it work. (*PM*)

This again suggests the relevance of 'from–to' analysis (see Chapter 6) in helping managers to put economic value on strategic thinking – what is it worth to shift from being 90–95 per cent UK-focused to only 55 per cent?

The key 'so-what?' from this section on value is again that strategic thinking adds value in a variety of ways, depending upon the context of the strategy – including emergent value, detergent value, the art of the possible, speed of decision-taking, and the value of change.

Context

This section covers:
- Mind-set
- Complacency
- Organizational thinking style
- Legacy
- Technology
- Growth
- Timing
- Acquisition
- Divestment.

Mind-set

The existing mind-set may be severely frustrating for strategic thinking:

> Our culture rejects certain knowledge skills like marketing, less so now, but information management, etc. [elaborates on change management]. (*LK*)

Complacency

More specifically, complacency acts as a major block against the value of strategic thinking:

> Complacency can set in. Rather than being dynamic and constantly changing then the complacency sets in and that's when we start to fall backwards. There may not be the will to change. (LK)

(This brings us back to the complacency of Dyson's competitors, especially Hoover, in the mid-1990s – see Chapter 3.)

Organizational thinking style

There are times when an organizational thinking style is viewed as a major inhibitor (and sometimes as an enabler). For example, at ZIFA we see that:

> Without doubt you meet people in the organization who are cynical about it. I do think that that kind of approach is still prevalent in some people. There are a lot of people who are still relatively open-minded and young, but there are still people within our business who are still relatively cynical about it. I think you need a more open-minded culture. (JR)

This thinking style is seen as being determined by leadership style, by structure, and by the spread of strategic thinking generally through the management population:

> The people side is also an enabler, and leadership. We have got a brand new leader in Barclays now and he is driving through a lot of change; he is an inspirational kind of character. (SL)

Legacy

At Barclays, the existing resources legacy is such that more challenging strategic thinking is restricted simply on grounds of perceived practicality:

> We have a legacy, which is a big constraining factor. We are really constrained by what we have got to work with, by our skills and by the infrastructure of the organization. (SL)

Again this is reminiscent of Hoover in the Dyson case. Having an old, brown-field industrial site in Scotland and over twenty existing product warrants meant it was hard (if not impossible) to think difficulty – at least until new management was appointed.

Technology

At Lex, we see that technology operates in a similar way to the resources legacy at Barclays. As the organization's competencies here are not technologically focused, this again inhibits the value of strategic thinking:

It is about where we are today, where are the constraints we have today, what are the things which are the enablers today, and how might they change, and over what sort of timeframe? What are the things that are coming into the environment, like technology? To think strategically today is to get a real grip on what technology will do to change the whole market-place. What implication does that have in terms of something being very global? (LK)

Growth

However, if the above issues were addressed, the value could be obtained and become manifest through additional growth:

The major value [in strategic thinking] would be our ability to grow. That is where the constraining factor is at the present time because we don't have a great strategic thinking capacity . . . (LK)

Timing

Appropriate timing is an interesting determinant of the value of strategic thinking. Strategic thinking done at an inappropriate time (relative to industry/organizational life cycles) may fail to generate value:

Timing is an issue – is the timing right? Because suddenly you can apply something like that rather than just think about it. (JR)

Timing is especially important to specific HR strategic breakthroughs, owing to their complexity and vulnerability to many internal organizational alignment factors.

Acquisition

Strategic thinking can add value through choosing the most appropriate pathway to corporate development – especially opting for acquisitions over organic development, or *vice versa*:

In one of our businesses we have grown and grown by acquisition, but the value of those acquisitions hasn't been assessed . . .. Other of our businesses have grown organically, but very few. The most profitable parts of our business have been grown organically. But it is only every now and again that we stop and consider that . . .. (LK)

Acquisition management is a key important area where either value can be created or destroyed – according to the quality of strategic thinking about what to acquire, how to acquire it, and how to implement it.

Divestment

Divestment (specifically), in a similar manner to detergent value, can add value through strategic thinking:

> An enabler too was the sale of a certain part of our retail group ... that in itself made a very big statement, and as a consequence of that we were recategorized on the Stock Market. As an enabler, in terms of mind-set and recruitment, then that is reasonably important. [Mentions new members of the Board] (*Anon*)

The key 'so-whats?' from this section are as follows:

- Once again, challenge of management of mind-set, thinking style and complacency is crucial in aligning strategic thinking to add real value – and migration away from an onerous legacy.
- Strategic thinking can add most value when it is well timed, and when it may be addressed to thinking laterally about investment and divestment options.
- The value of strategic thinking can also come from identifying new technologies and market growth opportunities that otherwise might not be spotted.

Thought value

The next section covers:

- Thinking space
- Thinking framework
- Thought alignment
- Competitive advantage
- Imagining the future (new category)
- Creative thinking
- Implementation.

Thinking space

'Thinking space' was very much on the minds of managers in relation to the value of strategic thinking. At Hewlett Packard, this realization appears to have had a profound effect on one senior manager:

> Just taking a day out to do strategic thinking does make a difference, out of the day-to-day environment. Often, and this is what it is like for most people in a sales organization, you end up with weekly, quarterly, annual pressure and targets. And you get really stuck into those – the grunt and grind, and the minutiae. And you don't get a chance to step back .... It's that helicopter

thing. Getting up in the helicopter and looking down. The thought that you are someone from Mars and have landed on Earth and doesn't have a clue – it gives you a completely fresh view. Looking from above – sometimes you catch yourself doing it. Sometimes I catch myself doing it in a meeting. I let them get on with it, and I go up, up. I have a look and listen. It is really good practice; you look at things from a completely different angle. (KS)

On one occasion, spending some time on strategic thinking does seem to have added considerable – and very tangible – value at Hewlett Packard:

That issue was a festering, gaping sore. Just sitting down and going through that [with a mentor], just taking me through that strategy grid [strategic option grid; see Chapter 8] and taking me out of my day job, it put the whole thing in context. (KS)

Thinking framework

At Tesco, one manager feels that the concept of 'strategy' could be broken down so that it can guide thinking at a different number of levels:

It helps me to consider a number of different concepts. It helps to have a clear framework and common language that can allow everyone to contribute. (PM)

Perhaps this quotation implies that it would be appropriate to think of strategy at the macro-, mini-, or micro-levels.

(The strategic thinking process used by Tesco has been employed extensively across the business. Examples include Tesco non-foods in the late 1990s. Arguably the incremental turnover generated by 2002 might have been in the order of £1 billion plus.)

Paul Mancey continues:

It gives us a framework to identify and agree where customer value and hence sustainable competitive advantage might lie. It also gives confidence to make decisions because the process is inclusive and thorough. Strategic thinking helps to explain why, rather than just giving what. (PM)

In sum, whilst strategic thinking does provide a thinking framework, the architecture of this framework needs to be elaborated, level by level, rather than left just at a vague and general level.

Thought alignment

Once again, strategic thinking may help to align disparate thoughts – which may then create economic value:

I knew I was going to be doing things, but I couldn't get a strong enough connection to what I was going to be doing to get the value we needed in order to meet the objective. A kind of light bulb went on with this particular idea. This would accelerate our progress towards the objective rather than just making a regular contribution, as I believe training and development does. It doesn't feel very exciting most of the time. (JR)

Here the alignment can come through completing a gap, and by giving an implementation imperative (thus aligning with the need to perform some action):

That one will definitely make it into implementation, mainly because I look after it! It has given me a focus on what we need to deliver next year. It just fits (from a timing and an ownership point of view) perfectly really. I was already grappling with the million things we could do in training and development – what can we do to really make a difference? That was a very welcome bolt out of the blue. This is the answer to what we need to do. Otherwise you can find yourself training and developing until you are blue in the face, but not being entirely sure what value it is adding. (JR)

Competitive advantage

Helping managers to think more clearly about competitive advantage is a very common theme amongst management, as we see in the following:

And it probably did highlight a specific thought which we had not thought before, which was – interestingly – it got us down into further detail, which was to have a strategy that increased the quality of our people. We highlighted one particular area that could give us particular competitive advantage. And that area was relationship management, so rather than train people in everything let us concentrate on the specific, because we believe it can give us a competitive advantage . . .. (JR)

Thinking about competitive advantage can be facilitated by benchmarking, providing that the benchmarks chosen are appropriate:

From that, the question was, 'which areas of non-food do you choose to get into first, and what will it look like?' And the process of the strategic thinking was to develop the framework to make choices and to understand benchmarks. Another important element is having benchmarks to beat. (PM)

Imagining the future

In-depth thinking about the future (and in an imaginary way) is explored as follows:

So someone's ability to think strategically is linked into their imagination, their understanding, their freedom to think and to consider what the art of the possible is, what the probable is. But it is not just like sci-fi, it is within a framework. (*LK*)

Creative thinking

One respondent feels very strongly that directors' roles should be more creative – and through strategic thinking:

A manager is very much about doing, a director is very much more about thinking about what the art of the possible is, and according to the level they are at. And it is that more of the time should be spent on the thinking rather than the doing. (*LK*)

You actually need to be lifted out of your normal frame of mind into a different structure and process and give yourself the permission to be different. That structured way of doing it works much better because it gives at the beginning, like a signal, the permission to do whatever you fancy. (*JR*)

Implementation

Implementation appraisal is, for one manager, an essential part of 'helicopter thinking':

So, being able to [often] go up in the helicopter, and then to come back and have landed on the ground, it seems to be pretty unusual to have that ability. People cannot seem to jump the divide . . .. The thing about the helicopter is that you go up, and then you come down, and for me it is about being able to go up and down, and up and down the scales. (*KS*)

Our Tesco manager also sees strategic thinking as integral with micro-strategies and implementation:

Strategic thinking can also be applied to internal ways of working, helping to free up time and resource for adding value activities. (*PM*)

So, strategic thinking – it would appear – can potentially facilitate strategy implementation, thus capturing more value from strategic thought.

The key 'so-whats?' from this section are that:

- Creating the necessary thinking space, using appropriate thinking frameworks and having the patience to align a number of disparate strategic thoughts are crucial to delivering its full potential value.

■ This value can be realized through exploiting present competitive advantage or by thinking about the future competitive advantage, by thinking creatively or by thinking about how implementation can be done in a particularly astute or cunning way.

Prioritization

This section covers:

■ Value through prioritization
■ Options
■ Resources.

Value through prioritization

Strategic thinking is seen as adding value through prioritization both at Tesco and at ZIFA:

> It is a way of prioritizing different activities, deciding to move into one market rather than another. (PM)

At ZIFA it is not seen as necessarily adding to the existing burden of implementation, but as refocusing it:

> It depends how excited they are really, when what you come up with isn't, certainly in my experience, it is not 'extra', it is 'instead of'. It is not on top of everything else we have got to do. (JR)

In conclusion, more structured strategic thinking helps to add value by prioritizing management agendas and through better resource allocation.

Options

Appraising specific strategic options is an area of significant value added (as in Tesco's experience, where the strategic option grid (see Chapter 8) is now used routinely to evaluate new strategic opportunities):

> And one of the techniques I use regularly [the strategic option grid] is the assessment of the attractiveness of various markets or options . . .. The strategic thinking approach that I take does not second-guess the answer. It is a tool to open up the debate. (PM)

Resources

At Tesco, key strategic projects are given high strategic priority, thus giving the organization a clearer focus than it might otherwise have:

> Tesco has a Customer Plan that lays out the key initiatives that must be achieved. These initiatives have well resourced project teams and receive a very high priority. (PM)

In summary, prioritization is a very important value-creating activity (for strategic thinking), and the strategic option grid in particular can play a powerful role in focusing managers on opportunities more likely to create real and sustainable shareholder value.

The key 'so-whats?' are as follows:

- Prioritization is a key vehicle for strategic thinking adding value
- But this presupposes that sufficient creativity in identifying options has been deployed.

Core process

Core processes contain categories on:

- Testing
- Facilitation
- Empirical feedback
- Strategic routines
- Communication.

Testing

Testing the strategic thinking helps to refine its value:

> A useful technique for us is a 'straw man' or an 'Aunt Sally'. A straw man is usually circulated before a workshop to kick-start a project and to start to gather the issues. The language of a straw man must be open and invite a contribution. (PM)

This shows how important it is to combine strategic thinking with innovative thinking processes, to maximize its economic value.

Facilitation

Facilitation is also seen as being generally very helpful in unleashing value at ZIFA:

> Before, we were coming up with a plan where we were pretty sure that our headings were correct, but what we were struggling to do was to get any sort of focus on the breakthrough areas. What happened on Thursday night was that our thinking became much more pinpointed on areas where we could make some extra value, to outstrip the market in some sort of

way. Where we could decide where we really, really want [laughing] to be, and make a difference, rather than just do the same things that everybody does, we might be able to do them that bit better. The focus on two or three areas was the breakthrough on Thursday night. (JR)

(Note: by 'Thursday night' JR was referring to a session facilitated by one of the co-authors.)

The above is an excellent example of where strategic thinking at an average level appears to have been raised to a higher level, and thus created significantly more value through facilitation (actually, through looking for the 'cunning plan' – see Chapter 6).

Empirical feedback

By actually implementing strategy and identifying the value added, this can add value through empirical feed-back:

It is interesting looking back. The Tesco non-food plan was based on strategic thinking. The aim of the plan was to become the positive choice for Tesco customers' non-food needs. Key issues included deciding which product categories to enter and how much space a category should receive . . .. (PM)

With the benefit of customer feedback and a trading history, space allocation is based on learning. (PM)

Strategic routines

By building in strategic thinking to organizational routines, this can help to increase its value, as evidenced by ZIFA:

And I think you almost need to make it something about how you do things in an organization. That you actually regularly go back and have those creative sessions, because you need to pull yourself out of the drudgery of the day-to-day more than we probably do. We tend to have little light bulbs that go on every year or two. I think we would benefit from making it a regular part of what we do and actually setting aside regular time for being more off-the-wall. (JR)

But at Tesco's, away-days are perceived as sometimes giving only an illusion of real strategic thinking – which should add value more on a day-to-day basis:

I think that there is a danger in leaving all strategic thought to away-days and seminars. Customer needs are changing constantly, and we are faced with options on a daily basis. 'No one tries harder for customers' is a core Tesco value. Although not necessarily a conscious thing, strategic thought and positive change are an everyday part of Tesco life. (*PM*)

So the appropriate kind of strategic routines may depend upon the experience the organization has with strategic thinking, and on its culture. For some, strategic workshops might helpfully signal 'we must do some new, different thinking', but for others this may not always be a good thing, perhaps signalling (inappropriately) that 'we are all going for a strategic holiday – for a day', and that we will not have to implement things subsequently.

Communication

Unless the strategic thinking is communicated step-by-step, its value may be diminished:

For me, strategic thinking makes sense and helps to explain decisions. Although there is also merit in the 'black box' revelation, it is riskier to invest in change that cannot be explained. (*PM*)

It is about the intuitive side, one of the Group MDs didn't know why he knew what he knew but he knew, and he would just intuitively know that we should buy that business. And he couldn't explain it to the rational colleagues that he had around him. So that inhibited his preparedness to share his thinking, because he just knew. And how many times did he make a mistake? They were minimal. But how much more could he have done [if he could have explained his intuition]? (*LK*)

The key 'so-whats?' from this section are as follows:

- Strategic thinking should always be refined, by internal critique and by the lessons from experience.
- It is at its best when it is built into regular organizational practice and culture, rather than made into peripheral, special exercises.
- Time is required to spell out the steps in the thought process.

Process drivers

'Process drivers' is an interesting section, as it drills down into many of the infrastructure issues that need to be addressed prior to getting the value out of a strategic thinking breakthrough in an organization.

This section covers:

- Leadership
- Ownership
- Agendas
- Defensive routines
- Distraction
- Time constraints
- Power (new category).

Leadership

Leadership is seen as being an important facilitator of strategic thinking:

> The people side is also an enabler, and leadership. We have a new leader in Barclays now and he is driving through a lot of change; he is an inspirational kind of character. (SL)

Ownership

At ZIFA, having the right people there (during strategic thinking) may help to capture its economic value:

> You need to have all the right people there, so they will become brought into the thinking actually at the time that it happens. And they tend to share the enthusiasm more than if it is an idea that happens at a meeting where only one or two people are present, and then you have to go through the experience of selling it and repeating the thought processes. Often that makes it die a bit; it loses spontaneity. (JR)

A lack of ownership can reduce clarity and cause dilution.

Agendas

To get maximum value from strategic thinking requires adjustment of management's agendas, as seen at Barclays:

> Dilution is quite a big issue .. ... You tend to find in organizations that there are quite a few people with a say and a voice. So they will have their pet projects, and you can have a bit of parochial influence, and this leads to dilution of outputs. (SL)

Defensive routines

Defensive routines can prove difficult, as illustrated by our Hewlett Packard respondent:

Strategic thinking can be frustrated by the team. In some cases the pace of change is going really fast. And some people say 'and this too will pass – we will drag it out as long as we can and it will have changed by the time we have to get to the end of it and have to implement it. Oh my God, this is too painful, how can I make this not happen to me'. (KS)

They say, 'let us get a bit more data'. But you have to have the courage of your own convictions. (KS)

Just often it is like marshmallows. Sometimes you have got a group of people sitting around the table like marshmallows. If you push them in they kind of blob out again. They blob about like marshmallows – it is marshmallow theory. If you hold them over the fire though you get a kind of chemical reaction. (KS)

Once again, defensive routines seem to impact covertly rather than overtly, making it slower and more difficult to turn strategic ideas into real action and change, and (by implication) reducing energy and enthusiasm.

Distraction

Both ZIFA and Lex highlight the loss of potential value through strategic thinking becoming diluted, perhaps through:

I think we don't follow through on it enough. And we try to follow-through on it in our own meetings, but you drift back. Your clever ideas and breakthroughs get a bit diluted at the next meeting that you are in, and you get very day-to-day and practical and the sales figures aren't where you want them to be. Or, right, you have got to batten down the hatches rather than taking the lid off and energizing, and that sort of thing. (JR)

We create distraction by people at the top of the organization starting new things: he will start that, and that, and that. And he will be creating distraction. (LK)

Time constraints

Without a pragmatic approach to strategic thinking, time constraints will frustrate its value:

In today's world, you know, we don't get a minute! But we can get a minute. With the e-mails and the Internet, and communication at every time of the day and night, the pace is getting faster and faster and faster – you don't get time to implement far-fetched or too academic or too theoretical ideas. You have got to be quick. *(KS)*

Power

Power, though important, is felt to be subservient to persuasion:

I don't think that strategic thinking is an exercise in power, it is an exercise in persuasion, but not power. *(KS)*

The key 'so-whats?' from this section are as follows:

■ Soft issues (like appropriate leadership, ownership, management of agendas, avoidance of defensive routines, destruction, running out of time and the inappropriate use of power, etc.) are just as important (if not even more) than the actual content of strategic thinking.
■ The outputs of strategic thinking need to be very simple and action-based, rather than complex, abstract and vague.

Supporting structure and skills

Following on from the last sentence, there is further strategic thinking infra-structure that needs putting in place.
This section covers:

■ Roles
■ Youth
■ Key appointments
■ Training and learning.

Roles

If managers see their role as doing, not as strategic thinking, they may not add value through strategic thinking:

We have a lot of people who think tactically, who are phenomenal doers. We have far fewer people who think strategically, and that would account for why our share price is where it is, why we haven't got many new technology businesses. What we are very good at is building up a body of knowledge and information and applying that. Our core competencies are in old technology things, and we do them well. [elaborates]. But what we want to be in the future is quite different to that. *(Anon)*

Youth

The length of time individuals have been in the organization, or in a particular position, might be either an enabler or a constraint of strategic thinking:

> You have a lot of long service [people], you have got traditional ways of doing things, and that can inhibit things. This constraint is diminishing because we are recruiting different sorts of people. (*LK*)

Key appointments

A key area (at Lex and Tesco) that might help to encourage strategic thinking is for key appointments to be made that will actively promote it:

> The last three appointments are people with sales and marketing backgrounds – who understand service delivery, and who are not [ex] Finance Directors. (*LK*)

> At Tesco we try to recruit people who share our values, which requires conceptual skills. (*PM*)

Training and learning

Training and learning might support strategic thinking skills (for example, those associated with leadership), providing the other parts of its supporting infrastructure are in place and are working well:

> Leadership is very, very important in strategic thinking. The previous leadership programme was around getting people to understand what leadership is about. The new programme is around leaders, and around managing change. We haven't had to do that in the past, but now we have to change. (*LK*)

> An enabler is the recognition of strategic thinking as an essential tool in the organization, and recruiting with the appropriate skills and training. (*SL*)

The key 'so-whats?' from this section are as follows:

- Strategic thinking needs to be seen as an essential part of a manager's identity, rather than a peripheral, nice-to-do perhaps once-a-year.
- All appointments that entail an element of strategic thinking need to be screened for that capability.

Supporting processes

This section covers:

- Project management
- Financial analysis
- Recognition
- Mentoring.

Project management

Project management is a complex area, and may not add value if implemented inappropriately. Project management might not necessarily help strategic thinking if it is focused primarily on just starting up new initiatives rather than on finishing what is in the pipeline:

> We have a lot of initiatives, projects, whatever, because we don't have strong project management skills. We are very imaginative – we start things, lots and lots of things – but very little actually gets completed. We don't see the value of these. (LK)

Project management also thus often requires a better process than previously – as at Tesco:

> As Tesco becomes more diverse, cross-functional projects are increasingly important. Cross-functional projects are not easy to deliver, and require effective sponsorship. We assemble a team to attack an opportunity, and then we move them on. (PM)

(Indeed, since 1996 Tesco has applied strategic thinking to its project management process through using a number of the implementation techniques that were expanded upon in Chapters 6 and 7.)

> If you try to do change on a business-as-usual basis, then you have people working part-time on it. People close to the business are essential for developing strategy, but they often don't have the experience to implement it. (SL)

However, at ZIFA there are concerns about project management resulting in overload – such are the organizational time constraints often in force:

> I think that's where it might get to become too difficult and then maybe you can potentially lose the value that you might have had. In fact, does it add workload, and I don't think it necessarily does mean that if you are doing it

'instead of'. But if you are making it into some kind of project-managed situation, then that does add more [difficulty]." (JR)

But Barclays' project management is seen as absolutely vital to help implement the strategy.

Conventional project management is perceived as being insufficient in itself. It also needs an injection of strategic thinking skills at a micro-level. (See Grundy and Brown, 2002a, for a practicable process.)

More effective project management thus may need to:

■ Incorporate strategic thinking as a more integral process
■ Necessitate (rather than being purely linear, detailed, and mechanistic) a much more fluid approach to applying project management principles – and an intuitive one.

Financial analysis

Financial analysis can provide an important steer to focus strategic thinking on areas of greatest value:

It also depends on what the organization requires in terms of payback and proving things like lack of ability to take risks. In any strategy there should be an element of real risk. (LK)

This picture is mirrored at Barclays, and has been assimilated within a process of 'managing for economic value' (with short- and longer-term trade-offs):

The economic profit target is a constraint, but it also puts the focus, the target that everyone tests their ideas against. (SL)

Whilst managing for value appears to be a helpful way of addressing the short- versus longer-term dilemma, it also poses new challenges for managers. These include:

■ Being creative in strategic thinking (otherwise it captures, at best, average economic value)
■ Managing and juggling with resource constraints, to deploy resources in order to get maximum value leverage.

Recognition

Recognition processes are also seen (for example at Tesco) as essential in encouraging managers to think strategically:

> Strategic thinking is all very well and good, but it is also vital to have effective performance management to support it. You have to ensure that people who deliver change through projects can have as fulfilling a career as traditional line managers. (PM)

Mentoring

Finally, mentoring might also be a helpful supporting process, although this requires finding an appropriately skilled, supportive, and politically neutral adviser – even someone from outside the organization:

> You do need someone to bounce your ideas off, because you need some help to get out of the context into a more objective way of thinking. Or just to get somebody to give you a different view. (KS)

> You could use somebody from inside the company I guess, a mentor or a coach. A relationship and trust would be needed. But I probably couldn't have dealt with that [specific] issue without getting some partiality, and avoid potential leakage as well. With most things which are really important, news travels really fast in our organization. You don't want to be sharing your thought process with someone who can pass on what your thinking is. You could find that the ideas turn into something which you hadn't intended, or might get misinterpreted, or which have implications in the business – you need to get outside. (KS)

The key 'so-what?' from this section is:

- Strategic thinking is not a stand-alone process at all, but needs to be married with operational, human resource and financial processes.

Soft value

This section covers:

- Clarity (of thought)
- Confidence
- Anxiety and stress
- Personal value
- Excitement.

Clarity

Once again, clarity is viewed as being a very important element of value. At Tesco, clarity has had a big positive effect, especially in helping make strategies happen (implementation) and in increasing organization speed:

> Tesco's success is based on clarity of what needs to be done and a personal responsibility to take the simple vision and turn it into reality. (PM)

At ZIFA, strategic thinking simply helps to link actions back to core objectives, and to providing a clearer focus generally:

> Strategic thinking adds value by linking what you are trying to achieve, i.e. the objective, and what you are doing. And I know that sounds really basic, but that's what it is to me. People go off doing things, which don't necessarily take them closer to their objective. (JR)

> Strategic thinking links the two things. And it also makes you think more creatively about how you can achieve the objective. (JR)

Great clarity is certainly one of the very big ways in which an HR strategy can add value – otherwise its purpose, and priorities, programmes and projects are primarily emergent.

Confidence

Linked to clarity is the category of confidence. At Tesco, confidence adds value by turning the latent value of a strategic thought into real value through implementation:

> Financial services are a good example of where Tesco has followed the customer into a new market. Having a practical approach has given Tesco the confidence to try things. (PM)

Anxiety and stress

The following example at Hewlett Packard highlights the severity of the effects of anxiety and stress when there are blockages in much-needed strategic thinking:

> It just completely wipes you out, in terms of your ability to concentrate on the day-job. And in my job a lot of it is about motivating people. People read every little sign, and if your mind is somewhere else, they know straight away. They interpret the signals as all sorts of things. So, that was worrying, and most of my team had spotted it. They were engaged in it, and the whole organization became paralysed. This had been going on for several weeks. (KS)

Personal value

The Hewlett Packard manager also illustrates how important strategic thinking has been in shaping her career:

Well, helicopter thinking has done me good, because it has helped make lots of career moves for me [laughs]. So, somewhere along the line one must see some correlation. I think helicopter thinking must have been one of the contributory factors. There are not a lot of people around who can balance the strategic and the tactical. There are a lot of people who can be very tactical, and there is another group of people who can be quite strategic. But getting the two things to come together is quite difficult. (KS)

Excitement

Strategic thinking can add value through generating a state of excitement – a quality possibly not easily found in many larger organizations today. Excitement (if suitably channelled) can then add value by translating into energy into action!

But I think it is hard to replicate the excitement that you feel about finding the breakthrough. Actually that can be quite time-consuming, to take them through the process which you have been through, especially if people are remote, and that can be quite hard work, getting them to the same place in their thought processes. (JR)

The key 'so-whats?' from this section are as follows:

- Considerable economic value can be gained by aligning and harmonizing managers' mental and emotional states about strategic issues, particularly reducing anxiety and stress, and building sufficient confidence to act.
- Another aspect of its value is to stimulate and focus a sense of excitement that will energize both specific individuals, and also the wider organization.

On the latter point, however, important caveats are that this excitement is not built up for inappropriate action, and that this state may wear off quite rapidly and may need further stimulus.

Summary of case study

To summarize again from the senior managers' interviews, we see the following.

Meaning

The words 'strategic' and 'strategy' are somewhat ambiguous, and warrant more precise definition. 'Strategies' themselves need to be broken down into macro-, mini- and micro-levels. Strategy is not easily differentiated from tactics in many managers' minds, and any true overlap between these two domains does confuse managers. This calls for a clear, agreed, and shared definition of what both 'strategy' and 'strategic' actually mean in the organization.

Business value

The business value of strategic thinking is manifold, but is often easier to harvest for detergent value and where change is involved, rather than for entirely new strategies.

Speed (of decision-making) and change are also generally perceived to be key areas of possible value.

Context

The context of the strategy is seen as a very influential factor, partly as a constraint (owing to the extent of pressures impacting on the business from many directions both externally and internally, e.g. due to the legacy). Such pressures do, however, put a premium value (if not an imperative) on strategic thinking.

Thought value

An emerging major theme in our research was the need for managers to give themselves much more thinking space – through strategic thinking as found, for example, in 'helicopter thinking'.

By giving a clearer thinking framework – particularly about competitive advantage – strategic thinking can add very tangible value to managers.

Creative thinking, particularly in terms of thinking about the art of the possible and also imagining specific futures, was potentially of particularly high economic value.

Strategic thinking was also felt to be best incorporated within and integrated into implementation, rather than being seen as 'blue sky'.

Prioritization

Prioritization was also seen as a huge problem for managers (as it is equally for HR managers), and as an area where strategic thinking could add considerable economic value (this was especially true in dealing with the problem of optimizing resource allocation, for example, by using the strategic option grid and/or AID analysis).

Core process

Facilitation was seen as a very important process, incorporating strategic thinking into everyday routines (we will go into this further in Chapter 13).

Also, without adequate communication much of the value of strategic thinking might never actually be realized.

Process drivers

Leadership was seen as a very important ingredient in facilitating strategic thinking – and especially so in helping to overcome defensive routines and to arrive a more strategic set of agendas.

Furthermore, managers could easily find that they had had a strategic thought stream but that their outputs had been diluted by organizational distraction and time constraints.

Managers also generally felt that gaining ownership was very important, which was unsurprising.

Supporting structure and skills

There was a significant stress on redefining senior managers' roles to make them (genuinely) more focused on the strategic (implying that this should be a key area for focus within HR strategies).

To help managers become more strategic, it was felt that younger blood was very important – along with appropriate intervention in the making of key senior appointments, and in supporting training and learning of senior managers. Notably, training and learning were seen as a small (if important) part of the equation. (This contrasts with some of those academics interviewed in parallel [the data are not presented here for the sake of brevity], who emphasized the significance of participating in MBA and similar level executive development programmes.) The authors believe that value creation (or destruction) through making a particularly important senior appointment is a very potentially significant issue within HR strategy. (This echoes the case of Arsenal Football Club in Chapter 1.)

Supporting processes

There was also a very interesting diversity of views from the managers on how (if at all) project management might help. Some felt that strategic ideas needed to be project-managed right through implementation in order to extract their value. One particular manager felt that introducing project management could be counterproductive, as in her experience it tended mainly to increase workload rather than to accelerate its implementation (but this might be a company-culture specific phenomenon).

Financial analysis was another mixed bag, with the Barclays manager suggesting that it could be very helpful (in targeting strategic thinking on value), but at the same time could constrain thinking. It was felt that recognition systems needed to encourage strategic thinking more directly to make it effective. Again, its role seems to be a function of specific organizational style – where an organization has a particular focus on 'value-based management', on balance this might well be a factor.

Finally, mentoring offered a useful opportunity to support the strategic thinking process, although there were some perceived difficulties in finding an impartial and competent mentor.

Soft value

Strategic thinking was felt to add considerable value by its direct impact on the individual – for example in giving them greater clarity and more confidence, and also by alleviating any anxiety and stress that had built up.

Overall lessons from the case study

This final section of the case study considers the key themes that came up, and the key implications for strategic thinking generally and for further enquiry. It also includes our final conclusion, returning to the question of 'what is the value of strategic thinking?'

Figure 12.4 shows us the full framework of influences on the value of strategic thinking. A number of things stand out from this:

1. Strategic thinking itself is a complex process, and one that has previously perhaps not been well understood.
2. There is a considerable diversity of ways in which strategic thinking can add (economic) value. Analysing these has now given us a way of targeting, monitoring and controlling whether it is actually adding value, and if it is not adding value, then why not. Each category of value explored gives a different area of value creation.
3. As strategic thinking is often associated with higher-level thinking, it may not be so obvious that it can be targeted economically. However, by taking it down to 'sets' or 'mini' strategies and breakthroughs, this should be possible. Also because many of these areas of value are at least partially intangible, the routes towards harvesting the value have perhaps not been very well explored.
4. Finally, getting the economic value out of strategic thinking requires considerable alignment of support processes in the organization, otherwise its latent value may never be captured.

Several key themes emerged from our study, including:

- The ambiguity of 'strategic thinking'
- Levels of strategic thinking

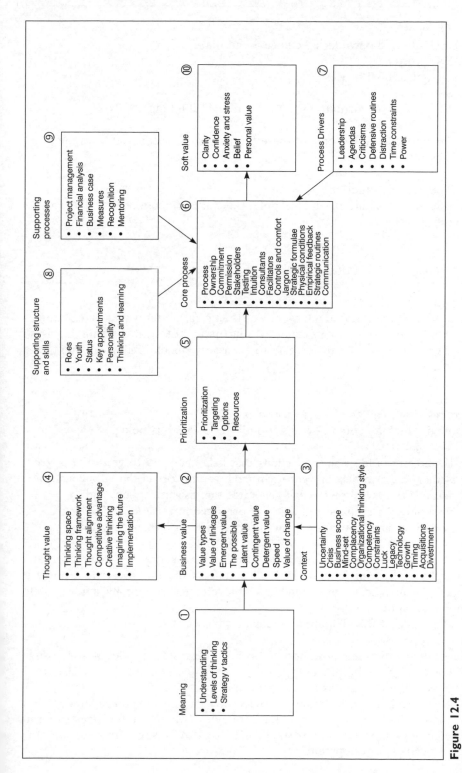

Figure 12.4
The value of strategic thinking: the big picture

① Meaning
- Understanding
- Levels of thinking
- Strategy v tactics

④ Thought value
- Thinking space
- Thinking framework
- Thought alignment
- Competitive advantage
- Creative thinking
- Imagining the future
- Implementation

② Business value
- Value types
- Value of linkages
- Emergent value
- The possible
- Latent value
- Contingent value
- Detergent value
- Speed
- Value of change

③ Context
- Uncertainty
- Crisis
- Business scope
- Mind-set
- Complacency
- Organizational thinking style
- Competency
- Constraints
- Luck
- Legacy
- Technology
- Growth
- Timing
- Acquisitions
- Divestment

⑤ Prioritization
- Prioritization
- Targeting
- Options
- Resources

⑧ Supporting structure and skills
- Ro es
- Youth
- Status
- Key appointments
- Personality
- Thinking and learning

⑨ Supporting processes
- Project management
- Financial analysis
- Business case
- Measures
- Recognition
- Mentoring

⑥ Core process
- Process
- Ownership
- Commitment
- Permission
- Stakeholders
- Testing
- Intuition
- Consultants
- Facilitators
- Jargon
- Controls and comfort
- Strategic formulae
- Physical conditions
- Empirical feedback
- Strategic routines
- Communication

⑩ Soft value
- Clarity
- Confidence
- Anxiety and stress
- Belief
- Personal value

⑦ Process Drivers
- Leadership
- Agendas
- Criticisms
- Defensive routines
- Distraction
- Time constraints
- Power

- Thought value
- Pressure and bewildering choice – the maze
- Prioritization
- Organizational process
- Soft value
- Vicious versus virtuous cycles (of strategic thinking).

The implications of some of these themes are now covered from the point of view of:

- The current situation
- The future situation and its potential value (including key linkages to other themes).

The ambiguity of strategic thinking

The current situation

A number of the respondents were less than clear about what strategic thinking was, and equally of its value. If the nature of strategic thinking is so relatively ambiguous, this is likely to be a very major inhibitor to capturing its value.

The future situation and its potential value

Strategic thinking could now potentially be defined as being:

> The stream of ideas and reflections that help managers to grasp the bigger picture, and also help prevent them from getting lost in the wrong kind of detail. It is a fluid process that generates the insights, options and breakthroughs required to move the organization at all levels forward through to implementation in an uncertain and changing environment.

Note that we have added 'at all levels' in the last sentence, and also 'through to implementation'. This reflects the findings that strategy is applicable at macro-, mini- and micro-levels, and is equally applicable to implementation.

The value of this definition would be that:

- Strategic thinking now occurs both within and outside of the formal strategic planning process
- It is therefore seen as being applicable at any level
- It is associated with streams of ideas (however partial and isolated) rather than necessarily with completed strategies (we call these 'lines of strategic thinking' – see Figure 12.5 for a visual representation – for an area of business development).

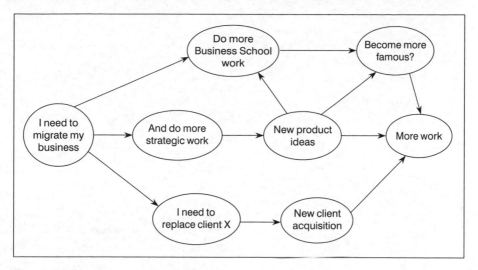

Figure 12.5
Lines of strategic thinking – an example

- It is linked with the idea of 'helicopter thinking'
- It is focused on choice (options) and action directed at breakthroughs (implementation).

The key linkages to our other strategic thinking themes include the following:

1. Because 'strategic thinking' has an unclear meaning, it is not necessarily associated with smaller-scale issues (mini- or micro-strategies).
2. Its ambiguity also hinders targeting its economic value.
3. The focus on 'breakthroughs' would help with incorporating it into prioritization (see Figure 12.6).
4. As it is now explicitly relevant to the individual, soft value may be enhanced (see Figure 12.7).
5. A more practical and immediate meaning might encourage a shift from a vicious to a virtuous cycle of strategic thinking (Figures 12.8 and 12.9 – see later).

Levels of strategic thinking

The current situation

It was felt by interviewees that strategic thinking might be held back because of the lack of clarity of strategy versus tactics. Also, whilst strategy might be clear at one level, it might be unclear at other levels. For example, there might be a clear business strategy but an unclear corporate strategy, or a specific breakthrough project might have a clear strategy but the business strategy may be unclear. This might result in considerable confusion amongst managers.

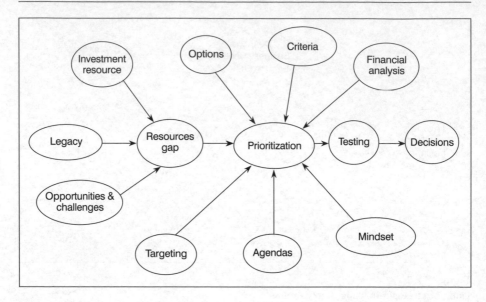

Figure 12.6
Prioritization

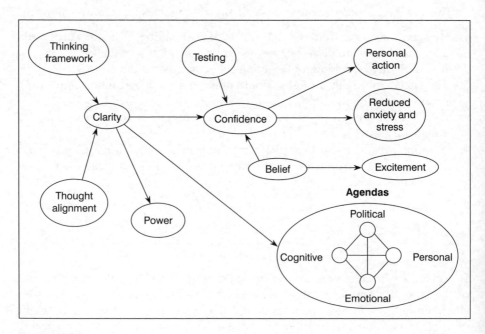

Figure 12.7
Soft value

The future situation – and its potential value

By linking the various levels of strategy explicitly (through the strategic thinking process), it might become easier to manage and extract economic value. This would occur through improved alignment of that thinking – across both issues and organizational levels. Indeed, a constant focus ought to be (in senior managers' minds) on thought alignment as a team, which would also help strategic team-building (see Chapter 11).

Thought value

The current situation

Our key findings here were that:

1. Strategic thoughts have a highly contingent value. Because of the fragmentary and incomplete nature of existing thought process, much of the value is currently lost – the process being hit and (mostly) miss – and is often perceived to be down to 'luck', owing to a number of weaker links (see below).
2. Weaker links appear to be:
   - Getting the more creative process going (which may conflict with mind-set, thinking style, culture and legacy) in the first place
   - Providing the thinking space – the appropriate physical conditions and initial stimulus to get managers to think higher-level and/or differently
   - Distilling the ideas into workable breakthroughs
   - Gaining buy-in
   - Securing sufficient resources (to harvest its value)
   - Mobilizing implementation effectively
   - Coping with jargon and with generic strategic prescriptions that may not be appropriate
   - Not understanding the potential and positive role of intuition.

The future situation and its potential value

By more systematic attention to the process of crafting strategic thoughts into an economically valuable form, strategic thinking could become more effective. Also, by increasing the likelihood and extent of business and personal pay-offs, strategic thinking might also become more fully brought into everyday routines.

Pressure and bewildering choice – the maze

The current situation

The interviews with the various managers highlighted graphically the difficulties of coping with change – from all directions. This makes prioritization difficult, and also undermines the preparedness to implement the strategy.

The future situation – and its potential value

Whilst there are no ready remedies for resolving these difficulties, improving the strategic thinking capability throughout the organization (and not merely at the top) could help managers to find their way through the maze more effectively. This could occur, for example, through:

1. Making key appointments, with a greater bias towards those who can think strategically and have a more strategically orientated personality.
2. Strategic thinking and mentoring.
3. Effective facilitation (see Chapter 13).
4. Bringing strategic thinking into regular routines, for example into project management.
5. Recognizing excellent strategic thinking – and its execution through breakthroughs – more formally, and rewarding it.

Soft value

The current situation

Soft value (for example clarity, belief, and reduced anxiety and stress) was seen as an important area of value by both academics and managers. Whilst clearly some soft value was being harvested, there was a lot of further potential to extract value from strategic thinking, both by individuals and by the organization generally.

The future situation and its potential value

In future, it might be possible to add more value by managers at a micro-level seeing soft value (and not just business value – and thought value) as being a primary target of strategic thinking.

In particular, the refinement and clarification of agendas – at cognitive, political, personal and emotional levels – would be seen as most helpful. More specifically, this would significantly enhance the perceived economic pay-off for strategic thinking, and thus the probability of managers engaging in it. This in turn would help them devote more thinking space to it, and also help the shift from the vicious to virtuous cycles of strategic thinking (see below).

A more conscious quest for the soft value of strategic thinking might also reduce anxiety and stress (and enhance the sense of excitement), thereby increasing organizational energy and the preparedness to act. It might also increase speed, which was viewed by both managers and academics as being an important benefit of strategic thinking.

Key linkages to other themes include:

1. Where soft value is actually captured, this might encourage a more strategically focused thinking style.
2. The vicious cycle of strategic thinking could shift to the virtuous.

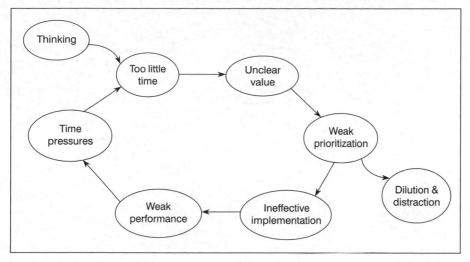

Figure 12.8
Vicious cycle of strategic thinking

Vicious versus virtuous cycles

The current situation

In most of the cases studied (except at Tesco and, to a lesser extent, Barclays), organizations seem to be locked into the vicious rather than the virtuous cycle of strategic thinking.

In the vicious cycle (Figure 12.8) there is relatively little effective strategic thinking. This results in unclear value, weak prioritization, dilution and destruction, and weak implementation and weaker results. This puts additional time pressures on managers, discouraging them from actually doing strategic thinking, thus completing the loop.

The future situation and its potential future

Potentially, in the future it might become possible to achieve a good alignment within the system of strategic thinking to the point where managers appreciate what it can do for them – at both business and personal levels. Besides this, by spending more time doing strategic thinking they might then become more effective, thus saving time otherwise wasted, and thereby freeing up more time for strategic thinking – thus creating a virtuous cycle (Figure 12.9).

Study conclusion – what is the value of strategic thinking?

Going back to our key question of 'what is the value of strategic thinking?', it was discovered that the economic value had previously been relatively

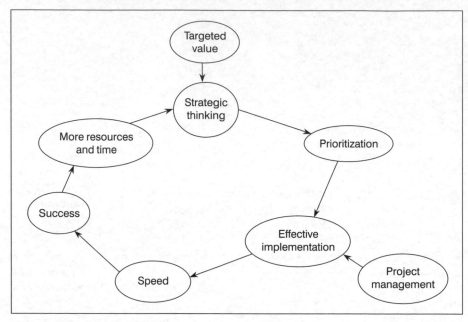

Figure 12.9
Virtuous cycle of strategic thinking

unclear. Not only was the strategic thinking process (and its underlying influences) not very well understood by individual managers, but even the definition of 'strategic thinking' itself was ambiguous.

Economic value can come from:

■ Business value, for example as deliberate strategy, emergent strategy or through change
■ Thought value, through creating alignment within managers' thoughts
■ Soft value, through building confidence, reducing anxiety, and through building appropriately focused excitement
■ Prioritization (see below).

Managers were also found largely to be in a maze of strategic bewilderment when decision-making. Here they faced prioritization issues without a very clear strategic thinking process, and with one where resource allocation and other pressures and constraints had a tendency to drive out the more creative aspects of the process. Indeed, it was not even particularly clear from the interviews as to who should be involved in the strategic thinking process, when and how, and whether it did or did not apply equally to implementation. This is a strong hint to organizations that they should explicitly communicate that strategic thinking is something that can and should be done at all levels, by giving people the encouragement, permission and thought-space to do it. Where any boundaries on strategic thinking *are* set, these need to be well communicated and justified.

So whilst strategic thinking might potentially add considerable value, the very partial, isolated and fragmented way in which it was currently manifest and disseminated meant that much of that potential value was lost. This potential value was further dissipated by softer constraints, such as the organizational thinking style, mind-set, leadership, dilution of outputs, organizational destruction, and a lack of the direct personal pay-offs of doing it. The 'so-what?' from this is that organizations need to question seriously whether they are genuinely interested in exploiting strategic thinking, and be more realistic about what needs to change to achieve this.

This suggests a useful equation for targeting the value of strategic thinking (derived from expectancy theory) of:

Effort = perceived probability of success × (business + thought value + soft value)

or

$$E = PV$$

where E = effort, P = perceived probability of success, and V = economic value.

A useful summing-up of the answer to the question 'what is the value of strategic thinking?' is that 'it is highly contingent, but potentially, with full organizational alignment, could be huge'.

This chapter gives plenty of pointers in terms of what needs to change in order to get real economic value out of strategic thinking. Unfortunately, organizations that are incapable of seizing this challenge could well end up in the following situation, depicted in Sun Tzu's *The Art of War*:

> So when the front is prepared, the rear is lacking, and when the rear is prepared the front is lacking. Preparedness on the left means lack on the right, preparedness on the right means lack on the left. Preparedness everywhere means lack everywhere.

War cannot be waged without some sort of target measures, so why do strategic thinking without targeting its economic value? Clearly, getting the economic value out of strategic thinking should be a major theme in the future HR strategies of leading organizations.

CONCLUSION

Strategic thinking is a prominent area for HR strategy and consultants to focus on. However, many organizations fail to address this, perhaps because it is assumed that managers do think strategically, or because it is labelled as an area that it is just too difficult, ambiguous and complex to address.

Strategic thinking initiatives are best begun by identifying the economic value that is required from them. Once that is clear, it is important to look at the various factors that are preconditions of strategic thinking adding value first, rather than laying on a smattering of *ad hoc* strategic workshops.

Once these various factors have been well understood (see Figure 12.1), then it is time to look at the various options for intervention to support it. These might include:

- Strategic thinking training (either for individuals or groups of managers, in company), hopefully focusing on live business issues, but where the main focus is learning.
- Strategic workshops aimed at addressing (and resolving) key business issues and dilemmas, where the primary focus is business (or HR strategy), the secondary focus is acquiring a process, and perhaps a tertiary purpose is learning.
- One-to-one support (or 'strategic coaching'), with key individuals facing very major challenges at MD/Director/Senior Manager levels.
- The transfer of the strategic thinking process, of a generic kind (for example as at Tesco) or for specific issues (as at the Royal Bank of Scotland Group for HR strategy, or at Nokia and Microsoft for implementation), or for scenarios (as at HSBC).
- The project management process (see Chapter 7) and facilitation support for these projects.

Key points

The key points from this chapter include the following:

- Strategic thinking can add distinctive economic value, particularly through thinking about the art of the possible
- Strategic thinking can also add considerable economic value by simply speeding up organizational decision-making and action
- The legacy from the past can unfortunately prove to be a major burden on strategic thinking, and needs to be let go of
- Strategic thinking can also add value through a widespread obsession with creating competitive advantage
- Imagining the future is one of the distinctive ways in which strategic thinking can add economic value
- Strategic thinking frequently requires facilitation to draw out its full value
- Where you put a value on strategic thoughts that you have had, this closes the loop of empirical feedback and is likely then to encourage further strategic thinking
- Away-days or strategic workshops can degenerate into becoming more strategic routines and rituals, and may supplant the important activity of thinking strategically as a continuous process

- Mentoring can help significantly to encourage, reinforce and amplify strategic thinking
- Confidence is one of the absolutely central ways in which strategic thinking can add value
- Because strategic thinking is apparently an intangible, its value is infrequently targeted; nevertheless, this value ought to be very clearly and specifically targeted
- Strategic thinking does have a clear meaning, but its present ambiguity dilutes a lot of its value
- Strategic thinking can add value at a variety of levels, and its value at lower levels can be considerable
- The value of strategic thinking is manifest in a variety of forms, from emergent and detergent value (sorting out past mistakes) through to its value in steering change
- Strategic thinking has value simply through clarifying thinking – this requires sufficient thinking space, and a framework for understanding how strategic ideas fit in through alignment of thoughts and through genuinely creative thinking
- Strategic thinking is of major help in prioritization – especially of key options
- Unless the appropriate support processes are in place organizationally, the value of strategic thought will be rapidly dissipated
- This requires skilful management of softer factors, such as agendas, and top management permission
- To encourage greater strategic thinking demands considerable organizational change, and more roles for younger, thrusting people.

In conclusion, there are very major opportunities as well as constraints in getting economic value out of strategic thinking. Whilst strategic thinking can add value in a huge diversity of ways, there is a major challenge in aligning the thoughts, behaviours, practices, and support processes of the organization in order to deliver this value.

A major constraint is the ambiguity of what 'strategic thinking' actually means. This ought to be an easy constraint to remedy, albeit one that requires extensive education throughout the management community. Perhaps strategy academics generally have some significant role in this?

PART 4

Putting HR strategy to work

CHAPTER 13

Becoming your own HR strategy consultant

INTRODUCTION

This final chapter looks at how you can develop as an HR strategy consultant, which draws together many of the process threads of this book.

Learning to think strategically is just one of the qualifying steps to becoming your own strategy consultant in the round. In addition to being able to understand, diagnose and resolve key strategic issues effectively, you will also need to be able to accomplish the more difficult task of carrying others within the organization with that thinking. Paradoxically, this can sometimes mean holding back from advancing your own strategic thinking too far – otherwise it may take too long for others to catch up. Also, there is a very real risk that you might close your mind off to thoughts and perceptions that may come from others.

In addition, your mind-set might be one of the Holy Grail strategy – that there is one single right and best strategy in any given business context. Usually there is more than one good strategy – and even where there is only one, there is invariably more than one way of implementing it.

In the final analysis, the process of strategy is more important than its actual content. If you are prepared to work hard to get the process right, then the content (and in particular the outputs) of strategic thinking will largely look after itself.

In this chapter we look at how to plan, implement and review a process of strategic thinking within your own team or organization.

THE ROLE OF THE HR STRATEGY CONSULTANT

Whilst there has been much criticism of the role of strategy consultants generally in the past, nevertheless it is unlikely that they would exist if they did not have a function. There are many that doubt their virtues, sometimes because of valuable scepticism and sometimes because of cynicism or envy. However, just because strategy consultants seem to have a function currently, there is no reason why they have to be a permanent feature of management. Indeed, it is our contention that at least some of their expertise can (and perhaps should) be exercised by managers. So, before we look at how the manager can be his own HR strategy consultant, let us look at how strategy consultants can add value generally.

The key ways in which an external HR strategy consultant can add value include the following thirteen activities:

1. Acting as an independent sounding board
2. Helping to set the strategic agenda
3. Asking the right questions – generally
4. Asking the questions that others dare not ask
5. Providing a process for thinking
6. Collating and interpreting data
7. Facilitating the thinking process
8. Generating or providing the teams with 'out-of-the-box' ideas
9. Acting as a catalyst for decision-making and for action
10. Critiquing the output constructively
11. Helping to identify blind spots
12. Providing energy and enthusiasm
13. Being a symbolic presence – to help people think and behave differently.

Some of the above activities may seem relatively self-evident – such as providing a process for thinking, and collecting and interpreting data. Others might be less obvious, such as the latter two points of providing energy and enthusiasm and being a symbolic presence. Being a symbolic presence is an interesting activity – this involves value being added by simply being there. Minimalistically, this presence sends signals that something different can happen and that it can happen in a different way from normal.

Also, note that some consultancies will focus on a relatively small number of the above activities – for example, on collecting and interpreting data. In our own case we would probably rarely be involved in collecting raw data ourselves, as we work principally as process consultants. This means that we primarily add value by facilitating the strategic thinking process. This is in contrast to the expert consultant, who is hired primarily because of his or her content expertise.

One area that we have not mentioned above, but that is often commented on by sceptical managers, is:

■ Helping to provide an official stamp on decisions effectively taken already by top management.

Whilst management is a political process, and this is not something that consultants can escape, this does not mean that the consultant should be used in a covert, political role.

Turning back to the role of the internal strategy consultant, all of the thirteen roles can be exercised by an internal manager. The activities that an internal manager might find it harder to fulfil are:

- Asking the questions that others dare not ask
- Critiquing the output constructively
- Being a symbolic presence.

Whilst not impossible, the challenge in these areas is perhaps greater for internal managers. This challenge puts more stress on their self-confidence, and indeed on their courage. Depending upon the situation, this may mean that internal strategy consultants may need to put the process first and thoughts about their longer-term career in the organization second.

Table 13.1
Internal strategy consultant questionnaire

	Very strong 5	Strong 4	Average 3	Weak 2	Very weak 1
What is my natural ability to see the very big picture?					
What is my ability to think outside the box?					
What is my ability in devising management processes?					
What is my level of political skills?					
What is my level of interpersonal skills – at senior levels?					
What is my ability in asking the right questions, and at the right time?					
What are my listening skills ability, and powers of observation?					
What is my ability to cope with the ambiguous and uncertain?					
What is my ability to handle personal stress under difficult challenges?					
What is the level of my all-round analytical ability?					
What is the level of my communication ability?					
What is the level of my own persistence and drive?					
Total score					

Paradoxically, success in this role is the ideal preparation for becoming a top manager. Alternatively, if managers succeed in this difficult role then there should be no shortage of job offers elsewhere!

Besides playing an official (internal) consulting role, every manager can also adopt this role by stealth, or informally. Consultancy facilitation ought to be an integral part of a senior manager's skill-set.

To check out whether you have the natural capability to become an internal strategy consultant (whether formally or informally), first complete the questionnaire in Table 13.1.

Next, calculate your overall score out of 60:

Score	Assessment
50–60	You might consider setting up your own consultancy (after some experience, internally or with another firm)
40–50	This may be a full-time internal role for you
30–40	You can add a lot of value through merely internal consulting by stealth
20–30	Don't give up! Work out a number of developmental activities to move this forward (especially pinpointing key projects or meetings as the vehicle for consultancy-by-stealth)

CULTURAL IMPLICATIONS OF STRATEGIC THINKING

This section looks first at the more general implications of having a strategic thinking culture, and then turns to HR in particular.

Strategic thinking probably does not come naturally to most organizations. Most companies are caught up in tactical everyday pressures, and the attention is therefore on managing a kaleidoscope of horribly fragmented issues (as seen in Chapter 11). This haphazard process is sometimes punctuated by attempts to take a quick look at the bigger picture, rapidly replaced by immersion in the detail once again. This situation is like letting air force trainees loose flying a helicopter for the weekend, but telling them to save fuel and that this can be accomplished by not taking off. Instead of soaring rapidly to their destination they therefore drive out of the airbase and onto the local motorway, doing a steady 65 kph. When stuck in a traffic jam they take off temporarily, but then land on the other side to resume their journey in the slow lane.

Whilst being overtly absurd, this helicopter scenario is precisely what many attempts at strategic thinking amount to. Because it is not apparent what strategic thinking can achieve, first attempts at it are woefully under-resourced. Consider the case illustration of a major European institution as an example.

Case study: a major European institution begins to 'think strategically'

One of the co-authors was recently asked to facilitate a strategic thinking workshop for a major European institution. The institution is very large and complex, and the 'mission' was to run a strategic thinking workshop pilot within a specific business area.

The author (acting as consultant) first suggested that it would be immensely valuable if the workshop programme were to be tailored to the institution's context, and to focus on specific issues. A visit was proposed, but on budget grounds this did not happen. Instead, the tailoring of design was done through a 15-minute telephone conversation, conducted partly by mobile telephone in a Cornish pub, and partly outside in the rain (as the signal was inadequate).

Notwithstanding this somewhat inadequate preparation (which also ruled out doing meaningful pre-work) the workshop ran exceptionally well. However, although it ran well, a number of constraining forces impeded its effectiveness:

■ The workshop was held in a very exclusive hotel, but in a conference room with no natural light (a 'strategic dungeon'). The consequence of this was that the participants rapidly lost energy and momentum in the afternoon.

■ The participants were served a three-course lunch with rich food and two or three glasses of wine. This took an hour and ten minutes, prohibiting any other form of exercise or fresh air (other than taken for smoking purposes).

■ The purpose of the workshop was not positioned internally at the start, even though the business unit's general manager was present as a participant. Presumably his (laudable) intention was to be 'one of the lads', but this meant that when difficult or sensitive issues came up the facilitator had to leave them substantially in suspense.

■ At the end of the workshop, the facilitator posed an open question as to what they might do next with the process, and once again there was no take-up on this theme. (This was notwithstanding the fact that the group had used the Champneys case illustrated in Chapter 8).

The above case is by no means unrepresentative of most companies' first attempts at strategic thinking. Had this been our own direct client (as it was the work came through another channel), we would have insisted on more suitable preparation and follow-through.

The case highlights the importance of getting some physical hygiene factors (the room) and the positioning of any strategic event right. In the above case study it was as if the client had not even begun to realize that to introduce strategic thinking effectively in an organization requires a considerable culture shift. It cannot be achieved with a quickie, one-off strategic event (which inevitably becomes more a form of strategic entertainment rather than something that shifts the centre of gravity of thought in an organization).

To examine what we mean by a strategic thinking culture, let us therefore reflect on what it might look like. Key characteristics might include the following:

- Key issues are not only clear on the top management's strategic agenda, but are also openly discussed and reflected upon within the levels of the organization.
- All staff (at whatever level) are encouraged to do strategic thinking at their own level – albeit within the bigger picture context.
- Strategic thinking is genuinely prized within the organization and is rewarded not merely through organizational progression but by individual recognition – both financially and non-financially.
- Strategic thinking is regarded as a critical management competence, and is supported through both individual and group training.
- Key teams within the business take relatively regular days out to address emerging strategic issues and also to think strategically about implementation.
- There is a culture of asking the unconventional question about 'why are we doing things in this way?', and a recognized process for dealing with new ideas once they come up.
- Key management processes are infused with strategic thinking rather than acting as brutal enemies. Particular processes that are aligned include business planning and budgeting, management reporting, senior management meetings, organizational change and restructuring, cost management initiatives, and performance reviews.

Is this a fabulous dream or a reality in your organization? Probably the former. Certainly most companies seem to be a long way from this ideal at present. Despite the hype of the learning organization over the last decade or so (see Chapter 10), relatively little progress appears to have been made in terms of injecting strategic thinking into core management culture.

So where does a strategic thinking culture need to begin? Well, we will avoid the conventional prescription that:

Strategic thinking must begin at the very top of the organization

if only because it may not take root initially at that strata. Sometimes it can blossom at the level just below board level, through ambitious, thrusting managers seeking to initiate development or change. This, we have observed, is frequently supported by a sympathetic and eager HR director, or other senior HR development staff.

Once some strategic thinking has been done and has borne fruit, then this can spread naturally both horizontally (to other senior managers with similar agendas) and vertically and directly to the top team. In our experience, in many instances the Board has seen successful attempts at deliberate strategic thinking lower down the organization as a significant opportunity for themselves – for strategic thinking offers the top team a welcome escape for intractable dilemmas and overly microscopic thinking.

On occasion, the CEO is the catalyst for a strategic thinking culture. However, when this is successful it is often accompanied in parallel by an infusion of strategic thinking across senior levels – as described above.

For strategic thinking to become truly embedded within the organizational culture, it thus needs a number of things. Borrowing from the idea of the culture web/organizational paradigm (Johnson and Scholes, 1987), we see shifts to the following as being necessary:

- *Structure*: strategic thinking is definitely not seen as only residing at the top of the organization
- *Power*: all staff are given some power to think strategically, within their domain of responsibility
- *Controls*: control systems based on financial and operational measures also reflect the strategic dimension
- *Routine*: organizational routines (such as meetings, reports, etc.) reflect the imperatives of strategic thinking (like root cause and option analysis, prioritization, etc.)
- *Rituals*: these are adapted to have a more strategic content – looking forward rather than backward (for cxamplc, company conferences)
- *Symbols*: managers are encouraged to use more strategic language, without this getting bogged down in artificial jargon
- *Stories*: real strategic thinking successes are captured and circulated in the organization – in management presentations or by the Intranet.

Strategic thinking is not merely a set of analytical processes that can be grafted easily onto existing management activities. Rather, it demands a rather different style – one that is lighter, more imaginative and open to thoughts that transcend any particular ownership and power base (this was underlined in Chapter 12, where potential value was greatly inhibited without cultural alignment with its imperatives).

This demands a number of important cultural shifts, as seen in the 'from–to' analysis (see Chapter 6) in Table 13.2.

By any reckoning, introducing strategic thinking into all or part of an organization inevitably implies some culture change. Implementing those changes requires consistency. For instance, if the planning process is redesigned and a different agenda set but without changing managers' expectations of what plans will be used and who will be judged against them, success will be fitful.

It is often helpful, in order to introduce a strategic thinking culture, to run a small number of strategic thinking workshops to equip staff with both the skills and the mind-set required. However, it is important that initiatives like these are not just isolated, and that they should be reinforced.

Within HR there are some special difficulties of developing a strategic thinking culture. This is because HR staff:

Table 13.2
Cultural shifts required for strategic thinking

From	To
Thinking driven by what worked in the past	Thinking driven by the possible and by the future
Top-down driven business planning	Thinking percolating freely through the organization
Really big issues not talked about	Big issues freely and constructively (other than cynically) discussed
Plans as 'comfort blankets'	Plans drive actual action
Obsessive and narrow financial targeting	Measured, balanced sets or organizational goals
Lip-service paid to 'empowerment'	Empowerment is genuine
A leadership environment, where 'what I say' is the strategy	Pluralistic ownership of the strategy

- Often feel less commercially knowledgeable and less confident in their ability to understand business strategy. The lack of a robust cognitive context undermines their confidence in thinking about HR strategy.
- Are not always particularly good at business analysis or at devising analytical processes. (Often they are drawn to HR because they perceive they have more 'soft' skills, rather than 'hard' skills.)
- Often feel less than highly influential in the organization, leading again to reduced confidence.
- Can be highly reactive and tactical in the face of HR issues – making strategic thinking about these issues a highly novel way of reflecting.

To be truly successful, the internal HR strategy consultant will almost certainly need to coordinate the training of HR staff to think strategically. This can be usefully combined with the process of actually compiling the HR/organization strategy, or through strategic workshops aimed at dealing with specific strategic HR issues.

DIAGNOSING AND MEETING CLIENT NEEDS

This short section summarizes how the techniques found earlier in the book can assist in meeting the needs of either internal clients (if you are in a strategic planning role) or external clients (where you are an external facilitator). We will focus on those that are most relevant. For diagnosing clients' needs, the valuable tools are:

- Fishbone analysis, for understanding the root causes behind a client's problem

- Wishbone analysis, for helping clients to think through all the factors that need to line up to deliver the value of any actions they now wish to take
- Stakeholder agenda analysis and the 'out-of-body experience', for understanding their deeper anxieties and drivers
- Scenario development and the uncertainty–importance grid, for helping the client to see around corners and to anticipate alternative futures
- Attractiveness–implementation difficulty (AID) analysis, for helping to prioritize client options (see Chapter 6).

An interesting feature of assisting clients to develop and implement their strategies is the management of the emotional boundaries around these strategies. A facilitator may put a lot of energy into helping a client reach a point where not only a decision but action too is possible. The client may then falter from moving ahead because of a combination of strategic, organizational and personal uncertainty.

When the client does not follow through at this point, it can be somewhat disappointing to the consultancy facilitator. Facilitators need to manage their own emotional commitment at this point. After all, their role is simply to set the decision-maker up for the decision, and not actively to force the decision. This is akin to the role of the mid-field player in football – if he puts the ball sublimely at the striker's feet and the striker then proceeds to knock it over the bar, then the mid-fielder has done his job.

The consulting facilitator's primary role is therefore to stimulate and challenge the strategic thinking of the client – whether internal or external. It is not primarily to come up with brilliant strategic ideas themselves.

This is an intensely political and also personally sensitive process (as seen in Chapters 11 and 12), and one that must be managed extremely delicately. As the client, however tough on the outside, can internally be extremely sensitive, there are almost unlimited possibilities for the process going off-course. Besides the more analytical technical techniques in this book, there is never a substitute for the exercise of judgement, foresight and skilful persuasion.

Such a combination of skills is hard (if not impossible) to package – although the more successful, larger consultancies manage still to exercise these skills as if the client is just dealing with one facilitator and not with a firm. Better still, the client makes very selective use of external facilitation, relying upon this on a just-in-time, rather than on a just-in-case, basis. In its state of complete perfection, this is achieved within and by the client itself. A life-saving technique here is to begin any workshop by asking 'what behaviour do we *not* wish to have (political, picky, personal, pedantic)?; having done this, the difficulty of facilitating a session will be halved as there will be at least some buy-in to a more harmonizing interactive process.

ORGANIZING FOR STRATEGIC THINKING

In the past many organizations have actually made the planning process the responsibility of a strategic planning manager, creating some interesting sounding job titles (and associated scepticism and perhaps cynicism). However, to place the primary responsibility for planning in the hands of one specialist staff member may dilute ownership of any outputs. Indeed, it can potentially build up major resistances to what would (in another process/structure) have been seen as perfectly sound ideas.

Rather than default to appointing a potentially full-time planning manager, with the attendant bureaucracy, a perhaps more cunning plan might be to project manage it through the existing management team – and preferably with facilitator support.

An HR facilitator would have a rather different role to an HR planner, as Table 13.3 illustrates.

Table 13.3
Differences between an HR planner and an HR facilitator

HR planner	HR facilitator
Issues the plans	Does not own or issue the content of plans
Focuses on planning process primarily	Focuses on thinking process primarily
Seeks a comprehensive picture and route to the future	Seeks to get the value out of a smaller number of lines of enquiry
Works through meetings and forms	Adds value through workshops
Is typically part of the management team	Is certainly not a member of the management team
Is internal	Could be either internal or external, dependent upon need
Is invariably full-time	Works on assignment or is part-time
Analytically skilled	Behaviourally skilled

This table contrasts quite markedly the role definition, skills-set and fit of planner versus facilitator. Here the facilitator focuses mainly on orchestrating the process of strategic discovery, rather than on the heavier task of planning administrator.

Sadly, it is hard to find the ideal blend of someone with analytical and creative techniques, and also the behavioural and political skills. Whilst it may be possible to find many of these skills through external consultants (with the advantage of them not being 'native' to the organization), this may cause the problem of looking like a 'nice-to-do' initiative.

Ideally someone needs training up to do the internal facilitation itself. Here it is actually more important that they have process and behavioural skills rather than either in-depth operational knowledge or MBA-level skills. Equally important is their inner political confidence – which might be non-existent if there is any possibility of future job security being threatened by how a facilitation process was handled.

In order to define your role as facilitator, it is necessary to select from a number of styles. A useful way of understanding these styles is to reflect on Figure 13.1, which displays two axes:

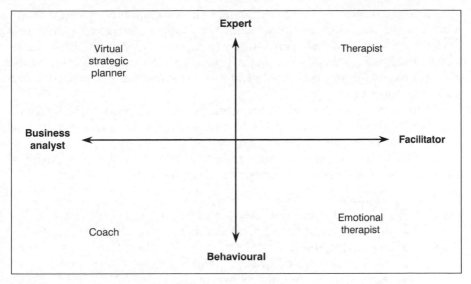

Figure 13.1
The consultant – different styles

- Expert versus process facilitator
- Analytical versus behavioural.

The 'expert' role can stem from your knowledge of the business, or of specific technical issues, or it can be an expertise purely in strategic thinking and analysis. The 'facilitator' role is concerned with management of the process, including time management, achievement of targeted output, managing the behaviour of the team, and controlling key stakeholders. There are also some practical aspects, such as chairing feedback sessions, setting the agenda for group work, and acting as scribe.

Different combinations of styles of facilitator can be defined as follows:

- Expert/analytical facilitator
- Expert/behavioural facilitator
- Behavioural/process facilitator
- Analytical/process facilitator.

The expert/analytical facilitator role is a very common one, and is one that an internal planner or an external consultant/adviser is inclined to play as a default style. The expert/behavioural role is often that taken by HR development people, where they are likely to make interventions that draw people in who are quiet, or to harmonize team behaviour. Such a facilitator is likely to play either in this role or in that of a behavioural/process facilitator. The analytical/process facilitator could be a former accountant or market analyst, or an external or internal management consultant.

Even when shown these different role styles and asked to reflect upon them, advisers/facilitators still tend to stick with their default styles – the ones that they are most used to. Unfortunately, the style adopted may not marry well with the specific situation at hand. For example, let's take a workshop focusing on a restructuring. This is likely to require a very heavy bias towards behavioural/process facilitation, due to the obvious sensitivities. Where the facilitator opts for an expert/analytical style, this may be inappropriate and counterproductive.

Where a workshop focuses on acquisitions, the main need might be for an expert/analytical style. Here an HR development person might not be able to deal with the variety of issues that may arise.

In order to identify your default facilitator style, we will analyse some of the key capabilities that go along with each of the styles as follows.

1. The expert/analytical facilitator has:
   - Knowledge of the business
   - Knowledge of possible technical solutions
   - Problem-solving ability
   - Analytical knowledge of strategic thinking
   - Integrative skills (seeing the bigger picture)
2. The expert/behavioural facilitator has:
   - Knowledge of the people involved (informal)
   - Knowledge of the people involved (psychometric)
   - Knowledge of team processes
3. The behavioural/process facilitator has:
   - Listening skills
   - Intervention skills
   - Influencing skills
   - The ability to provide energy to the group
4. The expert/process facilitator has:
   - Expertise in the strategic thinking process
   - Creative thinking skills
   - Questioning skills
   - Summarizing skills
   - The ability to provide inspiration to the group.

Another important area for the budding facilitator to be aware of is that of the issue recognition cycle. Figure 13.2 shows how this operates. During any workshop, new issues may well surface. A strong facilitator will be able to sense the potential of such an issue (either as a problem or opportunity), and of its implications on other issues or aspects of the business. Such a facilitator will also be able to think through:

- How long it might take to explore that issue
- What techniques might be helpful in analysing and discussing it
- How bumpy the process and associated behaviour might be *en route*
- Who might cause problems or be of help.

This demands very quick thinking, and a well-honed intuitive sense of the workshop dynamics.

Exercise 1

To assess your default facilitation style, consider the following.

How would you rate:

1. Which role you like playing?
   - Expert/analytical
   - Expert/behavioural
   - Behavioural/process facilitator
   - Expert/process facilitator
2. Which role others would see you as good at?
   - Expert/analytical
   - Expert/behavioural
   - Behavioural/process facilitator
   - Expert/process facilitator.

In getting up to speed with this level of facilitation, there is no substitute for lots of experience. Facilitation is never a boring task. On one particular occasion a team of eleven managers insisted on working together (without splitting into groups) for 2 whole days and an evening. They refused to go along with the facilitator's advice, making little progress and wearing themselves out. In 16 years of experience as a facilitator, this was a first.

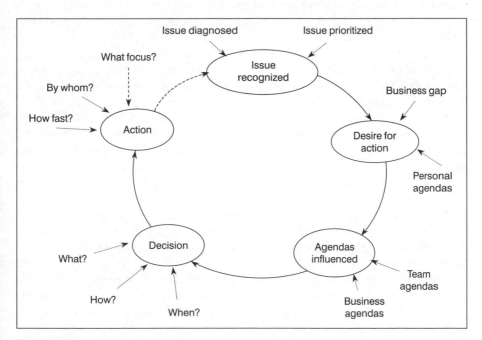

Figure 13.2
The advisory cycle – the client

On another occasion, the top manager in one organization told one of the authors that 'This will be the most difficult project you have ever undertaken'. Unfortunately, he neglected to say that it was he who was going to make it so difficult. A very strong, forceful manager by nature, 2 hours into the strategic workshop (when we were just finishing off checking out the current strategic position), he exploded volcano-style:

Tony, when is the helicopter thinking going to start, if we don't get airborne soon I will bloody-well take off in my helicopter for Japan and the Far East, where the real growth is!

[This workshop was in the mid-1990s, when the Japanese and Far East markets were in boom – and just before this boom turned to bust.]

Returning to Figure 13.2, the facilitator needs to recognize that even where an issue has been discussed in detail, there is no guarantee that any action will ensue unless all the preconditions for actually doing something are met.

A second area for thought is the simple logistics of running strategic thinking events effectively. Often the arrangements for such a process are determined by the managing director's PA's decision on hotel accommodation. It is not unusual for facilitators to be told that a workshop is to be run for 2 days in a hotel room without external light – hardly encouraging visionary thought. Alternatively, a 'workshop' might be planned for the top 30 managers of a specialist department, without thinking about whether this is actually viable or not (physically and intellectually), or whether it is significant that all the middle managers have been left out.

Where workshops are held on site, there are often inadequate catering arrangements (signalling that this workshop is not really that important), or managers drift back to mobile telephones and even to their e-mails between sessions, causing major distraction.

Before an event is held, its purpose and intended outputs (and next steps) need to be clearly defined in advance. When used, the facilitator should be appropriately positioned – and not be over-positioned. (One of the authors was once rather flatteringly described as being 'A leading European thinker', setting unrealistic and inappropriate expectations for the management team – who expected a cross between Superman and Einstein.)

It is also important to pre-define who will collate the outputs from a workshop. Unless these are typed up quickly, the sense and the immediacy are both lost. Ideally, the output should be available within 3 working days of the workshop.

In an effective, well-facilitated workshop, there can be quite a volume of output. Whilst the more critical decisions and analyses are probably contained in a dozen or so flipcharts (over a 2-day period), there may be another two dozen or so sheets of ancillary thinking, which provide helpful context. One of the central roles of the facilitator is to capture that thinking with a flipchart pen (or on acetate), so that the rest of the management team can have both their hands and their minds free. This part can be harder for an internal facilitator, who might make value-laden interpretations (either intentionally or unintentionally) of what is said.

 ## DELIVERING VALUE-DRIVEN OUTPUTS

Conventionally, many managers are happy to just see some strategic outputs rather than necessarily ones of the highest quality and value. As argued in Chapter 12, there should be economic value generated by specific strategic thoughts at each and every stage.

It is therefore a helpful learning discipline to set aside 5 to 10 minutes at the end of a strategic thinking session simply to put a value on some of the outputs. Whilst this value may be highly approximate and broad-brush, it is healthy to review whether real value has begun to come out yet or not.

This routine also helps to underline the need actually to implement the strategic plan, rather than just to have a number of temporarily exciting strategic thoughts.

To recap from Chapter 12, the major categories of the value of strategic thoughts are:

1. The meaning (of strategic thinking)
2. Business value
3. Context
4. Thought value
5. Prioritization
6. Core process
7. Process drivers
8. Supporting structure and skills
9. Supporting processes
10. Soft value.

LINKING TO HR STRATEGY IMPLEMENTATION

Having at last established some clarity of decisions and of key priorities, it is necessary actually to implement HR strategic breakthroughs. Many managers bemoan the lack of guidelines – either from business school thinkers or from management consultants – in how to approach this crucial phase of strategic thinking.

There are a number of important recipes to achieve successful links to implementation, and these are as follows:

1. Focus on a number of key HR strategic breakthroughs that are tangible and actionable (and not just broad-brush ideas).

2. Set some clear parameters on the outputs of the strategic breakthrough, for example in terms of:
   - Scale
   - Competitive benefits
   - Profitability and/or economic value
   - Shifts in capability.
3. Use the key implementation techniques of:
   - Fishbone analysis, for problem diagnosis (see Chapter 6)
   - From-to analysis, for exploring the scope of implementation (see Chapter 6)
   - Wishbone analysis, to examine what needs to line up to deliver effective implementation (see Chapter 3)
   - Force field analysis, for exposing the scale of implementation difficulty, possibly with the value-over-time curve (see Chapter 6)
   - Stakeholder analysis (and agenda analysis), for understanding who you need to communicate with and involve, who to influence and how to influence them (see Chapter 6)
   - Urgency–importance analysis and/or attractiveness–implementation difficulty analysis (see Chapter 6)
   - The importance–uncertainty grid, for exposing key implementation vulnerabilities and addressing these proactively (see Chapter 4)
   - Scenario story telling, especially for how future implementation might go well versus not-so-well, and also to work backwards from future implementation success (see Chapter 4)
4. Devise a set of key questions to work through.

Taking a closer look at the final point above, a typical list of questions to work through is found in the following exercise.

Exercise 2

For one area of implementing your HR strategy, at the corporate, business, departmental, project, team or individual levels:

1. Where this is a problem, and what are its root causes (fishbone)?
2. Where this is an opportunity, what is its vision, and what factors (both within and outside your control or influence) would need to line up to deliver this vision?
3. For this breakthrough, what is its targeted economic value? (Think about its likely net costs into the future.)
4. Where the breakthrough comprises a number of discretionary actions or activities, where are these positioned on the attractiveness–implementation difficulty grid?
5. What is your cunning plan now for implementing it?
6. How difficult will it be to implement? (force field analysis)
7. Who are the key stakeholders involved during the lifetime of this breakthrough?

---

8. Where are these stakeholders likely to be positioned, given your cunning plan, in terms of (a) attitude (for, neutral or against) and (b) influence (high, medium or low)?
9. How do these patterns of attitude and influence shift for different areas of implementation? (Here you might need to do separate stakeholder agenda analyses for each action or sub-project.)
10. Given the agendas of key stakeholders (use stakeholder agenda analysis), how might you influence them to (a) be more favourable, or (b) to reduce the influence of those who are against?
11. Given all of this thinking, what scenario stories can you tell about:
    - the implementation going very smoothly, or
    - the implementation being somewhat turbulent, or
    - the implementation going completely wrong?

DESIGNING AN HR STRATEGY WORKSHOP

HR strategy workshops can be used for a variety of HR strategic issues, including:

- Acquisition integration
- Balance of life
- Communication
- Culture change
- International development
- Management processes
- Performance management
- Recruitment
- Restructuring
- Succession and development.

Exercise 3

Based on the possible areas of workshops described in this book:

1. Do you presently run workshops in this area?
2. Should you run workshops in this area?
3. If you did, what would their targeted value be?

There follows some very practical advice on design, running and getting maximum value out of strategic development workshops.

Although workshops can generate disproportionate value (and vision), this value can be diluted considerably where:

■ There is inadequate pre-planning (of issues, process and outputs)
■ There is no facilitation, or facilitation is ineffective
■ There are no plans in place to deal with the output and to move it on into the next phase
■ There are no tools to help managers make progress (use the tools and checklists contained in this book).

Twelve key questions on 'how to run an HR strategic workshop' are as follows:

1. What is the objective of the workshop?
2. How does it relate to other initiatives?
3. What are seen as the key outputs (learning, problem definition, action plans, behavioural shift, etc.), how will these be documented and communicated, and to whom?
4. Who needs to be involved?
5. How will the workshop be identified/positioned in the organization, and by whom?
6. Who will facilitate, and is this person seen as competent and impartial?
7. Where should the workshop be held, and what facilities are required?
8. What are the next steps following the workshop likely to be?
9. What key barriers and blockages may arise, how will these be dealt with, and by whom?
10. What specific activities will be undertaken, and what will this input require?
11. How will these activities be broken down into discussion groups, and who will be in each one?
12. How long is it required to make substantial progress on each issue, and what happens if tasks are incomplete?

Experience shows that it is essential to consider all these questions at length, rather than rushing into a workshop on a particular issue with merely a broad agenda. The questions emphasize both content and process, and involve thinking through how these interrelate. They also involve analysing both current and future context, which provides high quality feed-in of data and is also of assistance in thinking through feedback into the management process in detail and in advance.

It is vital to structure the content of each HR strategy workshop to contain key questions. An example, for a bank, follows.

Morning:
1. What are our current capabilities, strengths and weaknesses?
2. What are our future external competitive challenges, and what is our future organizational vision?
3. What are the key gaps between where we are now and where we need to be? (FT analysis)
4. What are our key HR strategic breakthroughs/continuous improvements to address these gaps?

Afternoon:

1. How attractive/difficult to implement are these breakthroughs? (AID analysis)
2. For one key breakthrough:
   - What is the value added?
   - How difficult will it be over time?
   - Who are the key stakeholders, where are they positioned, and how can we influence them? (stakeholder analysis)
   - What are the key uncertainties? (uncertainty–importance grid)
   - What would the implementation implications be, and what would the direct and indirect costs be?

This workshop format is very similar to that used by the Royal Bank of Scotland Group as one of the elements of becoming HR consultants – and very successfully.

CONCLUSION

A key lesson from our final chapter is that you do not have to be a full-time consultant (either externally or internally) to be your own HR strategy consultant. Being your own HR strategy consultant merely requires a willingness to step outside the pure content of strategic issues and then to design, plan, target, resource and perhaps facilitate a strategic thinking process.

This requires some familiarity with a few strategic thinking techniques, sensitivity to organizational politics and agendas, and a structural process – one that includes at least some workshop elements. It does not require being Superman or Supergirl.

To summarize the key points of the chapter:

- The process of HR strategy is often more important to focus on than its content.
- An HR strategy consultant can add value in a diversity of ways – from being a sounding board to providing out-of-the-box ideas, and from being a symbolic presence and energizer to being a facilitator.
- Asking the right questions (and even unthinkable questions) is a key role, and one that it is hard for an internal manager to fulfil when operating within a conventional mind-set.
- An HR strategy consultant needs a variety of stretching competencies to fulfil this role – requiring training, development and (potentially) mentoring.
- Establishing a process requires being able to identify strategic issues, target the outputs, and select the necessary techniques.
- Data analysis needs to be focused on the situation and on the particular outputs sought, rather than spread thinly.
- The strategic thinking process needs to be project managed.

■ Strategic thinking requires cultural alignment with greater empowerment, especially within HR.
■ Even a facilitator's role is complex, requiring a number of different high-order skills.
■ A facilitator must be aware of the process of strategic issue recognition, and how to maintain the focus on a small number of issues.
■ A continual focus on 'what value is coming out' of strategic thinking is essential.
■ Very clear links to HR strategy implementation are always required.

Each workshop needs careful planning, structuring, key questions, targeted output, positioning, and project managing.

And finally . . .

We end this book with a suitably tough challenge for you. Suppose that you are a consultant who has always wanted to work in the Football Industry. You have chosen 2002 to seize this initiative for your 'Spice Girl' strategy of doing what you 'really really really want'.

Adam Crozier, the young and thrusting Chief Executive of the Football Association has recently resigned, amidst an environment of political dissent within the FA and between the FA and the premiership football clubs, and escalating office and project costs.

Wembley, a project costing over £700 million, is now in jeopardy following nervousness from a number of banks. There is also no certainty that Sky will actually even bid for the next FA cup, and there are rumours about a rival knock-out competition being staged just within the Premiership itself. Crozier has expanded the FA's head office significantly, which has a marketing department alone of 25 staff, and has tried to modernize the FA with uneven, mixed success. So what else could go wrong?

However, you see this as a 'mission impossible' and apply for the Chief Executive's job – as one of our authors actually did in November 2002:

Assuming you got the job, what competitive strategy would you pursue for the FA? What HR strategy would you pursue? How might the HR strategy actually *create* or *actively shape* the competitive strategy? How might the competitive strategy fall over if the HR strategy was not effective? And how does this link to economic value added by the FA?

Sounds daunting? Just ask:

■ What business will the FA be in, in future?
■ How might it add value? (business value systems)
■ What competitive breakthroughs are needed? (adding more value to the game, reducing costs, being more innovative?)
■ What HR strategy breakthroughs would achieve this, and how attractive–difficult might it be to implement these ? (AID analysis)

Geoff Thompson
Chairman
The Football Association
16 Lancaster Gate
London W2 3LW   8 November 2002

Dear Mr Thompson

Chief Executive – The FA

I noted that following a recent resignation the position of the Chief Executive of the FA is vacant. It may be that you are likely to find it difficult to get a suitable replacement. According to the Evening Standard (Tuesday 5 November),

> The successful applicant will have the business skills of Bill Gates, the patience of a saint and the hide of a rhinoceros.
> He (or she) will be able to deal with the criminally insane, terminally mediocre and insatiably greedy (who control professional football), and the elderly, infirm and incontinent (who sit on the county and amateur committees).

It continues

> We would frankly be amazed if anyone who is not already a resident of Broadmoor would actually want this impossible job.

I am sure that this picture is somewhat unfair, but almost certainly this is a job for Tom Cruise – were he to be available.

Well, you may well have found an unlikely and attractive candidate in the form of myself. I am an eminent strategist (and consultant, e.g. to Microsoft), facilitator of many missions impossible, turnaround specialist, guru on leadership – and expert in strategies for the Football Industry. I am also English, which might help this time (unfortunately this did not appear to help my previous applicant for England Coach, although I do get on well with Sven, who was coincidentally a witness to my recent wedding).

I would be delighted to hear how I can progress my application.

Yours sincerely

Dr Tony Grundy
MA MBA MSc MPhil FCA PhD

PS. As a back-up alternative, I would be delighted to help with your recruitment strategy and screening processes, which I am also expert in.

- Given assumed future competencies, what future competitive strategies for the FA would be feasible and attractive?
- How would you influence the disparate stakeholders both within and outside the FA?

Now you have read this book – and thoroughly digested it – we would ask that you send your ideas on a postcard to:

The New Chief Executive
The Football Association
16 Lancaster Gate
London W2 3LW

This might well give you some more exciting career options. As we said earlier of Winnie the Pooh's bumping downstairs:

Here is Edward Bear, coming downstairs now, bump, bump, bump, on the back of his head, behind Christopher Robin. It is, as far as he knows, the only way of coming downstairs, but sometimes he feels that there really is another way, if only he could stop bumping for a moment and think of it.

A. J. Milne, *Winnie The Pooh*

The literature linking corporate and HR strategy - an overview

HR strategy is often put forward as being a key means of achieving competitive advantage (Ulrich and Lake, 1990), and is seen as being a route to superior business performance. This is especially so where HR strategy is linked closely with corporate strategy. Where this is the case, the corporate strategy ought in theory to be easier to implement.

The literature is, however, scant in suggesting how organizations can achieve superior performance via HR strategy (Guest, 1993; Hegelwish and Brewster, 1993). In the past, HR strategy has either largely been handled mechanistically (an extension of manpower planning models) or has been viewed as emergent or simply incremental (Quinn, 1980).

Origins of HR strategy - and developments

First, we should briefly re-examine the origins of HR strategy. (As the main intent of our paper is to develop the conceptual linkages between HR and corporate strategy, this is a background review only.)

HR strategy was spawned from HR management (HRM) in the early/mid-1980s. HRM offered the attraction of doing for personnel management what competitive strategy had done for business policy, especially through the work of Michael Porter (1980, 1985). It offered a coherent and prescriptive framework for 'doing things in human resources'.

One way of showing how HR strategy may fit to any organizational conditions is by the link (or lack of link) to company mission (Hilb, 1993). For instance, HRM processes can be linked directly to mission (providing that 'mission' is well articulated - it is often not, according to Campbell and Tawadey, 1990).

Implementing (strategic) change is also a theme that has become increasingly prominent in relating HR strategy and corporate strategy, particularly over the last few years (see, for instance, Pettigrew and Whipp, 1991).

Another key theme is that of facilitating organizational learning (Kanter, 1983; Pascale, 1990; Senge, 1990; Pettigrew and Whipp, 1991; Argyris, 1991) - both for implementing change and also (more rarely) for formulating strategy (as in the use of scenario development as a learning process; see Grundy, 1993). But as Argyris (1991) has observed, there are many barriers and defences to open organizational learning. Organizational learning is also linked into organizational change, and into changes in structure (Brewster and Larson, 1993).

Within organizations there is frequently also a fragmentation of HR strategic programmes. For instance, the issue of developing strategic succession plans may be dealt with in relative isolation (for an alternative approach, see Grundy, 1997). Equally, management development strategy (if existing in a 'deliberate' as opposed to an 'emergent' form) may also be somewhat decoupled from higher-level views on HR strategy. (The root cause of this is that whilst management development is frequently owned by Training and Development [and managers], HR strategy is frequently owned by the HR Director. Depending on his or her personal skills, agendas and relationships, the obvious link within HR strategy may or may not be made.)

In summary, HR strategy may not have fulfilled its initial promise due to a combination of factors. For instance, it is evidently complex and less obviously tangible, its effects are relatively hard to measure, and it may not be clearly noted and interlinked within the organizational structure.

Corporate strategy and links to HR strategy – the literature

There are a number of analytical links between competitive strategy and HR strategy. These include:

- Portfolio theory
- Competitive strategy and the value chain
- Life-cycle analysis and types of strategy
- Competencies and strategic intent
- Strategy and styles.

Portfolio theory

A classic strategy tool is the Boston Consulting Grid. This plots market growth rate against relative market share. Here, a 'star' business requires more innovatory input than perhaps a 'cash cow'. The implication for HR strategy is that during the life-cycle of a business (or sub-business unit), the HR strategy and policies need to be adapted to changing conditions (Starkey and McKinley, 1993).

Competitive strategy and the value chain

In defining 'competitive position' for a specific business, HR strategy supports advantages such as skills, responsiveness, service quality, innovation, etc. More generally, Porter's (1985) generic strategies suggest that there should be more emphasis on innovation for differentiation strategies rather than for cost-leadership strategies. Likewise, there should be greater emphasis on process innovation within cost-leadership strategies. Focus strategies suggest greater specialization of distinctive skills.

The 'value chain' (Porter 1985) also positions human resources as central in determining how businesses compete on an ongoing basis. More specifically, Pettigrew and Whipp (1991) describe seven cases that illustrate the role of HRM in managing organizational change, showing how HR strategy is instrumental in adapting the value chain to a changing external environment.

Life-cycle analysis and types of strategy

Product life-cycle may also impact on HR strategies. Management style may need to change considerably depending upon the stage of the life-cycle, for instance.

With a 'prospector'-type strategy (Miles and Snow, 1978) appropriate to market growth phase, there is again a major emphasis on innovation and on marketing and strategic skills. However, a 'defender' (more a characteristic of a mature market) would place considerable emphasis on financial and related skills.

Competencies and strategic intent

A further concept is the notion of 'strategic intent' and the related notion of core competencies (Hamel and Prahalad, 1989, 1993). Strategic intent may help us to define the kind of competencies needed to enable the organization to compete in a distinctive and effective way.

Human resources are clearly a critical ingredient in any organization's key sources of competitive advantage (and equally, competitive disadvantage). Human resources figure importantly in the 'resource-based' theory of competitive advantage (Grant, 1991). Yet, oddly, they frequently play a secondary role in strategy formulation, relegated as part of the 'implementation' issues.

Strategy and style

'Strategic style' is another variable that may have an impact in shaping HR and corporate strategy links (Goold and Campbell, 1987). For instance, if an organization has a 'strategic planning' style this implies a relatively influential strategic apex and technostructure. A 'financial control' style implies a strong operating core.

There are therefore a considerable number of disparate linkages between corporate and HR strategy, which need to be unravelled in order to address the question 'how are corporate and HR strategy linked?'. Certainly there may be a very strong influence of human resource issues on corporate strategy itself, rather than HR strategy being seen as something that comes after the overall strategic direction has been set (suggested also by Holbeche, 2000).

Further reading

Guest, D. (1993). Formal perspectives in human resource management in the United Kingdom. In: A. Hegelwish and C. Brewster (eds), *European Development in Human Resource Management*. Kogan Page.

Holbeche, L. (2000). *Aligning Human Resources and Business Strategy*. Butterworth-Heinemann.

Starkey, K. and McKinley, A. (1993). *Strategy and Human Resource*. Blackwell Business.

Ulrich, D. and Lake, D. (1990). *Organizational Capability*. J Wiley & Sons.

References

Ansoff, H. I. (1965). *Corporate Strategy*. McGraw Hill.

Argyris, C. (1991). Teaching smart people how to learn. *Harvard Business Review*, **May–Jun,** 99–109

Bennett Stewart, G. (1991). *The Quest for Value*. Harper Business.

Bevan, J. (2001). *The Rise and Fall of Marks & Spencer*. Profile Books.

Brewster, C. and Larson, H. (1993). In: A. Hegelwish and C. Brewster (eds), *European Developments in Human Resource Management*, pp. 126–148. Kogan Page.

Campbell, A. and Tawadey, K. (1990). *Mission and Business Philosophy*. Heinemann.

Covey, S. (1992). *The 7 Habits of Highly Effective People*. Simon & Schuster.

Goldratt, E. M. (1990). *Theory of Constraints*. North River Press.

Goleman, D. (1995). *Emotional Intelligence*, Bloomsbury.

Goold, M. and Campbell, A. (1987). *Strategies and Styles*. Basil Blackwell.

Grant, R. M. (1991). The resource-base theory of competitive advantage: implications for strategy formulation. *California Management Review*, **53**, 114–135.

Grundy, A. N. (1992). *Corporate Strategy and Financial Decisions*. Kogan Page.

Grundy, A. N. (1993). *Implementing Strategic Change*. Kogan Page.

Grundy, A. N. (1994). *Strategic Learning in Action*. McGraw-Hill.

Grundy, A. N. (1995). *Breakthrough Strategies for Growth*. Pitman.

Grundy, A. N. (1997). Strategic human resource planning and development – in pursuit of the human advantage. *Long Range Planning*, **30(4),** 507–517.

Grundy, A. N. (1998a). *Exploring Strategic Financial Management*. Prentice Hall.

Grundy, A. N. (1998b). *Harnessing Strategic Behaviour: Why Personality and Politics Drive Company Strategy*. FT Prentice Hall.

Grundy, A. N. (2002). *Shareholder Value*. Capstone.

Grundy, A. N. and Brown, L. (2002a). *Strategic Project Management*. International Thomson.

Grundy, A. N. and Brown, L. (2002b). *Be Your Own Strategy Consultant*. International Thomson.

Guest, D. (1993). Current perspectives on human resource management in the United Kingdom. In: A. Hegelwish and C. Brewster (eds), *European Developments in Human Resource Management*. Kogan Page.

Hamel, G. and Prahalad, C.K. (1989). Strategic intent. *Harvard Business Review*, **Mar–Apr,** 63–76.

Hamel, G. and Prahalad, C.K. (1993). Strategy as stretch and leverage. *Harvard Business Review*, **Mar–Apr,** 75–84.

Hegelwish, A. and Brewster, C. (1993). *European Developments in Human Resource Management*. Kogan Page.

Hilb, M. (1993). The challenge of management developments in Western Europe in the 1990s. In: A. Hegelwish and C. Brewster (eds), *European Developments in Human Resource Management*, pp. 117–125. Kogan Page.

Holbeche, L. (2000). *Aligning Human Resources and Business Strategy*. Butterworth-Heinemann.

Johnson, G. and Scholes, K. (1987). *Exploring Corporate Strategy*. Prentice Hall.

Kanter, R. M. (1983). *The Change Masters*. Unwin.

Miles, R. E. and Snow, C. (1978). *Organizational Strategy, Structure and Process*. McGraw-Hill.

Mintzberg, H. (1993) *The Rise and Fall of Strategic Planning: Reconceiving Roles for Planning, Plans and Planners.* The Free Press.

Mitroff, I. and Linstone, H. A. (1993). *The Unbounded Mind*. Oxford University Press.

Pascale, R. A. (1990). *Managing on the Edge*. Penguin.

Pettigrew, A. and Whipp, R. (1991). *Managing Change for Competitive Success*. Basil Blackwell.

Piercey, N. (1989). Diagnosing and solving implementation problems in strategic planning. *Journal of General Management*, **15(1),** 19–38.

Porter, M. E. (1980). *Competitive Strategy*. The Free Press.

Porter, M. E. (1985). *Competitive Advantage*. The Free Press.

Quinn, J. B. (1980). *Strategies for Change – Logical Incrementalism.* Richard D. Unwin.

Rapport, A. (1986). *Creating Shareholder Value*. The Free Press.

Senge, P. (1990). *The Fifth Discipline – The Art and Practice of The Learning Organization*. Century Business.

Stalk, E. (1990). *Competing Against Time*. The Free Press.

Starkey, K. and McKinlay, A. (1993). *Strategy and Human Resource*. Blackwell Business.

Stein, D. (1996). *Essential Reiki*. The Crossing Press.

Sun Tzu (1971). *The Art of War*. Oxford University Press Inc.

Ulrich, D. and Lake, D. (1990). *Organizational Capability*. J. Wiley & Sons.

Index